THEMES IN SOCIAL THEORY

Series Editor: Rob Stones

This series explores how cutting-edge research within the social sciences relies on combinations of social theory and empirical evidence. Different books examine how this relationship works in particular subject areas, from technology and health to politics and human rights. Giving the reader a brief overview of the major theoretical approaches used in an area, the books then describe their application in a range of empirical projects. Each text looks at contemporary and classical theories, provides a map of primary research carried out in the subject area and highlights advances in the field. The series is a companion to *The Traditions in Social Theory* series, founded by Ian Craib and edited by Rob Stones.

Published

Forthcoming

TRADITIONS IN SOCIAL THEORY

Founding Editor: Ian Craib
Series Editor: Rob Stones

This series offers a selection of concise introductions to particular traditions in sociological thought. It aims to deepen the reader's knowledge of particular theoretical approaches and at the same time to enhance their wider understanding of sociological theorising. Each book will offer: a history of the chosen approach and the debates that have driven it forward; a discussion of the current state of the debates within the approach (or debates with other approaches); an argument for the distinctive contribution of the approach and its likely future value. The series is a companion to the *Themes in Social Theory* series, edited by Rob Stones.

Published

PHILOSOPHY OF SOCIAL SCIENCE (Second Edition)
Ted Benton and Ian Craib

CRITICAL THEORY
Alan How

MARXISM AND SOCIAL THEORY
Jonathan Joseph

MICRO SOCIAL THEORY
Brian Roberts

WEBER AND THE WEBERIANS
Lawrence Scaff

STRUCTURATION THEORY
Rob Stones

Forthcoming

POST-STRUCTURALISM AND AFTER
David Howarth

THE SIMMELIAN LEGACY
Olli Pyyhtinen

Politics and Social Theory

The Inescapably Social, the Irreducibly Political

Will Leggett
University of Birmingham, UK

First published 2017 by
PALGRAVE

Palgrave in the UK is an imprint of Macmillan Publishers Limited, registered in England, company number 785998, of 4 Crinan Street, London, N1 9XW.

Palgrave® and Macmillan® are registered trademarks in the United States, the United Kingdom, Europe and other countries.

ISBN 978–0–230–57680–3 hardback
ISBN 978–0–230–57681–0 paperback

This book is printed on paper suitable for recycling and made from fully managed and sustained forest sources. Logging, pulping and manufacturing processes are expected to conform to the environmental regulations of the country of origin.

A catalogue record for this book is available from the British Library.

A catalog record for this book is available from the Library of Congress.

Printed and bound by CPI Group (UK) Ltd, Croydon, CR0 4YY

For Jo

Also by the author:

After New Labour: Social Theory and Centre-Left Politics
The Third Way and Beyond: Criticisms, Futures, Alternatives (edited with Sarah Hale and Luke Martell)

Contents

Series Foreword

The latest books we've had the privilege of publishing in the *Themes in Social Theory* series – Will Leggett's *Politics and Social Theory* and Eamonn Carrabine's *Crime and Social Theory* – reaffirm the simple aim of the series, which is to deepen understanding of the role of social theory in the creation and validation of the most valuable empirical research in the social sciences. The series rests upon a belief that it is important to explore the vast terrain upon which theory and the empirical meet, and it extends an invitation to readers to share in this exploration. Each book takes on a specialised substantive area of research, and the books published so far have covered the fields of health, technology, international migration, human rights, the environment and nature, politics, and crime, with books in preparation focusing on gender and work, identity, and interaction within institutions. The task the books set themselves is to excavate the character of the interplay between social theory and empirical evidence in relation to key themes within their specialised field. I'll say more about this below.

The authors of the volumes in the series write clearly and accessibly even when the material they are dealing with is intrinsically difficult. They have a close knowledge of the relevant field, an enthusiasm for the kind of theoretically informed empirical research that has been produced within it and possess a flair for theoretical analysis. Within the general rubric of the series each author (or team of authors) has her or his own style and approach, and a distinctive authorial voice. This should translate into a sense of pluralism within the series as a whole, meaning that the investigation of the theory–empirical terrain will take on the broad and varied character required to push forward our understanding in the most open and constructive manner possible.

Each book in the series aims to bring together in one volume some of the most significant theoretically informed empirical work in that subfield. The substantive findings and arguments produced by each of the empirical studies highlighted are valuable and significant in and of themselves, and so will be clearly indicated. It is these fruits that are ultimately at the core of the enterprise, and without the creative, committed, combination of theory and evidence they would not have come into being. It is hoped that the books in the series will play their part in helping to bridge the harmful gap between theory and the empirical that is still too often present within the social sciences, and that they will not only be used on undergraduate and postgraduate courses to train and sensitise the next generation of social analysts, but will also be helpful more generally to researchers, citizens and activists. The books demonstrate that there is already a large existing literature in each subfield that has indeed combined theory and the empirical, and they go some way to clarifying the varying levels of descriptive, explanatory and critical power produced by these combinations.

The opening chapters of each book see authors reflecting upon the current state of theory in their field, and there have been a variety of approaches to this task. One of the most striking features of the latest three volumes to be published in the series has been that all the authors have felt the need to draw attention to the shortcomings of dominant current trends in their field, and to argue that a new framework of theoretical guidance is required. Each has offered a constructive way forward, whether in the form of a critically inspired synthesis of current approaches (*Environments, Natures and Social Theory*), a powerful insistence on the renewal of a more holistic, socially embedded, approach that can grasp the interplay between different forces, processes, and scales of activity (*Crime and Social Theory*) or the presentation of a new and imaginative guiding framework explicitly acknowledging the respective powers of social and political paradigms of analysis, and the need to draw from both (*Politics and Social Theory*). One of the previous volumes, *International Migration and Social Theory*, took a similar standpoint, arguing for a major renewal of current theorising in the field focused around a more sophisticated grasp of structure, agency and the practices resulting from their interplay.

These authors have felt the need to reflect deeply on how theory has framed empirical research in their field. The volumes include fascinating discussions on the tensions and divisions between different theoretical approaches, and on the historical trajectory of such divisions in terms of conflicts, attempted resolutions and new directions. The implications of all this for the production of particular types of empirical research, and for the emergence of key empirical case studies, is vividly revealed. Authors of these books have typically placed less emphasis on the precise details of how particular theoretical approaches, or hybrids of approaches, have been used in particular empirical studies. There seems to be something about the current state of the relationship between social theory and empirical research that makes the most pressing issue for authors that of theoretical framing itself, and of differences and tensions between framings. It looks like the authors intuitively see this as a necessary first step that must be taken before it is possible to settle into questions around the exact mechanics of application. Some authors also point out that much of the empirical research in their field is not theorised at all, meaning, in effect, that the ideas that organise and make sense of the empirical evidence are *ad hoc*, intuitive and unsystematic, making the research weak and unlikely to stand up to serious scrutiny. This is what Carrabine is referring to when he criticises the 'abstracted empiricism' of certain strands within criminology.

This apparently widespread need to rethink the most fundamental bases on which empirical research is carried out in different substantive fields was largely unanticipated. There are many reasons, however, why, on reflection, it isn't surprising. We are living through an age, the age of a globalised radical or late modernity, in which there is a colossal struggle between those for whom it is vital that respect is accorded to the question of the validity and adequacy of knowledge claims and those who believe it is possible to say and claim anything with impunity. There is a frighteningly arbitrary quality to the kinds of knowledge of the social world that are currently allowed to claim authority in the public sphere. Social thinkers are in the strongest position to resist and challenge the validity of weak, reckless knowledge claims. Constructing an appropriate frame for knowledge is an indispensable part of such resistance. The authors of *Environments, Natures and Social Theory*, highlighted the fragmentation of approaches in their field, the chronic oversimplification of approaches to particular issues, and the restrictions imposed on the funding and conduct of research by insufficiently examined ideologies. All of this points to the need to be more reflective about the theoretical paradigms and orientations that guide research. Will Leggett's notion of the 'irreducibly political' dimension of social life in *Politics and Social Theory* draws our attention to – amongst other things – the politics of all knowledge, and the need to scrutinise and assess the theoretical frameworks through which we approach and make sense of empirical evidence. It emphasises that all social life has a political dimension to it, one in which values, ideas and their contestation inform political agency and strategy. The absorption of series authors in the task of strengthening the theoretical frameworks that guide empirical research – in order that justice can be done to empirical realities – needs to be seen in this light.

In the midst of fragmented, contested landscapes, it is more important than ever to insist upon what that formidable American sociologist of the mid-twentieth century, Robert K. Merton, called the 'institutionalised vigilance' of intellectual life. By this, Merton meant the examination, appraisal, criticism and verification of knowledge claims by intellectuals and academic peers. Such vigilance needs to be rooted in an 'organised scepticism' that requires social scientists to invoke doubt in the first instance, and then to find all ways possible to fathom if that doubt is well founded. But it must be understood that such questions of validity always take place within a theoretical framework, and that this will direct attention to certain aspects of the empirical world rather than others. Strong theoretical frameworks can play a vital role of shaping the arena in which empirical evidence emerges, and in which, therefore, scepticism or validation necessarily takes place. Both the imaginative, systematic, creation of theoretical frameworks and the procedures of organised scepticism within these frames must be carried out through public scrutiny and criticism, within and by intellectual communities. These communities belong to the realm of what Leggett calls 'the inescapably social', which refers to those areas of social life that have preoccupied sociologists and social theorists: the macro social structures, institutions, norms, relations and practices in which things are made to matter by society, or, more insidiously, made not to matter.

This is the context for Eamonn Carrabine's concern in *Crime and Social Theory* that criminology, as it has begun to take on all the trappings and privileges of a discipline, is in danger of becoming entrenched in an intellectual world that is narrow and parochial, conformist and unreflective. In a highly accomplished and engaging account, Carrabine situates the strengths and weaknesses of contemporary empirical research within the broad contours of what he believes would be a more adequate theoretical framework. His expansive vision of what is needed reacts against: weaknesses that have accrued within the long historical formation of criminology over three centuries; sociology's initial, extended, indifference to the subject matter of criminology; and contemporary criminology's failure to consolidate the potential opened up to it by various threads of twentieth century social analysis, from Durkheim and the Chicago School to the 'new criminology' of the 1970s. The latter had held out the promise of a 'fully social theory of deviance', which has remained largely, wastefully, unfulfilled. Carrabine's analysis of current research within the subthemes of transgression, control, geography and representation is framed by an aspiration towards a combined sociological and criminological imagination. The analysis uses this frame to situate and explore cutting-edge empirical research under each heading. In the process, *Crime and Social Theory* begins to draw together the elements necessary to create a theoretical–empirical paradigm able to rise to the demands and forces of the age.

It is worth noting that the notion of 'themes' referred to in the series title in fact signals two kinds of themes. The *first* kind is *substantive* and refers to the overall theme of the respective volume – in the present cases, crime or politics – and, more subtly, to the subtypes of thematic content to be found within each of the different clusters of studies highlighted in each volume and indicated through the titles of the more substantive chapters. In *Crime and Social Theory* these are immediately apparent through the chapter headings we've just mentioned – transgression, control, geography and representation. The substantive themes of *Politics and Social Theory* are gathered around three organizing frames. These are: 'politics from above', where the state and governance are primary themes, allowing the practices of 'Washington', 'Wall Street', and so on, to come into focus; 'politics from below', where reflection on the theoretical themes of identity and participation inform Leggett's empirical focus on consumer identity in an age of economic austerity; and 'politics all around', in which the theoretical themes of culture, ideology and discourse provide an incisive way into some of the key characteristics of neoliberalism.

The *second* type of theme is *methodological*, and refers to the ways theory and empirical data are brought together within each of the studies highlighted. I prefer to refer to this set of themes under the label of *conceptual methodology*, rather than just 'methodology', in order to emphasise the ways in which particular theoretical ideas or concepts (and combinations of these) *should* guide more formal methods – such as interviews, observation, documentary analysis, surveys and so on – towards certain types of empirical evidence. Theories, and the interlocking concepts that make them into the theories they are, influence what parts of the world are selected to be of interest. The concepts, also, are shapes that direct us to look for the corresponding bits of empirical evidence, and they allow us to see how much of the (conceptual) shapes are covered by the available evidence, and how much of them remain uncovered, unsubstantiated. In these ways, the theories and concepts can be seen to have clear and identifiable methodological and empirical consequences.

It is relatively self-evident that the *key substantive themes* that emerge in, for example, Fernando de Maio's volume on *Health and Social Theory*– such as those around health inequalities and demographics, the functioning of the sick role, or the practices of pharmaceutical companies, will be distinct from those in other volumes, such as Karen O'Reilly's on international migration or Steve Matthewman's on technology. This is not to say there couldn't be fruitful overlap; it would be very easy to find theoretically informed research projects looking at the health implications of international migration or the use of technology in health care. However, it is to say that one might expect a series of distinctive thematic concerns to emerge from a focus on studies that have health as their primary concern. It is probable that the lessons to be learnt from the *conceptual methodological themes* can more easily be generalised across the domains of the different books in the series. Here, more commonality is likely to emerge across subfields in the ways that theory and the empirical are combined together, notwithstanding their different subject matters.

Each of the authors in the series takes it for granted that particular ways of framing, seeing, hearing, interpreting and understanding – to name just some of the ways we apprehend the world – are involved every time an empirical 'fact' is given that status by somebody. That somebody, in turn, may be any kind of everyday participant within society, deploying their own cultural and social standpoint on the world, whether they are a political power broker, a homeless migrant, a parent, an environmental activist or an academic researcher. Whoever does the apprehending will inevitably infuse the empirical facts they witness with their own perspectives, ideas and ways of seeing, just as they will do something similar in the ways they join the facts together into stories and arguments about the social world. Both aspects of their accounts will be affected, in turn, by the texture and contours of their personal biography, by their social positioning and by the interrelated cultures and subcultures they belong to. Embedded within their lived cultural experience are concepts, presuppositions and categorizations that can range from a mixture of the simply inherited and/or confused at one end of the spectrum to a mixture of the systematically reflected upon and/or analytically lucid at the other. Social theory looks to produce knowledge that sits much nearer the latter end of the spectrum than the former. It aims to identify entities, relations and processes in the social world that are sufficiently general to be usefully transposed from one situation to another whilst leaving space for the uniqueness of particular circumstances. At its most effective, it also strives to find ways of integrating these general concepts with the variations in empirical evidence one meets in the diversity of those specific, unique, circumstances.

The degree of rigour and intellectual seriousness implied by these standards, brought into close liaison with the imaginative ways of seeing that high-quality social analysis seeks constantly to renew, are what should make the activities and claims of the social and human sciences stand out. Our claim should be that the accounts we produce add something invaluable to public and civic culture, and to political life, something that damages and undermines less reflective, less systematic forms of knowledge. Social science has its own generic standards: standards that we need to ceaselessly explore, reflect upon and improve. The relationship between social theory and substantive studies is an especially significant part of this endeavour. It is only by resolutely pursuing this agenda that we can genuinely carry forward the ambitious aspirations of a public social science to make the contribution we so manifestly need it to make in the challenging years ahead.

Rob Stones
Western Sydney University
August 2016

Preface and Acknowledgements

This book has been a long time in the making. As the work unfolded, the social and political landscape was radically shifting in the ongoing aftermath of 'The Crash' of 2008. I consoled myself that most of the theorists I was engaging with had also been writing at times of profound social and political change – or at least tended to think they were.

The project has taken me to the heart of the society–politics relation, which has animated my thinking from undergraduate days to the present. In many respects, the book is a distillation of the ideas and people I have encountered over that time. I was very lucky to participate in strong traditions of integrating thinking about the 'social' and 'political' while a student at the Universities of Warwick, Essex and Sussex. Thanks are due to all of those who taught and studied with me at those institutions, especially my peers on the Social and Political Thought Programme at Sussex.

I've been privileged to work closely with colleagues in both sociology and political science at the University of Birmingham. Special thanks are due to my longstanding colleagues in Sociology: Ross Abbinnett, Justin Cruickshank, Andrew Knops and Therese O'Toole. And in particular Shelley Budgeon, for offering serious advice while simply refusing to take the whole thing too seriously. My undergraduate and graduate students, particularly on my Political Sociology option and our MA Social and Political Theory, have been a constant, lively source of inspiration for the themes across this book.

I'd like to thank Rob Stones for inviting me to undertake this project, and his sound advice and unflappable patience along the way. Lloyd Langman and his colleagues at Palgrave have likewise been very supportive throughout.

And Jo and Lois have been inescapably, irreducibly delightful.

Introduction

Social theory and political analysis: Suspicious neighbours?

From the nineteenth century to the present day, what we call social theorising has inevitably involved political analysis. Issues such as the role of the state, the nature of power and resistance, and the political means of social transformation are integral to understanding society. Despite this, I remain surprised at how sociologists and political scientists can regard each other's subjects as alien species. While sociologists are often deeply enmeshed in broad political questions, they can be reluctant to engage with mainstream political ideas and practices. At the same time, there is no shortage of political scientists who treat the whole idea of the social with deep suspicion: a half-baked realm of woolly theories and jargon about the next big 'change' (typically ending in the letters 'isation'). This is seen to detract from the business of understanding the machinations of elite actors, political institutions and the role of political ideas.

Of course, the majority of work and thinking lies between these (somewhat) caricatured extremes. Sociology and social theory cannot afford to ignore issues that are taken for granted by political scientists: the nature and concentration of power; interests and representation; and the institutions and mechanics of decision-making. Conversely, political science and political theory cannot avoid reference to the social: theories of large-scale social change; structured domination; the role of tradition and habit; and the origin and function of ideologies and social norms. This book argues for a dynamic relationship between social theory and the analysis of politics. There is an implicit dialogue throughout between social theory and political science, highlighting what the two disciplines can learn from one another, while retaining their distinctiveness.

The overarching focus of the *Themes in Social Theory* series is how social theory can enhance empirical research in a variety of settings: expertly written titles have included analyses of health (De Maio, 2010), technology (Matthewman, 2011) and migration studies (O'Reilly, 2012). Each of these examines the interplay between their core subject matter, social theory and societal relations. Each of these titles also encounters complex and fundamental issues in the process, and this book is no exception. When it comes to the relationships between social theory, society and politics, we face some quite distinctive challenges. This is partly because of the comprehensive (some would say universal) and contested scope of the conceptual and empirical field of 'politics'. But it is also because

1

of the ways in which politics enters into the constitution of social theory itself. Social theory's ways of seeing are irreducibly normative and political, and so it is important to foreground and analyse these characteristics.

A further challenge for this book is the degree to which the bodies of literature and styles of thought associated with social theory and political science have diverged (Sigelman, 2010). The book seeks to bridge this chasm in two primary ways. First, it reveals just how fundamental politics is to the perspectives adopted by social theory. Second, it demonstrates the power of social theory to illuminate both political reality and political analysis. Social theory has a self-consciously reflexive relationship to reality – historical and social, but also political. Social theorists are acutely aware of how theory enters, shapes and might even play a part in transforming that very reality.

The theoretical argument and contribution

Given these complexities, the book offers its own distinctive theoretical contribution: it foregrounds the society–politics relation, and develops an overarching conceptual frame for understanding it. Our argument is that accounts of social and political phenomena should keep what we identify as the 'inescapably social' and the 'irreducibly political' in view, as distinct but interrelated elements of analysis. The inescapably social refers to those factors which have preoccupied sociologists and social theorists: the role of macro social structures, institutions, norms, relations and practices. The irreducibly political denotes the political agency, ideas, strategy and contestation that these social elements are 'shot through' with, giving rise to their ultimately open-ended character. Sociology and political science have at times been guilty of neglecting the irreducibly political and inescapably social respectively. However, we cannot decide in advance of any empirical scenario which of the social or political might predominate: by keeping both in view we can analyse their interplay in specific conjunctures.

To this end, we shall find in what follows three key senses in which social theory interfaces with empirical political research and practice, sometimes simultaneously. The first is where social theory provides the resources for identifying and explaining a political entity. For example, we shall see how sociological theories of long-term processes of individualisation provide the backdrop for identifying new, 'do it yourself' forms of political activity. The second is where competing social-theoretical perspectives politically critique each other, as well as political reality itself: this aspect will be seen throughout where we use the major social-theoretical traditions to offer alternative interpretations of our empirical case studies. The third, often overlooked but most direct case, is where social theory is itself constitutive of a political idea or practice. This occurs, for example, where social-theoretical ideas are taken up by elite (or oppositional) political actors.

By foregrounding the significance of the inescapably social and irreducibly political as analytical categories, and highlighting these more specific senses in which social theory can inform political research and practice, the hope is that this book will contribute to developing a dynamic relationship between sociology and political science. Such a relationship is essential if we are to make sense of contemporary social and political phenomena in their complexity.

The structure of the book, and how to read it

Chapter 1 develops in more detail the analytical issues involved in studying the society–politics relation, and elaborates our key categories of the irreducibly political and the inescapably social. Subsequent chapters use this device to analyse how social theory interfaces with key empirical dimensions of politics: the nature of the state and governance (politics 'from above'); political identity and participation (politics 'from below'); and the political role of culture, ideology and discourse (politics 'all around'). In each of these chapters, we identify and analyse what classic and contemporary social theories have contributed to our understanding of the political phenomena in question. We then show the different ways in which social theory has informed specific empirical case studies. Each chapter concludes by considering what both the theories and empirical examples tell us about our overarching analysis of the society–politics relation.

In terms of the more specific content, Chapter 2 explores the state and governance as the classic site where politics and social theory have intersected. It charts the long-term shift from theory which sees the state as separate to society, to it being implicated in the detail of complex social relations in a way that blurs the state–civil society relationship. To illustrate this, we consider how accounts of rapid social change – most notably globalisation – led centre-left political parties to redevelop their conception of the state in the 1990s and 2000s. We then look at influential work from Scandinavia which captures the changing relationship between state and citizen amidst social complexity, and the rise of new culturally oriented governors and activists alike.

Chapter 3 elaborates these themes by examining what social theory has brought to our understanding of political identity, and the changing shape of political participation. We map how the long-term trajectory of theory – but also of the wider society and political discourse – has been from presenting stable selves with relatively coherent, fixed political identities and interests towards increasing fragmentation, fluidity and hybridity. In the last two decades, the key theoretical and empirical category here has been individualisation. We illustrate what is politically at stake in this shift with contemporary work on so-called 'political consumerism'. This refers to how people's identities as consumers are becoming increasingly politicised through, for example, ethical purchasing or more radical lifestyle changes such as 'downshifting'. Debates over political consumerism get to the heart of the politics of individualisation: are individual practices in the market sphere the basis of a new politics, or do they simply reflect the commodification of social and political identity within consumer capitalism?

The politics of identity are related to the wider political role of norms, values and ideas. These are present throughout the book and are dealt with head-on in Chapter 4. Here, we chart the increasing preoccupation with questions of the ideational in political analysis, the role of culture and, particularly, the move from the study of ideology to that of discourse. In our case study we address the status of neoliberalism: perhaps the most entrenched ideology in history, as well as the focus of key contemporary debates. We account for the ascendancy of neoliberalism across social and political life since the late 1970s, and how varied theoretical perspectives in ideology and discourse analysis offer different ways of grasping its character and the possibilities for alternatives.

The combination of addressing key theories, case studies and analysis of the society–politics relation means that each chapter is relatively long – but do not be daunted by this! While it is hoped you will read the book in full, it can also be read in sections, and for different purposes. This introduction and Chapter 1 offer a device for analysing the society–politics relation: this is both an original theoretical argument as well as a framework for empirical analysis, designed to be applied more widely. Subsequent chapters elaborate this argument, but also make particular contributions of their own. Theory sections form the first half of each substantive chapter. These can be read for insight into how social-theoretical themes and thinkers have been and remain relevant to the study of the state, political identity, or ideology and discourse respectively. The case studies and analyses that form the second half of each chapter can also be read in their own right. So, for example, discussions of political consumerism and participation, or the history and practice of neoliberalism, should prove informative in themselves as well as offering a distinctive social-theoretical perspective.

This overview raises a series of further questions that we will now address, before proceeding to our main chapters. What exactly do we mean by 'social theory' and is this the same thing as 'sociological theory'? What is the relationship between theory and the empirical research which informs our case studies? What specifically is the relationship of social theory to politics? And how do we justify what to include and exclude in a wide-ranging book such as this?

Definitions and boundaries

Defining social theory

One of the advantages social theory is held to have over the natural sciences is its *reflexivity*, or critical reflection upon the conditions of its own existence (May and Perry, 2011; Pels, 2003). This is embodied in sociology's own loose and pluralistic structure, which accommodates a range of competing – and some-times incompatible – perspectives. However, the flip side of this pluralism is disa-greement over apparently basic questions such as 'what is social theory'? Despite this, attempts to define social theory broadly agree that it has two main, distin-guishing objectives. The first – which is *not* the focus of this book – is theoretical reflection upon the purposes and possibilities of knowing about the social world at all. This is social science having a necessary conversation with itself about its role, and how it might deliver it. Intentionally or not, social scientists can't avoid engaging with these questions, and this book is no exception. However, here we shall not regard addressing these issues as social theory, but as the more special-ised domain of philosophy of social science (see e.g. Rosenberg, 2015). The latter is specifically concerned with questions of ontology (what is the social world?), epistemology (how can we know about it?) and methodology (how do we inves-tigate it?) – as well as the complex relationship between these different aspects.

This book is primarily concerned with the second sense of social theory usually offered in the literature, which can be summarised as something like: *theorising social structures, institutions, practices and ideas – and their impli-cations for groups and individuals – in the context of large-scale dynamics of stability and change.* Following Harrington (2005), this is what we might call *substantive* social theory, as opposed to philosophy of social science. It involves theorising actual social processes, as opposed to debating the possibility of doing so, and is thus necessarily related to empirical observation at some level (see also Turner, 2010: 29–35).

Theory and empirical research

Illustrating how philosophy of social science issues can't just be ignored, how-ever, the above discussion leads us to the relationship between 'theory' and the 'real world' – between theory and empirical research. Interrogating this relationship is central to the *Themes in Social Theory* series. For many – not least of all governments and major research funding bodies – the way to find out about the social world is to get out there, armed with appropriate research methods, and collect data. Some might therefore regard 'substantive' social theory as sounding suspiciously like an excuse to interpret the world from one's armchair. On this issue, I want to insist on the necessity of both theory and the empirical. Anything calling itself substantive social theory must clearly have an empirical referent. To be plausible, theory can't make assertions about reality which clearly contravene observation and experience. However, we also need to recognise that empirical research is theory-laden and dependent. We have increasingly sophisticated methods to collect and process informa-tion about a reality which is infinite and complex. But to describe such a real-ity, let alone *explain* it, we cannot avoid reference to conceptual categories, however rudimentary. The minute we do this, we are engaging in theory.

One of the most significant commentators on the inevitability of theory was Max Weber, a canonical figure in both sociology and political science. He recognised that the infinite and complex nature of social life had two unavoidable implications that lead researchers to theory. The first is the choice of what to study in the first place. Weber (1917) insisted on 'value-neutral' (objective) research methods and strategies. Nevertheless, he recognised that the act of choosing to study any particular area of social life introduces an unavoidable point of subjectivity, what he called the moment of 'value-relevance'. This inevitably calls on the experiences, objectives and values of the researcher, which are extrinsic to the 'purely' empirical aspects of the object of study itself. This goes to the heart of the ontological, epistemological and methodological debates that characterise the philosophy of social science.

The second, more substantive theoretical aspect Weber identified concerned making sense of reality once we have engaged it. We have to develop conceptual categories in order to classify and understand social phenomena; otherwise we are simply groping in a void of endless data. The specific means Weber (1922a) used to achieve this was the famous 'ideal-type': Weber himself developed ideal-types such as bureaucracy, charisma and status group. Ideal-types are necessarily based to some extent on the researcher's own experiences and observations of reality. This is unavoidable for, as social actors, we are always part of our own subject matter. However, ideal-types do not directly reflect a *specific* empirical instance of the phenomenon in question. Rather, they are a tool for the researcher, which she will accentuate in certain aspects for the purposes of a specific research question. So, when Weber (1922b) discussed charisma, he was using it as a tool to understand a specific form of leadership under certain types of social conditions.

Ideal-types can be used in the formation of hypothesis, and refined in light of empirical evidence, but they remain theoretical constructs, once-removed from reality itself (see also Parkin, 2002: 27–37). We shall encounter similar constructs across the work of the theorists – and empirical researchers – we discuss in this book. They range from, for example, Karl Marx's (1844) concept of alienation as capturing subjective experience under early capitalism, to Anthony Giddens' (1994) account of a creative 'autotelic self' in globalised, late modernity. Or from Emile Durkheim's (1893) nineteenth century vision of an integrating, 'organic' form of modern social solidarity, to Zygmunt Bauman's (2000) contemporary fears for a 'liquid modernity' that dissolves such social bonds.

Social or sociological theory? And how do they understand politics?

Having established broadly what we mean by theory, and why we believe it to be important and unavoidable, there remains the distinction between 'social' and 'sociological' theory. In practice – be that in primary research, textbooks or university syllabuses – the terms are often used interchangeably. However, it is social theory which is being explored in this book and series, so a word is necessary on why this term is being used. Sociological theory applies more strictly to the discipline of sociology. This tends to imply an unambiguous commitment to society as a verifiable object of investigation, separate to, for example, economy or state. Analytically, the main focus of sociological theory is *structure and agency*: the relations between macro social structures and the activities of individual and group actors (Mouzelis, 2008). Of the sociological canon, for example, Emile Durkheim's (1895) *The Rules of Sociological Method* outlined how 'social facts' have an existence of their own above individuals, while Weber (1922a) insisted on the analytical primacy of individuals, their intentions and actions. More recently, theorists such as Margaret Archer (1995), Pierre Bourdieu (1990) or Anthony Giddens (1984) have attempted formal synthesis of the structure–agency relation.

When it comes to more substantive theoretical analysis of society, as opposed to abstract models of structure-agency, sociological theory again adopts a more formalised and system building approach: it extrapolates models of society from the building blocks of the structure-agency problem. This was exemplified by the structural functionalism of US sociologist Talcott Parsons in the 1950s and 1960s. More recently, theorists working in a clearly sociological-theoretical tradition include George Ritzer (2001) and his meta-sociology, which models from the level of the individual to that of the global system; Anthony Giddens' (1990) institutional analysis of modernity; or Ulrich Beck's analyses of globalisation, individualisation and the relations between them (Beck, 2000; Beck and Beck-Gernsheim, 2002).

Why, then, do we sometimes describe social theory as distinctive from (but often overlapping with) these kinds of sociological theory? While there are no hard and fast rules here, those who deliberately talk of social as opposed to sociological theory tend to have two main reasons. The first is that in researching social life, they often draw on disciplines and traditions that lack a direct lineage to the classical sociology of those such as Marx, Durkheim and Weber. They may equally seek resources in continental philosophy, linguistics, cultural studies, literary or psychoanalytic theory. The second, related reason is that not only does social theory signify a broader disciplinary base but also a more contested understanding of the object 'society' itself. Note what the very expression 'sociology' implies: a logic of society, something perhaps envisaged quite mechanically in the manner of functionalists such as Parsons, or structural Marxists such as Louis Althusser (1971). 'The social', on the other hand, is presented as something less mechanistic and more fluid. At the extreme, social theory includes post-structuralist thinkers who refuse the idea of society as a concrete object of study at all (e.g. Laclau, 1990). Such thinkers prefer to invoke the social as a horizon of action and meaning which is open-ended and driven by human agency, not subject to any causal laws (see especially Chapter 4.) It is here that the significance of these perhaps over-elaborate distinctions to our understanding of *politics* becomes critical.

Marrying social theory and political analysis

In more traditional sociological theory, 'politics' tends to be elided with the state. It is understood as an analytically and empirically distinct level of a wider social system that also includes 'economy' and 'private sphere' (the family). On this view, politics is the means by which society takes strategic decisions about its direction (Parsons, 1951). In Chapter 1, we examine further how sociological theory has treated politics in this functionalist way. Such an approach can lend itself to a technocratic vision, characteristic of policy-oriented, reformist British sociology (Marshall, 1990). The state occupies a necessary, functional position, and levers can be pulled towards achieving political objectives in the wider society.

Social theory implies a different view of the society–politics relation. Here, society itself is politically formed. We can't point to some separate level or strata of 'politics': society is riddled with politics, of which a much broader conception is required. The state of course remains an important site of political activity – but so are all areas of social life. Consequently, there is less focus on the structural function of the state and elite actors, and more on social movements, culture and the everyday political activity enmeshed with the social (Nash, 2001, 2010). The theoretical backdrop to this broader conception of politics is a key feature of this book. It is also reflected in our case study examples such as the new political role of 'expert citizens' (Chapter 2), or the rise of 'political consumerism' and 'culture jamming' (Chapter 3). One would imagine that analysing political issues and practices would be integral to social theory as we have defined it. However, outside the subfield of political sociology and, arguably, increasingly within it, this is not the case. Social theorists can be remarkably silent on mainstream, 'bread and butter' political issues which concern political scientists, and which inform the media and public's view of what politics is. This is somewhat ironic, given the prominence of post-structuralist social theory which views *everything* as in some sense political. It is perhaps this 'discovery' of the ubiquity of politics that has led social theory – and especially cultural studies – to focus on more marginal political actors and practices; but this can be at the expense of bringing a social-theoretical understanding to mainstream politics. Consequently, some of the examples in this book are taken directly from the political mainstream: they include the way that modernising social democrats adapted the state in response to social change in the 1990s and 2000s (Chapter 2), and how the ideology and discourse of neoliberalism has become embedded among political elites and the wider society, from the 1970s to the present (Chapter 4).

Political scientists have had a similarly neglectful relationship with social theory. An obvious candidate for overlap is political theory. However, this is more concerned with conceptual clarification and normative questions, such as the relative merits of liberty and equality. Political science does focus on, for example, power, interests and institutions. However, it tends not to locate these in terms of overarching, substantive theories of social structure and social change, which could add a good deal to the analysis (Thornhill, 2009). For example, Colin Hay's (2002: 256) important overview of the discipline contains a concluding section which calls for 'An inclusive and post-disciplinary conception of political analysis'. However, this section makes no reference to society, the social or sociology, despite criticising a narrow conception of politics and warning against ignoring, 'the key exogenous factors, processes and mechanisms held (by others) to circumscribe the realm of feasible political agency' – which sounds rather like the domain of sociology (Hay, 2002: 257). However, there are clear exceptions in both political theory and political science. Post-structuralist political theory has a considerable following (Finlayson and Valentine, 2002). Like its counterpart in social theory, it draws on, for example, psychoanalysis or the discourse-theoretical approach of Michel Foucault. Feminist political analysis, too, is deeply enmeshed in questions of the social (Budgeon, 2011). Meanwhile, as the work of Hay himself and others demonstrates, political science has benefited from engaging with – and in many cases considerably advanced – the structure-agency focused sociological theory identified above (Bates, 2010; Hay, 2002: ch. 3; Hayward and Lukes, 2008).

Who's in and who's out?

Finally, it should be said that a book that addresses the potentially infinite field of 'politics and social theory' is necessarily selective. Here, the focus is to try and draw out the nature of the social–political relation in salient areas of political analysis. In terms of what is included and omitted, a number of things are worth noting. Regarding the key thinkers covered, I was struck by the ongoing relevance of the founding sociological 'fathers' of the nineteenth century: Karl Marx, Emile Durkheim and Max Weber. In particular, the implicit dialogue between Marx and Durkheim sets the scene for each chapter, and continues to illuminate our understanding of politics in its social context. Of later theorists, two loom particularly large: Antonio Gramsci and Michel Foucault. Gramsci is not typically considered part of the sociological canon, but his work is profoundly suited to grasping both what I have termed the inescapably social and irreducibly political. The fragmented and flexible character of his concepts also lends them to empirical application. With regard to Foucault, initially I assumed that, given his post-structuralism, he would if anything work against my attempt to sustain a conception of the social. However, like Gramsci, he has proven an exemplar of what it means to walk the 'tightrope' between the social and the political in theoretical and empirical analysis.

Of more recent theories, it is the sociological framework of reflexive modernisation and individualisation that provides a crucial reference point. This is unsurprising given that its key advocates – Ulrich Beck (e.g. 1997), Zygmunt Bauman (e.g. 1999) and Anthony Giddens (e.g. 1994, 1998) – have explicitly pursued the political implications of their social-theoretical accounts of modernity (Dawson, 2010). This has proven highly productive, even if they do not always give due weight to the irreducibly political aspects of social life. In a very different register, the post-structuralist, post-Marxist discourse theory of Ernesto Laclau and Chantal Mouffe is drawn on in detail in the final chapter, as an exemplar of what such a politico-centric form of analysis can offer, and for the way in which it challenges our understanding of the social. Finally, with regard to specific thinkers, this book is rare among contemporary analyses of social theory in that it does not incorporate the work of Pierre Bourdieu. However, as David Swartz (2013) has shown, the full political-sociological implications of Bourdieu's work are only now being explored.

In terms of key concepts, some readers may be struck by the absence of explicit debates on the nature of power. These animate political science, political theory and have been central to political sociology (Nash, 2010). Power is certainly present throughout this book – it is for example crucial to Marxist analysis, and a ubiquitous master concept in the work of Foucault and post-structuralists. However, at no point do I draw on the more formalised accounts of the 'power = a's ability to make b do x' variety, often inferred from Stephen Lukes' (1974) seminal essay. It is possible to imagine structuring this book around such categories, but we have found here that it is also possible to do without them.

Finally, with regard to the book's substantive focus and case studies, my own interests in the state, ideology and the nature of political identity certainly informed my selections. But the long shadow cast by the Global Financial Crisis of 2008 – and the subsequent economic, social and political turmoil amidst which the book was written – were also of course influential. In this context, classic themes such as the relationship of the state to capitalism (e.g. 'Washington and Wall Street') have acquired a new urgency (Chapter 2). Similarly, a less traditional topic, such as the politics of consumer identities (Chapter 3), is discussed with reference to how debates in this area have shifted in a climate of economic austerity. And, of course, analysis of the character, history and possible futures of neoliberalism (Chapter 4) now animate public as well as academic debate. At a time of such complexity and uncertainty, the case for better integrating social theory and political analysis is all the more pressing.

1

The Society–Politics Relation: On the Inescapably Social and the Irreducibly Political

Introduction

This chapter stakes out the significance of the society–politics relation, developing a framework for theorising both it and its empirical manifestations. This framework will be returned to throughout the book, but the intention is that it can also be taken away and applied more widely. At its heart are two key categories: what I label the 'inescapably social' and the 'irreducibly political' elements of any analysis of social and political phenomena. The inescapably social refers to the prior and ongoing social context that frames political activity. This includes historically produced social structures, institutions, norms and values, social relations and patterned practices. The irreducibly political denotes how those very social phenomena themselves are shot through with political activity: the play of interests, the role of decision-making and contestation over material and symbolic resources. These broad categories are useful in characterising how social theory orients itself to political analysis. In particular, the analytical distinction between the social and the political enables examination of their interplay, theoretically or empirically, identifying where one or the other might predominate and the implications of this.

In what follows, the importance and possible permutations of this relationship are analysed in more detail, with reference to dynamics in both sociology and political science. We point to the limits of socio-centric theories which marginalise the role of politics, and then the ways in which political agency has been reintroduced. By the same token, we go on to identify where politico-centric approaches neglect the social, and how this is itself reinstated. We then reaffirm the case for keeping both the social and political in view, before considering

11

the implications of this for critique, and a more politically engaged mode of enquiry. Throughout, the discussion revolves around themes which foreshadow our subsequent substantive chapters: political institutions (Chapter 2 on the state and governance); political agents (Chapter 3 on political identity and participation); and political ideas (Chapter 4 on culture, ideology and discourse).

The irreducible nature of politics

We begin by highlighting social theory's historical tendency to neglect or undermine political agency. We shall argue that, by contrast, it must acknowledge the irreducibly political elements of any analysis. This consists, for example, in contestation over the distribution of resources (such as through the tax and benefits system), or the struggle for a dominant interpretation of cultural symbols (such as a particular event, or media narrative of it). The form and outcomes of such political contestation – and indeed moments of agreement – are not predetermined and cannot be reduced to some overarching social theory or logic. Having reviewed such depoliticising tendencies in social theory, we then look at countervailing politico-centric perspectives; these challenge sociological reductionism and assert the primacy of politics. They can be found both within social theory itself and, more significantly, in political science approaches. Having considered the advantages of politico-centrism, we then conclude by looking at some of its own limitations. At the extreme – in a mirror image of sociological reductionism – it collapses the social into the political to the extent that everything becomes 'politics'.

The limits to a depoliticising social theory

It is no surprise that social theory has focused on social structures and processes above all others, including strictly political ones. That, after all, is what has marked sociology and social theorising out as areas of enquiry. However, certain tendencies within social theory have – either explicitly or implicitly – obliterated the space for politics altogether: social structures, processes and logic become everything, and politics is merely a secondary effect which can be 'read off' from them. More specifically, we shall see below how this has a marginalising effect on political institutions, political agents, political ideas and, consequently, the whole notion of politics itself. In illustrating this tendency, we shall focus primarily on two approaches that will appear in different guises throughout the book: structural Marxism and functionalism. These traditions are often presented as being *opposed* for precisely political reasons. Crudely, Marxism is associated with a transformative political project, while functionalism is portrayed as inherently conservative owing to its theoretical assumptions. However, what both perspectives share is a marginalisation of the role of politics in shaping social life.

Political institutions include formations such as the state and its various organs (see Chapter 2), the formal structure of political parties and other means of representation; and the organised political media (see Lowndes and Roberts, 2013). In social theory, what marks out the structuralist approach to institutions is that, rather than seeing them as historically specific, contested and open-ended, they are instead reduced to secondary effects of an overarching imperative or logic. This is starkest in the case of Marxism, where it is economic production – and the social relations that flow from it – which determines the character of all other institutions and practices. In functionalist social theory, there isn't the same determining centre to social life. However, what does come through is an organising social logic: the inherent societal need for order and stability, reflected in the structure of political institutions. Thus, the founder of functionalist sociology, Emile Durkheim, imagined the state as a 'social brain'. He also placed great faith in the role of professional associations and other civil society actors (Durkheim, 1950). This could be seen as an inversion of Marx, in that political organisations are given the leading role in managing society for the better, without being determined by economic relations. However, for Durkheim, the integrating role of the state was a matter of *functional necessity*, in the face of rapid social change which threatened cohesion. Societies had an underlying logic of social solidarity. The shape of political institutions would not be determined by struggle in which the outcomes were uncertain: there was an optimum balance of institutional arrangements which it was the job of the theorist to discover, and political actors to implement. This theme of functional necessity was taken to its extreme in the mid-twentieth-century structural functionalism of American sociologist Talcott Parsons (1951, 1969). For Parsons, political institutions were predestined to perform the core, universal function of 'goal attainment', that is, setting societal objectives. Identifying key sites of social integration remains a key feature of much contemporary social theory. This is most obvious in neo-functionalism (e.g. Alexander, 2006), but also appears in work that doesn't self-identify as functionalist, such as the analysis of the 'institutional dimensions of modernity' offered by Anthony Giddens (1990).

Beyond institutions, structuralist theory also depoliticises political agents – people – themselves. This occurs through presenting interests as being objectively formed, independently of the aspirations and actions of the agent him- or herself; through a tendency to see the agent as a 'dupe', prone to manipulation by powerful cultural and political forces; and, similarly, through seeing the agent as largely passive, that is, unable to shape social processes. The first of these, the question of the constitution of an interest, is particularly important to political action and is taken up in detail in Chapter 3. In socially reductionist theory, an individual's best interest is not something that she constructs for herself but, rather, is external to her. The classic version of this is Marxism, where political struggle is determined in advance by the social relations of production, and the inevitable historical showdown between owners and labourers.

Here, the task of individuals is to 'realise' their position within this schema. Consequently, the role of 'activism' is to make others aware of a grand plan which is already objectively true. At the extreme, this can manifest in the politics of quietism – or not engaging in active political struggle – as the objective historical forces will take care of themselves eventually. While this approach has had its heyday, its determinist assumptions remain evident in non-Marxist perspectives on the political agent. Thus, the modelling of how socio-economic conditions might be a predictor of voting and other types of political behaviour continues to dominate psephology, as well as media commentary. Even in rational choice theory, which supposedly gives sovereignty to the individual, the political actor is modelled on the assumption that she is able to calculate a fixed, optimum interest. This is predicated on a view of agents possessing a particular type of rationality, usually modelled on the maximisation of individual economic advantage. Indeed, this assumption is widely held by political parties and strategists, encapsulated in the famous slogan among Bill Clinton's presidential campaign team: 'it's the *economy*, stupid!' Today, this view persists in the so-called retail politics mode of campaigning. What these disparate approaches have in common is an understanding of an individual's interest being determined by structures – or against a criterion – which is external to them.

A second tendency – especially in critical theory – is to treat the individual as highly malleable, and subject to manipulation by (usually malign) forces beyond their control. In Marxism, this links to the question of objective interests: it was the distorting properties of ideologies such as the work ethic, or acceptance of inequalities as natural, which prevented workers from perceiving their true, exploited position. However, this was not seen as an obstacle to the revolutionary project, as the objective contradictions of capitalism would eventually lead to class consciousness. But as capitalism proved to be durable, and the early twentieth-century revolutionary impetus faded in Europe, the so-called Western Marxists theorised what was preventing the proletariat from rising. This included the Frankfurt School of critical theorists, who offered a pessimistic analysis of emerging mass consumption, communication and entertainment that was turning the masses into stupefied cultural dupes (Adorno and Horkheimer, 1944) of a 'one-dimensional' type (Marcuse, 1964).

Unsurprisingly, an agent who doesn't define his/her own interests, and is under the sway of various ideological pressures, suffers from the third tendency in reductionist accounts: powerlessness and/or passivity in the face of structural forces. At least in Marxism the agent would, ultimately, have to *become* an agent, take matters into their own (collective) hands and usher in socialism. A starker example of individual powerlessness is found in current social theory. The irony is that contemporary theorists tend to present late modern individuals as critical, informed and *reflexive* – processing, filtering and acting upon multiple, competing sources of information, and in so doing changing the conditions for future reflection and action (Giddens, 1984). However, the paradox is that these 'clever' individuals actually inhabit a world of rapid and constant change that they have no choice but to adapt to. The processes of detraditionalisation, globalisation and individualisation which characterise late modernity are themselves part of the *longue durée* of a modern project: this has been unfolding 'behind our backs' since the Enlightenment. The idea that history could be different – shaped by alternative political decisions or actions – is barely acknowledged. This is no better captured than in the title of Giddens' 1999 Reith Lectures: 'Runaway World' (Giddens, 2002a).

The third major area where structuralist social theory has marginalised politics is in the realm of ideas (which we develop in Chapter 4). Certainly for political theorists, and a good many political scientists, political ideas are crucial. Debates over what constitutes equality, liberty, justice, efficiency or the 'good life' more generally are integral to motivating political actors, provide the underpinning rationale for institutions and can reinforce existing practices or mobilise change. Within structuralist social theory there have been two contrasting ways in which ideas have been depoliticised. One version is in structural functionalism. Here, politics is understood in terms of its integrative function for the social system as a whole, and ideas in themselves are of secondary importance. Thus, Durkheim was not concerned about the specific content of political norms and values as such. Rather, it was the fact that they existed at all, and served an integrating purpose, which mattered. But the more notable relegation of ideas occurs in Marxism, and its account of ideology. For Marx, ideas were the reflection of – but not the basis for – practical human activity (for which read economic and class relations). In particular, Marx depicted ideologies such as liberalism as *distortions* of reality, which could only be grasped through Marxist political economy. Political ideas were always a reflection of economic relations, and the interests of the dominant class (Marx, 1846). The work of Louis Althusser (1971) was the ultimate embodiment of the structuralist, Marxist approach to ideology. Althusser identified a vast, ideological structure which, rather than being the outcome of political struggle, *determined* political identity in advance. It achieved this by 'interpellating' ('hailing' or 'calling') individuals to certain predefined subject positions. Thus, while Althusser's structural Marxism puts the power of ideologies at its centre, it is profoundly *depoliticising*: it presents us as dupes in the face of an overbearing ideological apparatus.

Politics fights back

In contrast to the socially reductionist approaches above, this book will argue that social theory needs to account for the *irreducibly political* element to social relations and institutions: a political moment that cannot be reduced to other explanatory factors such as the economy, or wider social norms. Social theory does a grand job of mapping the institutions, dominant ideas and key groups which frame political action. However, these need to be understood as sites of political contestation and struggle, and not as pregiven and immovable facts of nature. There are, of course, traditions of highlighting the primacy of agency (and therefore the possibility of politics) within social theory itself. But the main source of asserting the importance of the political is, unsurprisingly, political science, unencumbered by the need to foreground social structures. The case for the irreducibility of politics is presented here again in terms of conceptualising institutions, agents and ideas.

We saw above how a focus on the determining power of institutions may diminish the play of politics. The alternative, politico-centric view is to see institutions themselves as the outcome of ongoing political interactions. The classic statement of this position came, in fact, from one of the founders of sociological theory, Max Weber. For methodological individualists such as Weber (1922a), there was no mystery to institutions such as the state, which shouldn't be ascribed powers of their own (see Chapter 2). Rather, institutions are never anything more than the aggregate of the intentions and actions of the *individuals* who constitute them (Freund, 1972: 111–16). It is a short step from this assumption to a more politicised view of institutions. Rather than trying to identify in advance the (usually constraining) institutional properties that individuals must slot into, we can instead only understand something like 'the state' or 'party' by looking to the ongoing strategies and actions of concrete individuals and groups within them: in short to the *politics* of them.

A more radical critique of the institutional monolith comes from within post-structuralist discourse theory (see also Chapter 4). At the extreme, this refutes the objective existence of 'society' or 'structures' at all. Nevertheless, it recognises that an account of the apparent durability of institutions is required (e.g. the state, family or economy). The proposed solution is that 'institutions' should be seen as *sedimented politics* (Laclau, 1990; Torfing, 1999). All institutions and norms are the outcome of prior political struggles, and the insertion of a specific set of power relations: in the language we've used here they are irreducibly political. Over time, these relations may harden and become enduring, but this serves merely to obscure the fact that they are contingent: there was nothing inevitable about their formation; they could have turned out differently and still might in the future.

Perhaps the most important shift with regard to stressing the irreducibly political concerns the agent (see also Chapter 3). In socially reductionist approaches, we saw that the agent's sense of identity and interests could simply be inferred from social structures; that the agent was presented as vulnerable to manipulation; and that, as a result, they have little control over their wider operating environment. In stark contrast, we shall discuss here how more politicised accounts regard the agent as the author of their own identity, able to set and calculate their own interests; as possessing the capacity to resist domination; and (even if indirectly) as able to shape social and political outcomes.

The achievement of socially reductionist analysis was to overturn the figure of the asocial individual of classical political economy and liberal political theory: individual consciousness was instead presented as a product of social circumstances. However, this risked a view of a totally socially determined individual who was denied meaningful agency. In political theory and political science, we are more likely to find an agent with a fully formed set of interests, which they are conscious of and able to strategise from. We see this, for example, in a thought experiment such as John Rawls' (1999) *A Theory of Justice*. In trying to identify the most just form of society, Rawls posits the social arrangements individuals would choose from a hypothetical pre-social condition, with no knowledge of what their future social status would be (he concludes that they would choose an egalitarian society, as a kind of insurance). This type of calculating is explicit in rational choice theories, where the political scientist attempts to model the choices actors would make to further a supposedly coherent set of interests (see Eriksson, 2011). More widely, there is a well-established political science focus on the intentions and actions of various elite actors (e.g. cabinet ministers, senior civil servants). The underlying assumption is that individuals (or, at least, powerful individuals) certainly do matter and that their decisions can have much wider, 'structural' consequences.

Post-structuralist theory foregrounds the agent even more strongly, but paradoxically by doing away with the idea of a stable identity altogether. Individuals are not seen as possessing intrinsic essences – nor interests or identities as laid down by social structures – but as the intersection of a multiplicity of discourses that constitute a fluid identity. Of course, as we shall see in Chapter 3, there is a highly determinist version of this position (owing more to Althusser's idea of subject positions). But overwhelmingly the ethos, particularly in the study of political identity and action, is to stress the agent as actively constructing his/her identity from among the various discourses. Vitally, this is a never-ending process: there is no final closure where the identity and interests become permanent.

Politico-centric perspectives have a complex relationship to the role of political ideas, the third aspect of our analysis. One of the contributions of structuralist social theory was that it did offer a more politicised account of ideas than previous traditions. Originally, ideology was understood as the scientific study of ideas as entities that had properties in themselves. This form of theorising seeks inherent truth in concepts, and sees them as having independent causal powers upon the world (Kennedy, 1978). But theorists such as Marx, and later Karl Mannheim (1936), exposed the social and political context for ideas: they are bound up with the interests of social groups in a specific configuration of power relations (see Chapter 4). However, the extreme limit of socialised approaches was where the social production of ideas came to be seen as an automatic reflex of the social structure (e.g. in Althusser), taking away the sense of how they are politically contested. What post-structuralist understandings of discourse achieved was to maintain the insight that ideas are socially produced, while abandoning any necessary connection between ideas and particular agents or institutional arrangements. Instead, 'discourses' (the favoured term of post-structuralists) are contingent, free-floating formations of ideas and practices that are themselves *constitutive* of social and political life.

In contrast to social reductionism, this snapshot of politico-centric approaches conveys the importance of a space for politics. In opposition to a functionalist understanding of monolithic institutions and structures, politico-centric accounts see these as directly linked to the decisions and activities of agents. Such agents, rather than being the bearers and reproducers of a pre-ordained social and political structure, are able to construct their own identities, appraise what constitutes their own best interests and act accordingly. And rather than ideas being the mechanical expression of particular groups, or having inherent, transhistorical properties, they are the complex and contingent outcomes of political struggle. This is what we mean by the irreducibly political moment of social life. No matter how influential we believe structures to be – either macro entities, such as the economy or a dominant ideology, or more immediate ones, such as the rules of a political party – they must be understood at some level as the outcome of political interactions, and therefore contestable. This dynamism is analytically necessary in that it prevents a mechanical or static view of social and political life. But it is also politically significant: things could have been otherwise, and as such there is the ever-present possibility of political decisions and actions leading to *alternatives*. This normative dimension is explored at the end of the chapter. However, in the next section we argue that while it is essential to recognise the irreducibly political, we must not collapse everything into the political domain: the pendulum needs to also swing back towards the social and its effects.

The inescapable fact of the social

Extreme politico-centric approaches

Politico-centric approaches can go too far and obliterate the social (Thornhill, 2009). However important politics is, we shall argue throughout this book for recognition of the inescapably social element that has to be factored into any political analysis. The overly politicised approach generates two different extremes: the first, ironically, restricts our sense of what politics is, while the second expands our conception of the political to the exclusion of all else.

The first, restrictive approach arises paradoxically from an excessive concern with the immediacy of political action and agents. It is to be found in political science studies of elite actors, of the role of the political media and of the machinery of government and legislative process. By going straight to what, at a surface level, appears as the very heart of political power and action and staying there, it neglects the deeper social, cultural and economic forces that frame and influence 'high politics'. A common populist political tactic, used by parties or movements such as the

UK Independence Party (UKIP), or the Tea Party in the US, is to accuse the 'metro-politan elite' of being obsessed with the machinations of the 'Westminster Village' or the 'Washington Beltway'; this is counterposed to the wider, everyday struggles of 'real people'. To an extent, our criticism of a narrow focus on high politics is the analytical equivalent of this political tactic. Political scientists can get too hung up on the interactions of elites, and at worst this starts to resemble either descriptive political journalism (important though that is), or increasingly esoteric attempts to abstract and model 'rational' behaviour and processes.

By contrast, the second extreme version of politico-centrism expands the political, so that *everything* is seen as politically constituted. Interestingly, this has its lineage in post-structuralist social theory rather than political theory or political science. Social life is viewed as a field of discourses, with no necessary connection to any underlying principle or set of structures (Howarth, 2000; Torfing, 1999). Consequently, individual identity and political subjectivity are similarly free-floating, as there are no fixed structures to anchor identities or generate interests. The production and outcome of discourses are contingent, open-ended and always contestable. As such, everything is, in the language of post-structuralists, 'always already' political. What we imagine to be fixed social structures or social interests are simply sedimented forms of discourse, the political origin of which has been concealed over time (Laclau, 1990). The art of deconstruction is to challenge these taken-for-granted sedimented practices, reveal that they are the contingent outcome of power struggles and show that they could be different. Politics is thus a struggle over *meaning*, which defines what comes to be taken for granted with regard to 'institutions', 'identities' and 'values'. Vitally, this struggle takes place at all levels of social life, not just in an artificially designated 'political sphere'. Indeed, defining the boundaries of 'social life', 'polity' or 'economy' is itself a key political struggle.

Bringing the social back in

While recognising that the irreducibly political avoids sociological reduction-ism and introduces political dynamics, we should avoid the pitfalls of extreme politico-centrism. Specifically, we should maintain a sense of what we shall refer to as the inescapably social: something approximating to 'society' exists as the terrain upon which political activity takes place (i.e. it enables it) and, indeed, sometimes fails to take place (i.e. it constrains it). This can again be illustrated with reference to our themes of institutions, agents and ideas.

With regard to institutions, however much politico-centrism privileges the creativity of politics, we cannot avoid the brute fact of recursive social structures and processes which limit (as well as enable) what is politically possible. Such structures do not have to be equated with the economy as they so often have been – although there can be no doubting the central significance of economic factors – and they can also include traditions, values, roles, rules and ideas. These entities are more than the sum of individual intentions, and are prior to individual agents and acts of politics. In short, we inherit a situation which we have to deal with (Archer, 1995). Arguing over whether these structural arrangements were originally, at some point in the past, 'politically instantiated' is a distraction from this basic fact. More specific than macro structures such as patterned inequality, for example, are institutions such as the state or political parties. These entail roles and rules which are prior to the individual. More insidiously, they involve embedded norms and taken-for-granted ways of acting – culture – which also assumes structural properties (see Lowndes and Roberts, 2013). We can develop the effects of this in terms of our categories of agency and ideas.

In political analysis, it is the treatment of agency which, ironically, provides the most visible example of the need for a theory of structures. We saw that in politico-centric views, the agent is variously presented as a rational calculator, or as constructing identities in the 'supermarket' of the many discourses and subject positions on offer. The advantage of these approaches is to reinstate an active agent, capable of making productive choices, rather than the cultural dupe of reductionist theories. However, political identity construction does not occur in a vacuum: it is both constrained and enabled by the presence of structures that are more than simply the sum of individual choices. Most fundamentally, there is no escaping the common-sense fact that individual agents are born into a concrete situation. Their opportunities and worldviews are shaped by material circumstances and dominant norms. Combined, these material and cultural factors will impact upon not just the political subject positions available to individuals but, vitally, the content of the choices they exercise with regard to them (Bourdieu, 1990). In terms of political agency throughout the life course, early structural conditioning factors will continue to play a role, and be joined by the effects of others such as the institutional roles and rules one encounters. The degree of political agency an individual can exercise is shaped by their location within a distribution of positions, and these are determined by a structure beyond individual control. Thus, certain individuals have a degree of influence conferred upon them by a structure. This enables them to take decisions which may in turn have structural effects (e.g. the capacity of a president to go to war). Others within institutional structures, however, will have their agency restricted by the nature of their role and by rules (e.g. the soldiers ultimately subject to executive orders) (see Elder-Vass, 2010; Mouzelis, 1991).

Finally, turning again to ideas, we saw that in post-structuralist discourse theory, ideas have no inherent properties and are not anchored in any way. Instead, discourses are seen as (relatively) free-floating. Specific political tropes such as 'liberty' or 'equality' are empty of content: politics consists in the struggle to co-opt them to particular ends at particular times. While few would disagree with the premise that political values do not have inherent, transhistorical properties, the claim that 'anything goes' is more problematic. Analytical political theorists would rightly point to the demands of reasonableness, coherence and logical consistency. But in addition, two empirical issues with regard to the status of ideas indicate the need for a theory of social structures. The first is the relationship between ideas and interests. We do not need to suggest that social structures inevitably lead to individuals holding particular ideas, or some ideas becoming dominant. However, the recursive affinity between certain ideas or values, and specific interests or sets of institutional arrangements, suggests we cannot simply 'bracket out' the latter. Clearly, some ideas are linked to and systematically serve certain interests: it is not just coincidence that individuals occupying x structural location tend to hold y views *en masse*. For example, those who can be shown to benefit most from the operation of free markets and minimal state regulation typically subscribe to an ideology and policies which legitimate them.

We also need a theory of social structure with regard to understanding the plausibility and applicability of ideas. It is fine to talk of a proliferation of discourses about social and political life – but for a discourse to become politically effective, it needs to resonate with lived experiences (Hall, 1983; Leggett, 2013). The fact of social structures and institutions does not determine in advance the form or content of ideas or discourses. However, they do provide what we might call the horizon of possibility for which ideas will become available, and whether they are likely to take root. For example, radical critics of liberal democratic political culture argue that 'democratic debate' typically occurs on a playing field that has had its boundaries set in advance: dominant interests and assumptions about what is acceptable rule out certain arguments before they ever reach the table. This is approximate to what Stephen Lukes (1974) characterises as the agenda-setting, 'second face' of power. Looming over all of these issues is the possibility that *ideas themselves can constitute structures*. Narrower politico-centric approaches see political actors going about their business, calculating and strategising independently of dominant ideas, or even of possible 'group-think'. Similarly, post-structuralist, fully politico-centric perspectives imagine the entire social field as consisting of a number of free-floating and highly fluid discourses. By contrast, we are arguing here for recognition of the structural properties of ideas. This is to say that some assumptions and ideas become accepted as 'common sense': they endure over time, and they frame the conditions of action and exist prior to and shape individual actions – they have *structural* properties. Again, this is similar to what Lukes (1974) captures, this time with his 'third face' of power. At the extreme, this involves Marxist theories of 'false consciousness'. But such determinism is not necessary to simply appreciate the role of ideational structures upon individual worldviews.

The empirical interplay between the social and the political

We have outlined approaches which present a determining idea of the social – of which politics is simply another subset – and those which invert this by arguing that all institutions, ideas and subjectivities – indeed the social itself

– are politically constituted. The confrontation between these extreme perspectives revealed the strengths and weaknesses of each. The argument of this
book is that analysis of social and political phenomena needs to hold onto an
understanding of *both* these sociologically and politically informed traditions.
What is clear from our overview is that even the most sociologically determinist accounts at some point have to allow for the open-ended role of political
activity in social life. By the same token, we have seen that political activity
needs to be understood in terms of how it is enabled and/or constrained by
its social context. It is thus necessary to keep both the social and the political
in view, so that we can then examine the *interplay* between them in specific
empirical instances. So, as the substantive chapters of the book unfold and
we explore empirical case studies, we shall see that there may be moments
where strictly political actors, institutions or ideas play a leading role in determining the shape of the social. Conversely, there will also be situations when
political activity is secondary to much wider social forces. For now, let us take
some brief, general examples to illustrate more political or sociological types
of explanations.

The classic example of a 'purely' political moment delivering rapid social
change is revolution. Here we might consider how, notwithstanding long-
term structural conditions, a political movement and appeal for change
arises around particular agents and seems to develop a momentum of its
own. An example is the so-called domino effect of the rapid collapse of
Soviet and Eastern European state socialism after 80 years of relative stability. However, while there is a tendency to equate political action with such
moments of rapid transformation, political actors and projects can also
effect deep social change over a long period. In the UK, Thatcherism has
been described as just such a project: the deliberate, long-term remould-
ing of the state, polity, society and economy along neoliberal lines (see
Chapter 4). In everyday language, the deep social effects of this political
project are captured by an expression such as 'Thatcher's children': this
describes whole generations inculcated with the neoliberal ethos of possessive individualism. If we switch the lens to sociological explanations, in
which politics is secondary to wider social forces, we unsurprisingly tend to
find accounts of deep processes. In this vein, we might consider long periods of stability in the post-war industrialised societies. High employment,
steady economic growth and a more homogeneous social structure produced considerable agreement over how such societies should be governed –
a period of stability and the so-called post-war consensus (Kavanagh and
Morris, 1994). By contrast, determinist globalisation theories point to an
inevitable economic and/or cultural logic of globalisation which undermines the nation state: an example of rapid social change with dramatic
political effects (Albrow, 1996; Ohmae, 1995).

Maintaining both the social and the political as distinct analytical moments
enables the full range of explanations above. However, clearly, in each of those

generalisations, *both* the social and the political are in fact present. Thus, it is the complex interplay between social and political elements that will form the detail of any specific case: debates over interpretation will reflect how far one seeks to 'bend the stick' of analysis in either direction. So to take the same set of examples, we noted that the 'domino' collapse of Eastern European state socialism was an exemplar of where, in a revolutionary situation, political dynamics can take on a life of their own. However, this is clearly a limited view. A more sociological account would identify the structural preconditions of the calls for reform that generated such a critical mass. One such explanation is the longer-term development of an educated, critical and aspirational middle class. Ironically, this was a result of the relative success of the education systems in the state socialist countries that were now being challenged. At the same time, citizens' aspirations were fuelled by the impossibility of insulating a country from global cultural images, facilitated by the communications revolution (Giddens, 1994). Or, to take our example of Thatcherism in the UK, while most analysts would grant a degree of coherence and conscious ideological intent to the Thatcher project, they would also look to sociological factors to understand why it was able to be implemented in that particular historical period. These included the emergence of a less collectivised, more aspirational working class following the decline of traditional manufacturing industry. This put pressure on the statist social democracy of the Labour Party and resonated with the possessive individualism of Thatcherism (see Chapter 4).

By the same token, it is clear that our examples of sociological perspectives on historical change need to account for its political dimensions. Thus, political analysts have challenged the uncritical idea of a blanket 'post-war consensus', derived from relatively homogeneous and stable social conditions. Instead, they have pointed to the distinctive, opposing political worldviews among elites who still clashed in the post-war period (Kerr, 2001). Others have adopted a more politicised account by suggesting that any 'consensus' simply represented a balance of power – or stalemate – in the political relations between social classes (Devine, 2000). Similarly, those sceptical of characterising contemporary globalisation as an unstoppable 'juggernaut' claim that it is a highly political project: it is enacted by specific elite actors, seeking to free up global markets (Harvey, 2005; Sklair, 2001).

These broad examples illustrate the need to maintain an analytical distinction between the social and the political. At the same time, neither a 'purely' political or sociological account is likely to suffice, as neither can ever be entirely eliminated. Consequently, determining how far to lean towards the social or political is central to deploying social theory in political analysis. This means, in any given example, identifying where strictly political activity may be secondary to wider social forces, or where political action takes a leading role. By maintaining this dual focus, we are unlikely to be led to a determinist position in which the political is wholly the outcome of the social, or vice versa. A further argument is that it is impossible to specify in advance the character of the relationship between the social or political. There is no theoretical, *a priori* way of claiming that one or the other aspect will predominate: substantive empirical cases need to be taken on their own merits. The objective is to keep both the social and the political in view, and then bring them to bear upon specific examples. This fits with the wider aim of this book – and the series of which it is a part – to understand the implications of adopting certain social-theoretical positions in empirical cases.

Critique, social theory and political analysis

> Q. *'How many sociologists does it take to change a lightbulb?'*
> A. *'It's not the lightbulb that needs changing; it's the system!'*

Any book considering the study of political phenomena cannot avoid the issue of political values and commitments in the research process. This is the case even if such concerns are ultimately dismissed, and it is claimed that an objective approach is possible. The values issue is especially acute in dealing with the relationship between politics and social theory, where critical social theory contemplates what a *desirable* society would look like. The assumption of this book is that an entirely neutral or value-free social science is impossible but also that, in thinking about the relationship between politics and social theory, it is in any case undesirable: social theory should strive to be critically engaged. This critical mindset need not be allied to any specific or value-based agenda (although it can be). But deploying what C. Wright Mills (1959) famously identified as the 'sociological imagination' involves interrogating social norms and practices, and suggesting immanent or possible alternatives (Levitas, 2010). Such a critical approach is also the best route to a publicly engaged social theory. Public actors and private citizens adopt prescriptive positions as a matter of routine: for social theorists to do so is simply to participate in that ongoing dialogue about what makes the good society (Burawoy, 2005). An important caveat is that this is not intended to open the door to social theory as a relativistic free-for-all, in which everyone is expected to do battle, and attempts at objectivity are scorned. On the contrary, both theory and empirical research can be more or less systematic and rigorous, some accounts more accurate, and some arguments more insightful. But what we broadly come to see as objective, accurate or compelling is *itself part* of the politics of doing social science and social theory. To recognise this is what sociologists understand as reflexivity about the research process, and one's place within it.

Sociology and political science have different traditions – and stereotypical labels – with regard to their attitude to critique and advocacy. There is no doubt that sociology – and social theory in particular – is historically perceived to be more politically 'radical' than political science. However, the reality is of course more complex. For some on the political left, sociology became too (small c) conservative (Burawoy, 2005; Gouldner, 1973). On this view, the desire to present objective empirical research to policymakers lends itself to a technocratic managerialism, embodied in the post-war welfare state or, more recently, in public audit and target-setting, all of which rely on sociological knowledge. Those seeking a more transformative politics were thus often drawn to *social* (as opposed to the more conventional sociological) theory, with its influences from Marxism, continental philosophy and some forms of psychoanalysis. These influences also opened up cultural studies as a discipline which has self-consciously positioned itself against the perceived conceptual, methodological and political conservatism of mainstream sociology (McLennan, 2006). Equally, political science has its politically radical currents: Marxist and feminist political science, for example, as well as an increasing engagement with critical social theory. And, of course, it is political theory which is most likely to be found offering systematic advocacy for a certain normative position (e.g. equality or liberty).

The reasons for the political stereotypes ascribed to the disciplines of sociology and politics go back a long way, are complex and reflect longstanding patterns of working, institutional development, personnel and prejudice. No doubt there are grains of truth in the caricatures. However, the assumption of this book is that no field of enquiry – be it sociology, social theory, political science or political theory – has any *inherent* tendencies towards a more or less critical attitude, or this or that political persuasion. Nevertheless, we can here outline the possible normative political implications of extreme social reductionism, and then politico-centrism.

Sociological reductionism and depoliticisation

Socially reductionist approaches see political action as determined by, or at least secondary to, macro social structures and processes. As we have seen, one such tendency is to be found within Marxism: ironically, this can lead to depoliticisation, as the structural contradictions of capitalism are supposed to take care of themselves, rendering 'politics' superfluous. But Marxism is not the only culprit. Contemporary social theories of late modernity can also relegate politics in the face of overarching world-historical social forces. The most striking examples are theories of economic and cultural globalisation we have referred to throughout. In such work – which often criticises Marxist determinism – global capital and consumer markets, global brands, the decline of manufacturing, the rise of flexible working and an increasingly individualised public are treated as inevitable and overpowering features of late modernity. This neglects the political constitution – along largely neoliberal lines – of some of these apparently autonomous late modern processes. By this we mean that the role of conscious political decisions in apparently 'self-propelling' social processes – perhaps informed by ideological agendas – needs to be accounted for (Benton, 1999; Rustin, 1989).

The depoliticising effect of this is apparent in subsequent claims about the declining capacity of nation states to manage core parts of their economic and social policies. Instead, the best they can apparently do is to create conditions favourable for competition in the global market and knowledge economy. Needless to say, governments have found that this analysis provides useful justification for their own *laissez-faire* economic and social policies. What accounts of a 'runaway' late modernity tend to shut down, then, are critical debates about alternatives. These could involve, for example, state intervention in developing greener, more equal forms of economy and society. Thus, just as for Marxists communism represents the end of history, so in contemporary social theory there is the depoliticising implication that a globalised, individualised and cosmopolitan world was always the destiny of modernity.

Politico-centrism, self-interest and relativism

We have argued throughout this chapter that the corrective to sociological reductionism is an injection of politics: outcomes are not predetermined but contested and always 'up for grabs'. One might think that approaches which privilege political agency are best placed to develop a critical perspective and political programme. However, politico-centrism itself needs to be supplemented by an account of social context in order to have *critical* purchase, and provide a basis for any political strategy. Here, we shall point to limitations that emerge from different strands of politico-centric approaches in this respect: assumptions about the nature of individual action and self-interest; a tendency towards relativism which weakens critical capacity; and, in both of those instances, a lack of an account of the social basis for political programmes.

There is a long tradition of characterising the political realm in terms of the ceaseless struggle for power among self-interested individuals. This appeared in Machiavelli's (1532) ruminations on the dark arts of political leadership in renaissance Florence. It was also evident in Thomas Hobbes' (1651) work during the English Civil War, when he concluded that man's (sic) 'natural' state was a 'war of all against all', in which life was to be 'nasty, brutish and short'. In the twentieth century – inspired by Max Weber – Joseph Schumpeter's (1943) political sociology pointed to the inevitability of rule by competing elites. Later, the elaborate modelling of rational-choice approaches attempted to map the strategies of calculating political actors. More recently, there are interesting echoes of Machiavelli and Hobbes in how post-structuralist political theory has foregrounded power struggles: politics consists in decisions about, for example, inclusion and exclusion, which are always acts of power and designate 'friends and enemies' (Mouffe, 2005).

Such images of the political help to capture its dynamism and fluidity, and reinforce the message that, if nothing else, politics is about power and contestation. However, this presents limits in terms of developing a critical perspective and political strategy. Firstly, such approaches have inbuilt assumptions about what politics consists in: essentially the machinations of (typically) elite actors. This militates against a view of politics as being concerned with the transformation of wider systems; for example, challenging structural inequalities, or bringing about changes in social attitudes and practices. This is reinforced by the way actors in politico-centric approaches appear motivated by little more than ambition and self-interest, in a ceaseless power struggle. No doubt this can coincide with – and arguably on occasion even enhance – a transformative political project. However, this is a view of politics as consisting in the schemes of power-hungry individuals. It implicitly endorses individual or small group action over the collective activity that wider social and political transformation might require.

Politico-centrism also contains an implicit relativism, which poses further problems for the idea of critique and transformation. In the hard realpolitik tradition that comes down from Machiavelli, the content of political ideas and visions of the good society is secondary to their primary function of achieving and maintaining power. Arguments over the desirability of equality or liberty, or one form of society over another, are simply part of the politician's repertoire in the constant battle they are engaged in. The same would be true of appeals to evidence (such as social statistics) about 'what works' in terms of policy. Whether the data accurately reflects social or economic reality is irrelevant: it is a means to the end of achieving the upper hand in a ceaseless political game. This relativism is more directly evident in post-structuralist political analysis. Here, the aim is to deconstruct all claims to universal values, or the invocation of evidence about social reality, as an effect of the operation of power. Values such as 'equality' or 'freedom' – which in their differing ways are key resources for critique – are presented as merely 'signifiers'. These are devoid of content in themselves but provide the symbolic raw material which political actors struggle over in their power game (Laclau, 1994). A notorious illustration of how such assumptions can manifest in political practice was a remark later attributed to President George W. Bush's Senior Advisor, Karl Rove. Rove denigrated critics in 'the reality-based community' who 'believe that solutions emerge from your judicious study of discernible reality', and thus fail to grasp how the powerful 'create our own reality' (Suskind, 2004).

Thus, while we might assume that politico-centrism provides the necessary corrective to an uncritical sociological reductionism, it too can lend itself towards perpetuating the status quo. The image of politics as a serpent's nest of the power-hungry encourages cynicism or apathy. This is instead of fostering a more engaged and critical attitude – one that draws on values and evidence in assembling a critique of the present, and asking what might be done to transform or transcend it.

The space for critical theory

In this section, we have stressed the inevitability and desirability of a normative, critical dimension to social and political analysis. We saw that sociology
and political science carry their own disciplinary baggage in terms of percep-
tions of their political character. Although neither can be judged as inherently
'progressive' or 'conservative', we have discerned some broad political implications of either socially reductionist or politico-centric modes of analysis: these
logically follow from the general critique of these two extremes outlined earlier. Thus, despite sociology's leftist political reputation, its more reductionist
forms can be depoliticising, disabling of critique and fatalistic towards the
status quo – or external laws of social development. Politico-centrism brings a
revitalising dynamism to sociological approaches, foregrounding power, contestation and open-endedness. This is vital for the development of a critical
analysis and mindset, the precondition of which is that things could always be
different. However, politico-centrism can carry particular assumptions about
self-interest, power and agency. These may result in a narrow focus on elite
politics and its apparatus, at the expense of collective possibilities for transforming social, economic and cultural structures. It can also imply a relativism which marginalises the role of values and evidence in developing political
critique and action.

It is no surprise that we shall conclude this section – and the chapter
– by arguing for a synthesis of sociological and political traditions of critique, drawing on their strengths while circumventing their weaknesses.
This would avoid the fatalism of reductionist social theory, by maintaining
a space for political agency to challenge the status quo. However, in so
doing it must also avoid extreme, Machiavellian realpolitik. Political analysis needs to maintain the broader conception of politics that the sociological imagination can offer, as well as a sense of possibilities for collective
action. And in order to be effective, even the most scheming practitioners
of the political dark arts need to ground their strategies in a hard-headed
analysis of prevailing social, economic and cultural conditions. A critical
theory should thus embody a productive synthesis between the sociological and political imaginations. As Antonio Gramsci (1971: 172) – a political leader and theorist – observed:

> The active politician is a creator, an initiator; but he neither creates from
> nothing nor does he move in the turbid void of his own desires and dreams.
> He bases himself on effective reality...a relation of forces in continuous
> motion [...]

However, as has been stressed throughout this chapter, the final merits of
either a socio- or politico-centric approach – or ideal combination between

them – cannot be decided in advance: they need to be explored through analysis of substantive political areas. To this end, each chapter that follows analyses the key social-theoretical perspectives on specific political topics – the state, identity/participation and ideology – and considers empirical case studies to illustrate their applicability. In each chapter, both the theory and empirical accounts are evaluated using our categories of the inescapably social and irreducibly political.

2

Politics From Above: The State and Governance

Introduction

This chapter begins our examination of social theory and substantive areas of politics. It considers the role of the state: the main site of political analysis 'from above'. The state has been central to political science and political sociology, understood through a core of three broad classic perspectives. The most closely related of these are those which focus on the role of elites in controlling the state (Evans, 2006; Parry, 1969), and a Marxist tradition which, while also interested in elites, understands the state in the context of wider capitalist social and economic relations (Hay, 2006; Jessop, 2004). The third, pluralist tradition, sees the state as a relatively neutral body or arena: this reflects and can resolve competing social interests, with no outright capture by any particular group (Smith, 2006). The Marxist perspective has the most overlap with traditions in social theory, and will be taken up in more detail here. However, the other classic political science approaches also contain a social referent, supporting the argument made in Chapter 1 concerning the inescapably social in political analysis. Thus, pluralist theory is predicated on the fact of social complexity and diversity: it is this which necessitates a pluralist polity. And even elite theory, which foregrounds the qualities and strategies of power-seeking agents, acknowledges the socialisation of elites themselves, as well as the social mechanisms through which they are able to exercise control (Bellamy, 2004).

While recognising the importance of these elite and pluralist traditions, the task of this chapter is to detail perspectives which explicitly locate the state and government in their wider social context. The first part outlines some major social-theoretical traditions in this respect. It begins with the canonical work of Max Weber. However, Weber will here be presented as, ultimately, a leading influence upon politico-centric perspectives. We shall argue, perhaps controversially, that while Weber provided important resources towards a more sociological account, we need to look to others among the classics for a more fully socialised conception of the modern state. We find this firstly in the functionalist perspective originating with Emile Durkheim. For Durkheim, the task of both social theory and political practice was to promote an underlying unity between the institutions of the state and wider society. We then consider the strongly contrasting Marxist tradition, which understands the state as a product of inherently antagonistic capitalist social relations. While Marx himself did not offer a systematic account of the state, debates among subsequent Marxists have generated a substantial body of state theory. The key contribution of another – somewhat renegade – Marxist thinker, Antonio Gramsci, is then considered. Gramsci's work is a possible model of how to give due weight to the high politics of the state, but in terms of its complex relationship to not only the economy but also culture and civil society. Going beyond Gramsci, the post-structuralist account of state power – exemplified by Michel Foucault – collapses the state–society distinction altogether. We see how for Foucault – echoing much of our Weberian starting point – *all* social relations are relations of power, and society itself is a permanent object of government.

The second part of the chapter explores the relationship between more recent social theories of the state and contemporary governance and politics. It outlines the political implications of key social theories of late or reflexive modernity, developed since the early 1990s. Many of the assumptions of this macro social theory underpinned a significant shift in the political science and public policy literature – from 'government' to 'governance'. Two case studies, embodying different aspects of this shift, are then presented. These exemplify the different ways in which social theory interfaces with the empirical political world, as discussed in the Introduction. There we noted how social theory can describe empirical political phenomena, critique it or even be constitutive of it. Our first case study is the attempt to reimagine the role of the state in the face of globalisation. This was embodied in the Third Way political programme inspired by Bill Clinton's New Democrats in the US, and adopted by modernising centre-left parties around the globe in the 1990s and 2000s. The most notable of these was Tony Blair's New Labour Party in Britain. New Labour provided a perhaps unique example of the extent to which social theory can be constitutive of political practice: the party explicitly adopted the social-theoretical analysis of British sociologist Anthony Giddens. The second case study draws on work from Scandinavia. It details new types of political subjectivity and relationship between 'governors' and 'governed'. In this instance, the same social theories concerning the transformations of late modernity (such as individualisation) are drawn on. However, this time the theory provides the context for academics to identify and explain new types of political actor, rather than inform political practice.

We assess these recent literatures and case studies by returning to the critical insights of the theoretical traditions considered in the first part of the chapter. In so doing, we shall be illustrating the remaining sense of social theory's interface with politics: as offering different standpoints for critique. We shall see how, although written decades prior to theories of reflexive modernity and allied concepts, the work of Marx, Durkheim, Gramsci and Foucault enables a critical appraisal of contemporary empirical examples of political practice. Finally, we conclude by considering what social theories of the state and governance tell us about the wider social-political relation we mapped in Chapter 1, and our categories of the irreducibly political and inescapably social.

Social theory, state and civil society

Weber, state-centrism and violence

Max Weber is often the first port of call for those defining the state in both sociology and political science (Hay and Lister, 2006: 7–9). He should thus be an obvious starting point for our purposes. However, when the key aspects of Weber's analysis are distilled, the extent to which they demonstrate the value of *social* theory to understanding the changing modern state is, arguably, surprisingly limited. Here, we shall instead use Weber as an exemplar of a top-down view of the importance of the state as an institution – or a set of practices – in itself. We will see how Weber certainly gestures towards more sociological aspects of the modern state, but argue that he does not ultimately deliver on them.

In his famous lecture, 'Politics as a vocation', Weber (1918a: 78) offers a stark and brutal definition of the nature of the state as, 'a human community that (successfully) claims the *monopoly of the legitimate use of physical force* within a given territory'. He notes that in modern society, 'the relation between the state and violence is an especially intimate one', and that, '[t]he state is considered the sole source of the 'right' to use violence'. The emphasis on the centrality of both violence and the defence of territorial integrity provides a striking contrast to, for example, Durkheim's understanding of the state as primarily a moral entity, or Marx's concern with the reproduction of capitalist relations (although the latter, of course, may involve violence). However, it is Weber's views on what the state consists of, how we should analyse it, and what this implies about politics, that sets him most strikingly at odds with more socio-centric approaches. Weber was a methodological individualist. He was philosophically committed to the idea that social life had to be understood via the actions and intentions of individuals, not some other strata (e.g. institutions, or social structures) that have properties of their own (Freund, 1972: 111–16). This is clear in the language he uses above of the state as a 'human community', i.e. of concrete individuals and their actions. Given this ontology of the state, Weber (1918a: 77–8) is clear that it cannot be understood with reference to its supposed *ends*, or functions. Rather, for Weber the state can only be analysed in terms of its specific means (violence). Ultimately, for Weber, there is no mystery to the state: it amounts to individuals struggling for power and prestige among themselves, and wielding that power over others: 'a relation of men dominating men' (1918a: 78; see also Freund, 1972: 113–14).

This outline indicates why Weber is the key reference point for politico-centric accounts of the state, to be found in political science in general, and elite theories in particular. As Kate Nash (2010: 9) suggests, '[t]he autonomy of the political at the level of the state is central to Weber's political sociology'. Weber's insistence on 'the autonomy of the political' rather begs the question posed at the outset: what is sociological about Weber's political sociology? However, we also indicated that Weber did at least gesture towards the social context of the state. Here we shall note two ways he did this: his focus on the nature of domination and consent, and his account of the role of bureaucracy and rationalisation.

Having described the state as 'a relation of men dominating men', Weber sought to conceptualise the nature of that domination in some detail. He argued that, in contrast to the simple, negative exercise of power 'over', domination involves the genuine, sustained *consent* of those who are being dominated. The securing of such consent amounts, for Weber, to legitimate authority (Parkin, 2002: 74–5). By opening out the account of the state towards the citizenry in this way, the state–society relation is being explored. Weber next constructs three ideal-types of the forms legitimation can take. 'Traditional' authority is the invocation of pre-existing values, practices and hierarchies: 'we've always done it this way' (e.g. monarchical rule). 'Charismatic' authority relies on citizens being persuaded that a leader has exceptional qualities – typically in moments of crisis – and that following them will be transformative (e.g. subsequent to Weber's work, Hitler) (see Weber, 1922b). 'Legal-rational' authority is the invocation of codified laws, rules and regulations (e.g. the rule of law in liberal democracies). Weber does not see any historical sequence to these ideal-types: they can be present at different times in different regimes, and co-exist within a single regime. However, in modern societies the legal-rational type predominates (Freund, 1972: 229–34; Giddens, 1971: 156–63).

The highlighting of legal-rational authority reflects the second main area that adds a more sociological dimension to Weber's account: the inevitable bureaucratisation of politics. In his broader socio-historical work, Weber describes the long-term rationalisation of social life. Where this interfaces with his account of the state is in his view that, in increasingly complex and differentiated modern societies, only bureaucratic forms of administration can provide predictability, stability and therefore efficiency. Weber did not use 'bureaucracy' in the derogatory sense of today's popular parlance. Rather, he was the first theorist to systematically detail the characteristics of modern bureaucracies: including in the political sphere (Weber, 1922c). Such was the centrality that Weber gave to the rise of bureaucracy, that he is characterised as supplanting Marx's concern with control of the means of production, with a focus instead on the control of the means of administration. As Giddens (1972: 35) notes, Weber inverts Marx as:

Rather than generalising from the economic to the political, Weber general-
ises from the political to the economic: bureaucratic specialisation of tasks
(which is, first and foremost, the characteristic of the legal-rational state) is
treated as the most integral feature of capitalism.

Weber's focus on the means of legitimation/consent, and the encroachment of
bureaucracy in the context of wider societal rationalisation, thus offers a more
recognisably sociological aspect to his account. However, some important caveats
remain: these draw us back towards the top-down state, consisting of the machinations of elite individuals. Frank Parkin (2002: 76–80) makes three important
and interrelated critical observations. First, having identified a series of ideal-
types, Weber shows little interest in understanding the *mechanisms* of securing
the consent of citizens. Second, Weber does not analyse what domination might
look like from the perspective of the dominated: a curious oversight, given his
commitment to the 'interpretive understanding' of social life. Third, reflecting
Weber's focus on action and what state actors do, consent and legitimate authority are treated uncritically. The implication is that if elite actors are successful in securing their objectives, then the relation is one of legitimate authority.
We can add that with regard to the rise of the bureaucratic state, Weber was
clearly attracted to charismatic leadership as a means of countering overbearing
bureaucratic rationality. With this yearning, 'for the desert winds of charisma to
blow through the disciplinary society' (O'Neill, 1986: 43), Weber returns to the
power-seeking agency of elite individuals. This is in contrast to subsequent theorists who share Weber's concerns over bureaucratic domination. More socially
focused, critical theories look instead to challenge rationalisation through countervailing democratic institutions, collective social and political movements and
cultural subversion (e.g. Marcuse, 1956; Ritzer, 2015). Nevertheless, as the book
proceeds we shall see some of the important linkages that continue to be made
between Weber's work and a variety of more recent research programmes, most
notably that of Foucault (Nash, 2010: 11; O'Neill, 1986).

Durkheim: state and social harmony

Emile Durkheim was perhaps *the* 'founding father' of sociology, and for him
the function of politics was, in total contrast to Weber, to enhance social
integration. However, Durkheim (1950) by no means saw the state as secondary to the social. On the contrary, the state amounted to the 'social ego' or
'brain' of society. Durkheim (e.g. 1893, 1897) saw the main threat to modern
societies as anomie, or the normlessness that an increasingly atomised and
individualised society can exhibit. His *Professional Ethics and Civic Morals*
was based on a series of lectures spanning 1890–1900, first published posthu-
mously in 1950. In these lectures, Durkheim grants a key role to the 'secondary associations' of civil society, as a means of giving disparate individuals a

sense of the social beyond themselves. In particular, given the increasing centrality of work to people's lives, Durkheim placed great hope in professional associations and guilds. Certainly in late nineteenth-century societies such as England and Germany, these organisations did far more than just represent worker interests: they also provided extensive educational and cultural functions. However, while these were an important means of drawing individuals into society at the ground level, they could not achieve social integration on their own. For Durkheim, it was the sheer diversity of civil society associations – celebrated by those who saw them as a buffer against an over-mighty state – which also made them an imperfect means of integration. Durkheim was concerned that, left to their own devices, secondary associations would replace the individual ego with a 'corporate ego'. This threat was embodied in organisations representing particular (rather than universal) interests, such as trade unions (Durkheim, 1950).

Durkheim didn't want the nightmare of a Hobbesian 'war of all against all' among individuals to simply be replaced by a battle between organised interest groups. Consequently, he grants a leading role to the state in unifying disparate interests. In so doing, Durkheim understood the state in a much more activist way than liberals who saw it as 'holding the ring' between competing groups. Durkheim (1893) believed that the complexity of modern societies made their constituent parts *interdependent*, and this was the basis for cooperation and social solidarity. However, the tendency in modern societies – under the sway of *laissez-faire* economics and politics – was towards individualism, and therefore anomie. So the purpose of the modern state was to make manifest what Durkheim believed was an underlying (or, in his term, 'organic') form of social solidarity. Thus, in addition to its function of harmonising economic relations, the symbolic aspects of the state were also important for generating a sense of solidarity: public symbols, rituals, a legal code and so on (Durkheim, 1912). The ways these symbolic aspects were taken up by later Durkheimian theorists are outlined in Chapter 4, on culture and ideology.

With regard to our analysis of the society–politics relation, Durkheim offers an interesting model. On the one hand, he is the sociologist *par excellence,* who sees within industrialising societies an underlying logic of interdependence, and therefore the basis of social solidarity. In Durkheim's (1895) language, this interdependence is an objective 'social fact', rather than a matter of political contestation. However, Durkheim did not think that this social reality would simply will itself into being: he identified liberal individualism as a political obstacle to the realisation of social solidarity (Bowring, 2016). Thus, the state, in partnership with secondary associations, was to be the *active vehicle* for achieving solidarity. Indeed, Durkheim (1950) went further and spelled out the desirable political character of the modern state: civic republican, with a social democratic intent. It is notable that Durkheim is not ostensibly led to these political positions because of a preference for their moral worth. Rather, he saw them as the best *means* of delivering the state's necessary function of promoting social solidarity. We shall see in due course that this technocratic, social-theoretical understanding of the state was echoed by sociologists and politicians almost a century after Durkheim.

Marxism: state and social conflict

Like Durkheim, Marx focused on how forces beyond a narrowly defined state shaped politics. However, whereas Durkheim pointed to a logic of social integration, to be embodied in the relationship between the state and civil society, for Marx both state and civil society were subordinate to *economic* relations. Marx had a base-superstructure model of society. Here, the 'action' occurs at the level of the base or economic infrastructure. This consists of the means of economic production (for example factories, technical knowledge) plus, vitally, the specific form of social relations (classes) which these give rise to. The class structure is simply divided between those who own the means of production, and those who do not. Within capitalism these are the bourgeoisie and proletariat respectively. All the other major social institutions and practices (the superstructure of society) are determined – or at least shaped – by these social relations (Marx, 1859). Critically, the character of these relations is antagonistic: capitalists are locked into a zero-sum game with workers, in which they try and maximise profit by increasing working hours and suppressing wages (Marx, 1849). These conflictual, exploitative social relations come to be reflected in the social superstructure. Thus, the character of institutions such as the state, family and wider culture is determined by the nature of society's economic base.

The most significant contrast with Durkheim is that there is no long-term prospect of the state successfully managing, let alone resolving, social conflicts. For Durkheim, conflict was a pathology which reflected society's failure to recognise underlying interdependence. Marx inverts this analysis: conflict is the true condition of capitalist societies, and it is outbreaks of consensus or stability which are the illusion. Ultimately for Marx, this can only be resolved by the transition to communism (Marx and Engels, 1848). This would be a form of society where the means of production were fully developed and communally owned. The result would be the end of class antagonism and, by implication, the end of politics and the state itself as previously understood.

Marx was of course aware of the state's role in protecting the interests of the capitalist class and reproducing the capitalist economy and society. But given his wider theoretical framework, in which the importance of politics and the state is marginalised, it is no surprise that he never developed a systematic theory of the state. Instead, Marx's reading of the state has been inferred from his various historical and political writings (Miliband, 1965). In the twentieth century, Marx's predictions about the collapse of capitalism failed to materialise, and the system proved remarkably adaptable. Later Marxist thinkers thus sought to develop a more systematic theory of the state, its complex relationship to civil society and role in reproducing capitalism. From this now voluminous body of Marxist state theory, we shall focus here on three key perspectives: the state as the *direct instrument* of the ruling class; as the *structural guarantor* of the wider capitalist system (which may go against the short term interests of the capitalist class); and as *relatively autonomous* from the system, this latter perspective being embodied in the strategic-relational approach to the state.

Instrumentalism

The 'orthodox' Marxist position is that the state is the direct instrument of ruling class power. This was the position Marx and Engels (1848: 475) adopted in the *Communist Manifesto*, in which they claimed that, 'the executive of the modern State is but a committee for managing the common affairs of the whole bourgeoisie'. The best known modern exponent of this approach is British theorist Ralph Miliband. Writing in the late 1960s, Miliband (1969) drew on empirical evidence to argue that the British state remained 'captured' by the bourgeoisie. Cabinet ministers, members of parliament, the judiciary, civil service, military and business elites were drawn from the established upper-middle classes, with the elite public schools and Oxford and Cambridge universities serving as a training ground. Despite any superficial political differences between members of the ruling class, they held in common a belief in the naturalness of the capitalist system, and the necessity of promoting the interests of capital. Miliband pointed, for example, to the success of organised business in defining its own particular class interest as the general national interest. The crucial point was that capitalist dominance was maintained by the direct presence of members of the bourgeoisie – or at least those thoroughly socialised into its worldview – in key state positions: a question of agency, or personnel (with echoes, in that respect, of Weber). More recently, an apparent reconsolidation of this traditional elite power – that many thought had become diluted – has led to a renewed interest in instrumentalist-type accounts. In the UK, for example, there has been a striking preponderance of upper-middle-class products of Eton College, many with close personal ties, in the senior reaches of the Coalition and Conservative governments from 2010.

Structuralism

The structuralist Marxist account of the state bypasses the question of agency, and sees the state as an objective entity which functionally and mechanically meets the requirements of capitalism. Vitally, this occurs independently of the class background and worldviews of the individuals who occupy state positions. This was the argument made by Nicos Poulantzas in a famous, polemical debate with Miliband's instrumentalism in the *New Left Review* (Miliband, 1970, 1973; Poulantzas, 1969, 1976). On the structuralist account, to define the state with reference to individual capitalists is to deny the objective reality of the institution, as well as of the wider social classes and logic of capitalist accumulation which determine its function. The structuralist approach addresses some of the limits of instrumentalism, in particular what happens when key individuals are not drawn from the ruling class, or do not share its worldview. For example, how do we account for occasions when the state appears to act against the capitalist class, but still maintains the long-term maintenance and reproduction of capitalist relations? In theory, the instrumentalist approach struggles with this question. But in the structuralist account, the answer lies in the wider system requirements of capitalism; the state is 'destined' to fulfil these requirements regardless of the intentions of specific actors. There is something about the structure of capitalism which generates outcomes favourable to its own reproduction. The point here is not just that the business lobby is able to use its power to *define* the national interest. Rather, the reliance of the state upon capitalist actors – to generate jobs and the revenues to fund public services – means that the business interest *is*, in large measure, often the national interest. However, as with all structurally determinist theories, this one neglects the capacity of political action to promote – or challenge – capitalist relations.

Beyond the impasse: state managers and the strategic–relational approach

The instrumentalist–structuralist debate on the state was overdrawn, with both Miliband (1977) and Poulantzas (1978) ultimately seeking a more nuanced account (Hay, 2006). A way needed to be found to allow for the fact that the ruling class (or its ideology) does not permanently occupy the state, for example during periods of socialist government. In addition – in governments of various political hues – key decisions are sometimes taken against the preferences of capitalists: almost every piece of post-war social democratic legislation (e.g. trade union rights, progressive taxation, regulatory regimes) was made in the teeth of resistance from the business lobby. But any new approach needed to be able to account for this without analytical recourse to the logic of a 'capitalist system', which the state and political actors were destined, consciously or not, to reproduce.

Poulantzas' use of the concept of 'relative autonomy' offered a more satisfactory approach. In wider Marxist theory, relative autonomy recognises that the social, cultural and political spheres can, albeit in a capitalist context, generate outcomes of their own – they have relative autonomy from the economic. On this view, the social superstructure should not be seen as absolutely determined by economic relations, although such relations are nevertheless still, in Althusser's (1965) famous formulation, determining 'in the last instance'. Poulantzas (1968) had used relative autonomy to explain how state actors are able to exercise political agency, but in a *relative* manner which will still ultimately protect the interests of the capitalist system. This could explain occasions when the state acts against the wishes of capitalists, with various regulatory or social policy interventions: it takes such action because capitalists, trying to make a 'quick buck', may jeopardise system stability.

While, at face value, relative autonomy seems to indicate a common-sense way beyond instrumentalist and structuralist state theory, its use by the early Poulantzas steered it towards the latter. There was still the sense that the capitalist system was both predetermined and (ultimately) all-determining. Later interventions tried to move decisively beyond this theoretical impasse. In an important piece with the telling title, 'The ruling class does not rule', Fred Block (1987a; see also 1987b) tries to specify exactly *why*, despite the separation between those who manage the state and 'practising' capitalists, the former still consistently take decisions which promote capitalism. His answer agrees with both Poulantzas and the later Miliband that the state is indeed structurally dependent upon the jobs and revenues generated by capitalism. But Block adds a *political* dimension. He argues that state managers consequently have more of a stake in the successful performance of capitalism, and its long-term maintenance, than individual, quick profit-seeking capitalists. Block's achievement is thus to account for the agency of state managers and their political imperatives, relatively autonomous of the ruling class, but within a (capitalist) structural context which frames that agency (Hay, 2006).

The analytical potential of relative autonomy reached its fullest expression in the *strategic–relational* approach developed by Bob Jessop (1990, 2007). A surprising omission in the above Marxist accounts is the role played by class (and other) conflicts in shaping the form and content of the state – a lack of dynamism. To address this, Jessop draws on the work of the later, less structurally determinist Poulantzas (1978), as well as Antonio Gramsci (see below). Jessop defines the state not as a fixed, objective reality (as in structuralism), nor just in terms of ruling class actors (instrumentalism), but as an open-ended site of struggle. Any fixity, or concreteness to the state, is the crystallisation of previous strategies and struggles. Vitally, these struggles create a terrain which is more favourable to certain types of strategy than to others: state institutions are therefore 'strategically selective'. The state is the outcome of the relations between the strategies of actors and the institutional context that arises as a result; it therefore creates a partial (selective) terrain for further strategies and so on *ad infinitum* (see also Hay, 2006).

On this analysis, capitalist interests tend to be favoured not because of an inbuilt stabilising mechanism within capitalism, or just the direct actions of state elites. Instead, the theory suggests that the capitalist class is able to tilt the balance of social and political forces in its favour, and in so doing create a playing field more favourable to its interests being met. However, there is no inevitability to this outcome. The key to the strategic–relational approach is that political struggle is ever present: there remains the (at least theoretical) possibility of a reversal of fortunes, and strategic gains in the interests of workers or other groups.

Gramsci: state and civil society

The strategic–relational approach echoes and explicitly draws on the work of an earlier, pivotal figure in understanding the state–society relation, Antonio Gramsci. Gramsci produced the majority of his work as a political prisoner in

Mussolini's Italy in the late 1920s and 1930s. However, his collected *Prison Notebooks*, with their ground-breaking reconstruction of key elements of Marxist theory, were not widely available in English until 1971. Gramsci's advocates argue that he represents a 'missing link' in Marxist theory, offering more advanced insights on industrial societies than the theoretical cul-de-sac reached by structuralists such as Althusser and Poulantzas several decades later (Laclau and Mouffe, 1985). Thus, interestingly, Gramsci's work speaks to various theoretical issues addressed in the late twentieth and twenty-first centuries, but is preoccupied with the social and political context of the 1920s and 1930s. Below we consider Gramsci's key contributions of theorising the state as operating on a complex and contested social terrain; indicating the ways in which it intermeshes with the institutions of civil society; and revealing how this generates deep-seated power that extends to controlling 'common sense', but also offers the resources for resistance and transformation.

What is the state?

Gramsci's first major contribution lies in his definition of the state, which he does not see as a static set of institutions and actors that sit above society. To be sure, the state is relatively durable and a condensation of ruling class power. However, this reflects a wider, ever-shifting balance of social forces and is therefore a precarious, 'unstable equilibria' (Gramsci, 1971: 182). Vitally, for Gramsci (1971: 206–75) the state can only be understood in terms of its relationship to civil society, although teasing out this relationship from the fragmented passages of the *Prison Notebooks* can be challenging. Gramsci envisages civil society as a complex of institutions and practices – such as the church, press, trade unions, political parties, the family and cultural organisations – which exist between the relations of production (economy) and the apparatus of the state (Gramsci, 1971: 56*n*; Simon, 1991: 70).

In this model, the state itself is imagined in a dual way. On the one hand, Gramsci identifies – for methodological purposes – 'political society', by which he means the traditional, coercive and legal state functions of legislature, judiciary, police, army and so forth. However, he also offers the more expansive, original idea of the *integral state*, which comprises political society *and* civil society (Gramsci, 1971: 262–3). The reason for this move is to capture the expanding face of the modern state (Burawoy, 2003: 215), and how in addition to the coercive apparatus of political society, the ruling class seek to dominate – and mobilise consent – through the diverse institutions of civil society (Morton, 2007: 89–95; Simon, 1991: 72–3). Gramsci thus highlights how the modern state involves solidifying *consent* in the cultural realm, as much as exercising traditional forms of coercion:

> the State is the entire complex of practical and theoretical activities with which the ruling class not only justifies and maintains its dominance, but manages to win the active consent of those over whom it rules. (Gramsci, 1971: 244)

State and civil society

Gramsci dramatically expands our conception of state power – but also of possibilities for resistance. He famously uses the First World War as a metaphor, and contrasts the form of state–society relation in Western, industrialising societies with that confronted by the Russian revolutionaries in the East. There, the Tsarist state could be likened to a 'fortress', which needed to be confronted head-on in a 'war of movement': a revolutionary overthrow. In the West, however, the labyrinth of civil society was more like a series of trenches or fortifications. Either extending or resisting state power involved a protracted and dispersed 'war of position' across the many sites of civil society. There would be no 'storming of the Winter Palace' moment as in Russia: political struggle in modern societies involved a battle at the level of culture, a battle for hearts and minds to define 'common sense' itself (Gramsci, 1971: 229–39). Gramsci described this as the struggle for hegemony, for the ability to define society's dominant ideas, aspirations and worldviews. This meant that the objective of governing was more than just coercing citizens into following orders: it was about actively creating certain types of citizen. As a Marxist, Gramsci still saw the most fundamental objective of state power as being the reproduction of capitalism. However, this was now to be understood as a project occurring across all levels of society, with an active role for the state in making the modern worker. This process was illustrated in Gramsci's (1971: 279–318) extended observations on 'Americanism and Fordism'. Gramsci marvelled at how America was developing not just new factories, working practices and contract laws, but also the culture and worldview of the workers and consumers who would live this next, mass stage of capitalism, typified by the car factories of Henry Ford.

Domination and resistance

On one level, Gramsci's all-embracing account of the range and subtlety of state rule looks daunting for the activist seeking to fundamentally change society. The ruling class not only dominates the state, but has extended it to wage a culture war across society, moulding individual worldviews to meet the next phase of capitalism. However, Gramsci insisted that the relations between state, civil society and economy were not mechanically determined, and that civil society in particular remained open-ended and contested. Precisely because it is built out of everyday life, culture and tradition, civil society is a fertile ground for intellectuals to link their grand 'philosophies' to people's lived experience (Gramsci, 1971: 5–23; Olsaretti, 2014). This led Gramsci to take far more seriously than previous Marxists conflicts over, for example, gender, religion and nationalism. To more orthodox Marxists, these struggles, extraneous to class relations, were at best a distraction and at worst 'backward'. But for Gramsci, any successful political project had to speak directly to multiple, everyday, common-sense struggles (Hall, 1982).

So civil society was certainly the site upon which the state – and by extension the bourgeoisie – attempted to exercise hegemony. But it was also the best hope for generating a new, socialist common sense. Indeed, in Gramsci we see early signs of the idea of civil society *against* the state (Burawoy, 2003) that was, ironically, to later become so crucial in bringing down state socialism in Eastern Europe. On Gramsci's analysis, the route to socialism involves cultivating a broad-based, socialist common sense, and expanding this in a way that would gradually diminish the need for a coercive state. This was in contrast to revolutionary strategies which envisaged 'seizing' and then utilising the state apparatus. It suggests that the diminishing of the oppressive state would not be an automatic reflex of the communal ownership of the means of production (see Marx, 1875), but would result from the full fruition of civil society.

Subsequent theorists have debated the extent to which Gramsci truly broke from Marxist reductionism (Laclau and Mouffe, 1985), and the fragmented nature of his writing lends itself to ongoing (re)interpretation (Davidson, 2008). Gramsci certainly provided the tools with which Marxism could take the whole social and cultural terrain seriously as both an object of state power *and* the best means of superseding it. However, Gramsci saw himself as still working within an orthodox Marxist paradigm. This was evident, for example, in statements about the need for cultural forms to meet the requirements of the 'productive forces' (1971: 258), or his insistence on the primacy of the 'fundamental social groups' (bourgeoisie and proletariat) within the struggle for hegemony (1971: 5, *n.1*). It would take a much later generation of post-structuralist theorists to finally collapse the conceptual distinctions between state, society and economy.

Foucault: power, knowledge and governmentality

Michel Foucault laid the basis for a post-structuralist understanding of the state and political power. This does away with sociological or Marxist ideas of a logic of the social, or requirements of the mode of production. Instead, it focuses on power relations constituted by agency, practices and especially discourse (of which more in Chapter 4). Foucault was not strictly a social theorist or political scientist, but an historian and archaeologist of ideas. The most significant of Foucault's many insights is that power should not just be understood as negative (in the sense of denying freedom), nor as a 'thing' which a 'powerful' actor simply wields over a less powerful one. Rather, power should be understood as *productive*, that is, it is what motivates and enables agents to act at all (Foucault, 1980, 1983). Power is not some by-product or unfortunate anomaly in human affairs: it is absolutely integral to them. Power is constitutive of all action and, indeed, society itself.

In terms of the state–society relation, the significance of Foucault's work is best captured by his desire to, 'cut off the head of the king' in political analysis (Foucault, 1976: 89). By this, Foucault meant that theorists had fixated on the image of the ruler: one who possesses a thing called power which they wield 'over' subjects. But with his account of power as productive, Foucault wanted to shift the analysis to how power actually constructs subjects and definitions of normal conduct in multiple settings. So, rather like Gramsci, Foucault moved the focus away from the traditional confines of the state. Through his wide-ranging historical studies, he examined how the hospital, school, factory, prison and other social institutions contributed to the construction of 'normal' or 'deviant' behaviours and subjects. In the modern period, claims to technical expertise became critical to empowering certain actors to impose definitions of appropriate behaviour. With this insight, Foucault turned the spotlight upon social scientific knowledge itself, as a key tool in the productive exercise of power. Thus, it was only on the basis of data on, for example, the population and health, productivity or human emotions that objects such as 'patient', 'citizen' or even 'economy' could be ushered into being. Vitally, from the point of view of government, such objects could be *acted upon* (Foucault, 2007, 2008).

Methodologically, Foucault's approach inverts the traditional treatment of power and authority. Foucault does not look to elites, offices of state or an abstract institutional analysis. Instead, he sees power operating throughout society, and this encourages a bottom-up approach to unearthing techniques of control. Although Foucault is often highlighted for the centrality he gives to discourses in constructing power, it is in fact through the material artefacts of everyday life that he encourages us to see power acting upon our bodies and consciousness. Thus, Foucauldian researchers are interested in items such as the operations manual, accounting procedures or the methods of processing hospital patients: apparently mundane tools of bureaucracy become integral to capturing the flows of power across social life (Dean, 2010; Miller and Rose, 2008).

With specific reference to state power, Foucault's most influential work was a series of lectures in 1978 turning his attention towards 'governmentality' (Foucault, 2007). Here, Foucault sketches out the relationship between ideologies, governors, technologies and the production of subjects. In particular, developing the core insight that power is productive, Foucault outlines how, under (late) modern conditions where individual autonomy is so highly prized, 'autonomy' itself can be seen as an aspect of power. This counterintuitive idea, along with the vocabulary of governmentality, has been developed by a subsequent generation of Foucauldian researchers, most notably Nikolas Rose. In a seminal article on 'Political power beyond the state', Rose and Peter Miller (1992) apply Foucault's problematic to neoliberal forms of governance. They develop Foucault's repertoire by linking 'political rationalities' (what we might call ideologies) with 'technologies of rule' (the people, ideas and processes that deploy governing programmes), and again identify expertise as the bridge between programmes of rule and everyday life.

Understood through this lens, contemporary neoliberalism is not just the latest phase of capitalism, as Marxists would argue. Rather, it is the attempt to construct a specific form of autonomy and to make it *governable* (see also Chapter 4). The wider social-theoretical claim is that contemporary government has shifted from industrial disciplinary forms such as the factory or the school. With increasingly complex and diverse social and cultural practices, power must operate *through* the choices and aspirations of citizens themselves, upon the cultural terrain. This shift to a politics operating through our values is labelled by Rose (1999) as an 'ethico-politics', which elaborates the disciplinary politics of the early modern period. This theoretical approach has led to a proliferation of Foucauldian investigations into how we are increasingly exhorted to govern ourselves, for example through lifestyle magazines and a burgeoning 'self-help' industry (Blackman, 2004), or even subtle 'nudges' from government to change our behaviour (see Leggett, 2014).

Foucault's contribution was revolutionary. Philosophically, the understanding of power as a permanently shifting relation, as productive, and as constitutive of social life turned on its head much thinking about the state–society relation. Specifically, by seeing all relations and practices as an effect of power, Foucault effectively collapsed the state–society boundary, and radically expanded the object of enquiry for state theorists. All social institutions and practices are sites of power struggle, and there is apparently no limit to the types of artefact that might tell us something about how subjectivities and power relations are constructed. However, sceptics suggest that Foucault may have posed more questions than he answered. If power is effectively everywhere, is it a useful concept? The account of ubiquitous power underplays recursive, structural power such as that represented by the state. Indeed, Foucault's position waters down our understanding of the state *per se*, as in his schematic it can be nothing more than an artificial attempt to draw together or condense the complex web of power relations (Curtis, 1995). The increasing Foucauldian focus on autonomy and the productive aspect of power may also neglect the ongoing existence of brutal, 'negative' power that is routinely exercised by some (more structurally powerful) actors over others (see e.g. Agamben, 2005). Thus, surveillance, torture, imprisonment or what Marx (1867: 899) simply referred to as the 'silent compulsion' of life under capitalist relations are still very much in evidence. This underplaying of contemporary forms of material repression is ironic, given Foucault's original concern with the way in which bodies in modern societies are subject to multiple forms of *physical* discipline.

Contemporary social theory and governance

The traditions discussed above each offer a different way of understanding the state–society relation. In this section we consider a more contemporary body of social-theoretical work, associated in particular with British sociologist Anthony Giddens, although similar themes are pursued by social theorists such as Zygmunt Bauman, Ulrich Beck and Manuel Castells. Giddens' work is notable for not just describing the background conditions to contemporary politics but for also having been taken up by elite political actors. The theory is therefore itself constitutive of empirical political change. We outline the implications of Giddens' account of late modernity for politics in general, and governance in particular. We then look at how these social-theoretical assumptions have become embodied in the political science and policy literature, particularly in terms of describing a shift from 'government' to 'governance'.

The consequences of this shift are then explored in two case studies, illustrating theoretical debates over the changing relationship between state and civil society. The first example embodies how social theory can be bound up with political practice. In the late 1990s and 2000s, many centre-left political parties around the world significantly shifted their account of the state, as part of a wider 'modernisation' programme. This crystallised around the idea of Third Way politics, which had been explicitly developed in Giddens' (1994, 1998) social theory and political analysis. Taking the UK case where the Third Way was most pronounced, we examine how Giddens' sociological arguments profoundly influenced Tony Blair's New Labour Party and governments: their understanding of the electorate, the role of the state and its changing relationship to citizens. This latter aspect is developed in the second case study, drawn from empirical work in Scandinavia in the 2000s. The study explores how the relationship between governors and citizens is becoming increasingly blurred. Here the theoretical influence is a similar body of ideas – concerning the transformations of late modernity such as globalisation and individualisation – to those that informed new theories of governance and the Third Way. However, rather than directly influencing political practice, the theories are used by academics to enable the identification of new ideal-types of political actor among 'governors' and 'governed'. The case studies are then assessed, drawing on the more traditional perspectives covered in the first part of the chapter. This illustrates how the wider social-theoretical canon – including the classics – can provide resources for critically interrogating contemporary political practices. In the light of these discussions, we conclude by returning to our core problematic of the state–society relation – and our categories of the inescapably social and irreducibly political – outlined in Chapter 1.

Reflexive modernity and political analysis

The early 1990s gave rise to a body of social theory which rejected claims that we live in a postmodern era. Postmodern theory pointed to an 'implosion' of the social institutions, identities and values of modernity, amidst the endless play of cultural signs in a mediatised age (Baudrillard, 1980). By contrast, social theorists such as Ulrich Beck and Anthony Giddens argued that rapid social change is leading to a radical transformation *within* modernity: they prefer to talk of 'late' or 'reflexive' modernity (Beck *et al.*, 1994; Giddens, 1990). At the core of this account lie processes of economic and cultural globalisation. The economy has 'gone global' in the form of instantaneous capital flows facilitated by new information technologies, global markets and the mobility of both multinational corporations and labour. In this context, it is impossible for nation states to continue to manage their economic and social policies in isolation. Instead, the task of governments is to create favourable conditions for international investment (e.g. through low rates of taxation), and to equip workers for competition in a global 'knowledge economy' which they can no longer be protected from. This means investing in education and reskilling throughout the life course, and orienting social policy towards economic efficiency, prioritising labour market flexibility (Beck, 2000; Giddens, 2000).

However, for social theorists such as Giddens, it is the cultural and social aspects of globalisation which have the most significant consequences for governments and the state–society relation. Giddens (1990) sees the information revolution as intensifying the *reflexivity* of social actors. With the late modern proliferation of information, individuals, groups and institutions have no choice but to constantly monitor, process and act upon it. In so doing, they alter the conditions for further monitoring, processing and acting and the cycle goes on *ad infinitum*. Giddens (1984) refers to this as the reflexive monitoring of conduct, which becomes characteristic of agency in late modernity. A key consequence of heightened reflexivity is widespread *detraditionalisation* (see Heelas *et al.*, 1996). Again, given the proliferation of competing narratives about the nature of social life, 'traditional' accounts of the world which justify themselves self-referentially (e.g. 'listen to me because I'm your father') become increasingly hard to sustain. Instead, narratives and ways of living must be 'dialogic', that is, they must be prepared to enter into a conversation with competing accounts and justify themselves through reasoned argument (Giddens, 1994).

For Giddens (1994, 1998) and others (notably Bauman, 2001; Beck and Beck-Gernsheim, 2002), the most significant aspect of detraditionalisation is the way in which it both encourages, and is reinforced by, *individualisation*. Reflexivity and detraditionalisation tend towards releasing individuals from binding social structures and practices; individuals become increasingly detached from, and questioning towards, ideas and practices which may previously have been taken for granted. This in turn reinforces detraditionalising pressure. In the light of these processes, sociologists have grappled with a perceived shift from identity as being something which is largely inherited to something which is constructed, complex and fluid (see Chapter 3 for an extended discussion). This, and the individualisation thesis more widely, presents new dilemmas for the classic sociological problem of order: under such individualised, fragmented and fluid conditions, how is something like community – or even society itself – still possible?

Political implications: from government to governance

While tending not to use the social-theoretical jargon, political scientists have similarly charted how social change has reframed politics, specifically in the form of a move from 'government' to 'governance' (Pierre and Peters, 2000; Rhodes, 1997). Here, government refers to the traditional idea of an executive that rules over the economy and society, able to pull levers from the centre in order to achieve policy outcomes. The high point of this model is regarded as the 'command and control' post-war Keynesian welfare state. Governance theorists see globalisation and social complexity as having resulted in a 'hollowing out' (Rhodes, 1994) and disempowering of the state. This occurs from above, in the form of transnational political, economic and military practices and organisations such as the UN, IMF and NATO, as well as supranational blocs such as the EU. But the state is also squeezed from below in the form of an increasingly complex, diverse and individualised citizenry (Kooiman, 2003). This is evident in the decline of deference (an aspect of detraditionalisation), as well as the re-emergence of sub-national actors, allegiances and disputes. The latter have implications ranging from calls for greater devolution, to the revival of local ethnic and nationalist conflicts (Kaldor, 2012).

Under these conditions, command and control government is undermined, and the shift to *governance* involves the state entering into new forms of governing arrangements. The governance literature implies there is no universal form that the state should take in complex societies. However, there is a clear bias against command and control, which is seen as unwieldy. To a lesser extent, relying on markets and privatisation as a solution is also criticised: this is seen as an abdication of the state's necessary steering and public interest functions. Instead, governance theorists point to the emergence of flatter, horizontal, *network* forms of organisation. Through these, the state partners with the various bodies and forms of expertise that exist in a complex civil society and economy, for example NGOs, voluntary associations and business (Sorensen and Torfing, 2007).

The ethos of governance is 'weak power': the state sets frameworks for action, can regulate and even 'nudge' (Sunstein, 2014) actors in certain directions. This type of state does not command and control: it governs, but 'at a distance'. Successful network governance involves drawing on diverse forms of expertise, policy learning and experiments with new forms of democratic engagement, in order to mobilise individual citizens and groups (Bevir, 2010; Newman, 2005). This is not just because democratic innovation is seen as a good thing in itself (although it generally is by governance theorists) but because under complex social conditions it is a *prerequisite* of successful governance. As with social theorists such as Giddens, governance writers tend to describe the emerging new paradigm at the same time as advocating it (Newman, 2001). It is clear that governance theorists were dissatisfied with the top-down state of the 1950s and 1960s, but are simultaneously uneasy about the push for market-based solutions associated with the neoliberal experiment of the 1980s and 1990s. Network governance is seen, at its best, as an effective means of governing complexity while also facilitating democratic renewal: a win-win. Below, we examine two case studies which embody many of the assumptions offered by both social theorists of reflexive modernity, and those modelling the shift to network governance.

Case study 1: An active state in a changing world – the Third Way

What came to be known as Third Way politics is a striking example of social theory directly shaping political ideology, strategy, rhetoric and policy: under such circumstances social theory becomes constitutive of key aspects of the political world it analyses. Following a series of election defeats at the hands of Mrs Thatcher, the British Labour Party embarked on a modernisation process in the early 1990s. A rebranded New Labour developed a political strategy and model for the state, strongly influenced by sociological accounts of late modernity. This was explicit in the Third Way programme for centre-left parties offered by Anthony Giddens (1998, 2000, 2002b), and taken up directly by Prime Minister Tony Blair in his pamphlet of the same name (1998). Similar ideas had been deployed in the US by Bill Clinton's New Democrats (Jaenicke, 1999; Weir, 2001).

In the UK, the Third Way was based on a critique of stylised versions of the first two 'ways': the socialism and social democracy of the 'old left' (associated with the post-war British Labour Party, for example), and the free market neoliberalism of the New Right (associated with Thatcherism). While the old left rightly focused on social cohesion and combating inequality, it neglected individual aspiration and stifled innovation with a command and control state, extensive public ownership and 'cradle to grave' welfare benefits. The neoliberals were right to point to the dynamism of markets in unleashing innovation and encouraging individual responsibility. However, they by turns were criticised for tolerating excessive inequality and undermining social cohesion. The Third Way was presented as a synthesis of the strengths of these previous traditions, rhetorically achieved by the use of 'and' instead of 'either/or' (Driver and Martell, 2002). Thus, rather than favouring unconditional rights (old left) or seeing individuals as solely responsible for themselves (new right), the Third Way talked of a balance between rights *and* responsibilities. Similarly, rather than the top-down state of the old left, or the minimal state of the new right, the Third Way sought an *enabling* state: encouraging individual responsibility, but facilitating and offering support when individuals can't help themselves (Giddens, 1998).

A sociological political project

These developments in centre-left thinking were not derived primarily from political philosophy, or just a crude calculation about what is popular with voters.

Rather, the Third Way was based upon social theories of a 'changed world', as offered by Giddens and the governance theorists discussed above (Finlayson, 2003; Leggett, 2005). Thus, 'rights and responsibilities' is a response to individualisation, and the need to tie citizens into a new social contract if cohesion is to be maintained. Similarly, classic Labour concerns such as addressing inequality were reframed in terms of 'fairness', but not because of an *a priori* value-driven commitment to such a goal. Rather, in a global knowledge economy, excessive inequality and a lack of social cohesion damage economic efficiency (see e.g. Brown, 1994). New Labour politicians – and particularly Tony Blair – certainly did make appeals to political values, but the calls for a new type of governance were mainly presented as a necessary response to inevitable social change. Those who failed to grasp this, on either left or right, were part of the 'forces of conservatism', as Blair (1999) labelled them. The Third Way critique of the old left and the new right was not just that they had the wrong political values, but that under radically changed social conditions both failed to grasp the new role of the state. Economic globalisation means governments are unable to shield their social and economic policy from the global economy. Accepting this, the Third Way argued that the old left policies of generous welfare, high marginal taxation and Keynesian demand management hamper the openness, flexibility and competitiveness that modern economies require. At the same time, the 'sink or swim' *laissez-faire* attitude of neoliberalism failed to appreciate that governments need to invest in the supply side of the economy (Blair, 1998; Giddens, 1998, 2000).

The assumption that governments must adapt to the facts of economic globalisation underpinned specific New Labour policies. Government should create as attractive an environment as possible for businesses to locate and operate in the UK. Low rates of business and income tax at the top end, as well as deregulation of banking and financial services, indicated that these sectors were seen as at the leading edge of globalisation, and would generate the revenues to fund public services. Social policy was envisaged as positively reinforcing economic competitiveness, evident in the centrality of paid work. Measures such as the minimum wage, working families' tax credit and New Deal for the long-term unemployed were all designed to be seen to make work pay. This was coupled with a drive to improve the workforce's skills base so as to be able to compete against emerging nations in the global knowledge economy (see Coates, 2005). There was thus intensive intervention and targeting to try and raise school standards, an expansion of further and higher education places and incentives to encourage reskilling. Large-scale social policy interventions – such as the Sure Start programme investing in young children from poor families – were aimed at preventing a generation being 'left behind' by the pace of social and economic development (Driver and Martell, 2002). Of course, many such measures had long been advocated as progressive causes by those on the political left, and New Labour claimed them as such when addressing leftist audiences. However, the dominant discourse was of economic flexibility and development, to meet the realities of a new global knowledge economy (Fairclough, 2000).

Other aspects of the New Labour project addressed the state being squeezed 'from below', by processes of detraditionalisation and individualisation also described by social theorists. This necessitates a new form for the state and its relationships with the wider society, as advocated by the governance literature. Governments are confronted with a citizenry which is less deferential, more demanding and diverse than in previous generations. Such citizens are impatient with 'one size fits all' public services delivery, demanding individually tailored services on more consumerist lines (Chapman, 2007; Giddens, 2007). For New Labour, the re-imagining of citizens as individualised consumers began with election strategy (Gould, 1998). Party modernisation was built on focus groups and polling data. This positioned voters as consumers of political products, with the hope of making the New Labour brand the most desirable to key constituencies (Finlayson, 2003). It was out of such analysis that voter marketing categories, so redolent of the New Labour era, emerged in the form of, for example, 'school gate mums' and the ubiquitous 'hard working families' of 'Middle England' (Moran, 2005).

In government, assumptions about individualised consumers, not content (under detraditionalised conditions) to 'accept what they're given' from bureaucrats or professionals, were embodied in the Blairite drive for personalised public services (Blair, 2001). This was evident in the 'patient choice' agenda, enabling patients to decide which hospital, appointment time or clinician to use (Dixon *et al.*, 2010). Indeed, the final manifesto of the New Labour era, under Gordon Brown, continued to promise that, '[a] bove all we will build public services that are more personal to people's needs' (Labour Party, 2010: 5). In terms of the delivery of services, New Labour mirrored the governance literature call for a 'network state' that should enter into 'horizontal' arrangements with other providers (Bevir, 2010). There was increased use of public–private partnerships and private finance initiatives, as well as management consultancy and private sector personnel. The space created by abandoning direct government delivery of services, while avoiding outright privatisation, was filled by extensive target-setting and auditing (Prabhakar, 2004). The drive to make public services more customer-driven and responsive resulted in feedback mechanisms such as patients grading their medical providers, or the National Student Survey in universities.

The analysis of an individualised citizenry did not only lead to policies aimed at choice and empowerment: it was also the basis of disciplinary interventions. The Third Way discourse of rights *and* responsibilities involved a contractual understanding of the state–citizen relationship: welfare support, benefits and rights were to be conditional upon the fulfilling of certain obligations (Blair, 1998; Giddens, 1998). This ethos informed the New Deal for the unemployed, in which benefits for jobseekers were conditional on them actively looking for work. It was similarly evident in innovations such as contracts between schools and the parents of difficult pupils. In addition, a host of disciplinary measures were aimed at those who don't 'play by the rules', including Anti-Social Behaviour Orders (ASBOS), curfews, on-the-spot fines and threats to have benefits or housing rights removed (Perri 6 *et al.*, 2010). Public sector workers, too, were the main object of the relentless target-setting and audit culture which accompanied New Labour's version of network governance. To all these constituencies, claims of a new type of 'enabling' network state, which was 'steering, not rowing', were questionable.

Case study 2: Citizens as co-governors: culture governors, expert citizens and everyday makers

The example of the Third Way illustrates how social theory has directly shaped political strategy and ideas about the state, predominantly among political elites. Our second case study shows how academic researchers have used a similar macro-theoretical backdrop, but as a means for empirically investigating new types of political actor emerging at the state–civil society interface: such actors challenge the politics–society distinction altogether. Scandinavian societies have seen a number of experiments in local democracy which reflect theories about politics in reflexive modernity. In Denmark, Henrik Bang was one of a number of political science academics exploring the political impact of the processes identified by social theorists such as Giddens. In particular, this research programme sought to specify how the macro context of reflexive modernity, and its attendant dynamics of individualisation and detraditionalisation, impacted upon how individual citizens understand and engage with the state (Bang, 2003, 2005). Bang's own research included use of survey data and discourse analysis of the policy and 'mission statement' documents of government and other organisations. But the primary method was qualitative interviews with state actors, activists and 'everyday' citizens, used to draw out their imaginary of the state–citizen relation in general, and their particular political orientation towards and practices within it. The result was new ideal-types for imagining the state–citizen interface. Bang's work examines the interactions between, 'a highly politicised and culturally oriented new management and administration and a strongly individualised and consumption-oriented new citizen' (Bang, 2003: 241). He begins with the observation, common to contemporary social theory and Third Way politics, that late modern societies have become highly differentiated in terms of their institutions, complex in their functions, and pluralistic in the practices and worldviews of their citizens. The result is that states cannot operate on the command and control model of earlier modernity. We have seen that this observation is the common starting point for accounts of the transition from government to governance: a shift from a bureaucratic and hierarchical state machine to a flatter, network organisation in which the state partners with various actors.

Culture governors

Bang (2003, esp. 2004, 2005) identifies how, aware of these changes, a new breed of manager has a novel understanding of political authority and effective action. Such individuals are to be found in all spheres of social life, and not just the narrowly political. These 'culture governors' lack ideological allegiances and have a fluid, project-based identity oriented towards problem solving. They are highly pragmatic, and will partner with a range of (ideally like-minded) individuals and organisations to achieve their objectives. Culture governors do not legitimate themselves with reference to traditional institutions such as parliaments or parties, or formal norms and procedures. Instead, they appeal directly to individuals, using the language of empowerment and 'best practice' in order to get the job done. Crucially, culture governors understand that in the age of cultural differentiation and complexity, rulers need to:

> attempt to socialise and regulate people's conduct in an indirect manner by working on their identities and thereby their values, feelings, attitudes and beliefs via a variety of new interactive modes of dialogue and co-operation. The aim is to get them freely and willingly to employ their self-governing powers to help the system connect and deliver in an effective manner. (Bang, 2003: 247)

Culture governors thus work on the terrain of people's identities, experiences and values: they 'get inside' people's emotions and heads and have to pay attention to the ' "small tactics" of lay people in the political community for making a difference' (Bang, 2003: 248). Culture governors can operate both in and against the traditional system: they occupy key positions, are often close to centres of power and are well connected; but at the same time they are willing and able to bypass traditional structures, procedures and norms to get the job done on any specific issue.

Expert citizens

If the culture governor is the new face of political management from above in complex societies, who are they are targeting? Whose knowledge are they mobilising in civil society, or from below? Bang (2003, 2005) identifies the 'expert citizen' as an intermediary figure between the elite network of culture governors and the lay populace, but one whose sympathies lie with the former. The expert citizen is the ideal counterpart to the culture governor – keen to be 'enabled', while possessing the specialised, local knowledge which culture governors seek to mobilise. A good example is found in the field of UK health policy. Here, 'expert patients' are those whose working knowledge of, say, how to manage chronic long-term conditions, often exceeds that of medical practitioners and policymakers. Where once the expert patient, and patient interest groups, might have been viewed as oppositional and trying to put pressure on policy from 'outside', now they are actively courted in policymaking and delivery. Patient interest groups are incorporated into formal decision-making processes, and at the local level the Department of Health even developed an Expert Patients Programme to draw on patient knowledge in delivering care solutions (Coulter and Ellins, 2006).

Everyday makers

Still more important to the long-term maintenance of the political system, while also more challenging for culture governors, are the many individuals in civil society whom Bang (2003, 2005) identifies as 'everyday makers'. Like culture governors, everyday makers are 'post-ideological', impatient with traditional political processes, norms and forms of representation, and operate with a flexible, project identity. However, unlike culture governors, everyday makers are not seeking to expand their sphere of influence towards a long-term agenda, or to co-opt other actors to serve their objectives. Instead, they are the embodiment of the very complexity, fragmentation and differentiation of modern societies that ideas about governance are premised upon. For the everyday maker, political activity, in as much as they recognise it as being political, is indistinguishable from their own 'project' of identity construction: it is grounded in the texture of their daily lives, problems and experiences. Everyday makers may well be informed by a strong (often global) ethic or set of values. But these are not seen as something which can be represented by the political system, and nor is the system seen as something which they will try and input into from the outside. Rather, in their complex and busy lives, the ethos of the everyday maker is summarised by Bang (2003: 262) as being based on principles of:

> Do it yourself
> Do it where you are.
> Do it *ad hoc* or part-time.
> Do it for a concrete reason.
> Do it alone or in joint action with others.
> Do it for fun but also because it is a worthy cause.
> Do it preferably together with other lay people but draw on experts if need be.

Everyday makers don't have an 'oppositional' mentality, '[they] don't have anything against working closely together with public authorities concerning the solution of their daily life problems – *but* only as long as it contributes to their own practices of freedom' (Bang, 2003: 263).

The work of Bang and others identifies evocative new forms of political identity and relations. Drawing on the same social-theoretical literature as the Third Way, it indicates how the key features of reflexive modernity such as increased individualisation, detraditionalisation and social complexity impact upon the mindset and practices of both 'governors' and 'governed', in a manner that begins to blur the state–society relation as traditionally understood. Interpreted positively, culture governing is a recognition of the need to incorporate the aspirations and experiences of the public (e.g. expert citizens) into governing processes. Additionally, everyday makers indicate how – in contrast to concerns over citizen apathy – individuals are often engaged in multiple civic minded activities, but not embarrassed about regarding them as part of their individual project of identity construction (of which more in the next chapter). Bang's work was also prophetic, as the trends it identifies have subsequently intensified (see Bang, 2009). In seeking to supplant New Labour in the 2010 general election, David Cameron's Conservative Party (2010) put citizen capability at the heart of their manifesto launch in the form of the 'Big Society' (Kisby, 2010). Echoing early Third Way ideas of an enabling state, and also inspired by Barack Obama's 'Yes we can' vision of citizen-driven social renewal, Big Society was presented as a radical response to an over-centralised British politics. Civil society actors would be actively encouraged to roll back the state for themselves by 'expanding' society through, for example, being empowered to set up their own local schools.

However, while also recognising the radical potential of a more individualised politics, Bang and others are aware that power relations, stratification and the risks of exclusion, manipulation and domination do not simply disappear (see e.g. Li and Marsh, 2008; Newman, 2005). New political practices and configurations of the state–society relation will pose new challenges for democratic politics. In view of this, we conclude below by returning to the theoretical traditions discussed in the first part of the chapter, as a resource for critically evaluating our case studies. In so doing, we arrive at a third sense of how social theory interfaces with empirical politics: as a means of critiquing the very political practices which, as we have seen, it can also be constitutive of and interpret. Finally, we shall draw on the analytical issues identified in Chapter 1, to assess what the changing nature of governance tells us about the wider society–politics relation.

Reading the state and governance through social theory

Our case studies drew directly on contemporary social theories of late modernity and their implications for governance. In many respects these reflect a functionalist tradition of sociological analysis, typified by Durkheim, in which the 'problem of order' is paramount. The logic is that as societies change, political-institutional arrangements need to catch up in order to maintain equilibrium. But the other traditions of state theory which we considered in the first part, such as neo-Marxism, offer a more critical perspective. In some unlikely respects, there are similarities between Marxism and theories of reflexive modernity and the Third Way. They share an approach which deterministically infers political arrangements from claims about the economy and society. They each also assume that society progresses through pregiven stages, ultimately arriving at a destination in which the 'old' social tensions and conflicts disappear. However, whereas for Marxists this end-state was the transition from capitalism to communism, theories of reflexive modernity and the Third Way describe fundamental shifts *within* capitalism.

The starting point of the Marxist critique is precisely this claim that power relations and social conflict can be 'flattened out' within what is still a capitalist economy and society. Rather than seeing economic globalisation as a 'fact of life' that governments must respond to, Marxists analyse it as a process of capitalist restructuring necessary to restore profitability on a global scale (Callinicos, 2001). In explaining the precise character of this restructuring, the division between instrumentalist and structuralist versions of Marxist state theory persists. For those who tend to see the state as the instrument of the capitalist class, neoliberal globalisation was enacted by what Leslie Sklair (2001) identifies as a 'transnational capitalist class' of business and political elites, consciously pursuing their class interest. More specifically, the prevalence in New Labour of those from the business world, management consultancy and the culture industries suggested that the New Labour project represented the ascendancy of a particular managerial elite, both within the capitalist class itself and in the institutions of governance (Gilbert, 2000). Alternatively, a structuralist Marxist account would share with 'hyperglobaliser' neoliberals the view that globalisation is inevitable and has a logic of its own. However, in the Marxist version this is understood as the inherent tendency of capital to expand in the quest for profitability. In so doing, as Marx and Engels (1848) predicted in the *Communist Manifesto,* an ever-mutating capitalism dissolves traditional practices and ideas across the globe. On this reading, the modernisation of centre-left political parties such as New Labour was a reflex response to capitalist restructuring, and simply highlights the limits of mainstream democratic politics (Callinicos, 2001). Ironically, this suggests a fatalism about political agency that again echoes the determinism of the Third Way itself: arguments over political values and choices are academic in the face of wider structural constraints.

For both types of Marxist account, the Third Way was a vehicle for the commodification of social life, where the state opens up society for capitalist profiteering. For Marxists, the old left social democratic institutions and policies of the welfare state, while not perfect, at least protected people from – or even sometimes challenged – this encroachment by the market. However, the Third Way 'reconciliation' of social justice and economic efficiency in reality made the former subordinate to the latter. Thus, paid work became the primary objective of social policy, schools and universities became sites of 'entrepreneurship' and the wider public services subjected to privatisation in the name of greater efficiency. Third Way claims that left and right are redundant were only possible in a period of sustained economic growth such as the 1990s and early 2000s. (Apparent) rising prosperity, consumer affluence and high levels of employment served to mask the underlying tensions and imbalances in the economy and society brought about by global capitalist restructuring (see Brassett *et al.*, 2009). On this view, Third Way talk of being 'beyond left and right' was hubristic. This was embodied in New Labour Chancellor and then ill-fated Prime Minister, Gordon Brown, infamously suggesting New Labour had 'abolished' the boom and bust cycle of capitalism. The Global Financial Crisis and its aftermath sharpened class conflict once more, and exposed the precariousness of such claims.

Given this concentration on economic restructuring, Marxist theory has little to tell us about the new kinds of governor–citizen relations described by Bang and others. The changing state is understood by Marxists as a vehicle for marketisation. This is evidenced in increased use of private-sector partners and profitability criteria, embodied in figures such as the culture governor. As for other ideal-types such as the everyday maker or expert citizen, on a traditional Marxist reading such categories misrecognise the enduring political relevance of class. If a Marxist researcher was interested in such new types of subjectivity in the first place, they would likely try and link such apparently fluid and 'do it yourself' biographies to an underlying set of class relations (see Li and Marsh, 2008). For a richer account and critique of the new political subjectivities that emerge through state restructuring, we might turn to the Gramscian and Foucauldian perspectives also discussed in the first part of the chapter.

Gramsci argued that economic development necessitated the construction of a new type of subject – or 'collective man' (sic) to meet the requirements of a changing mode of production. The economy did not just take care of itself – politics, ideology and culture had to intervene to mould worker worldviews and practices. Crucially, for Gramsci, subjectivities would be forged through civil society and its complex relationship to the state. Thus, we saw how Gramsci (1971: 279–316) was fascinated by the rise of Fordism in America, because it was creating a disciplined, productive and consumption-oriented subject. The flexible, 'wired-worker' in the knowledge economy invoked by Giddens (2000) and New Labour was the latest instalment of what mid-twentieth-century sociologists referred to as 'industrial man' (Kerr *et al.*, 1960). In terms of governance, Gramsci (1971: 106–114) stressed that to ensure long-term control, ruling elites needed to know when to make concessions. Seen in this light, network governance and the rhetoric of partnership and empowerment is not just a functionally necessary feature of late modernity, as much of the governance literature implies. It is also part of a political *strategy*, diffusing opposition to economic restructuring and its social consequences. It achieves this by promoting a positive image of new modes of working and governance, and the democratic, 'empowering' possibilities for those who participate in them (Boltanski and Chiapello, 1999; Davies, 2011).

Foucault's insistence that power is productive could be seen as developing Gramsci's insights into how the state is deeply involved in producing a new type of 'collective man'. In a Foucauldian critique of the Third Way, Nikolas Rose (2001) points to the centrality of 'community' to its discourse in this respect. Community tended to be warmly invoked in Third Way rhetoric as either a set of 'authentic', pregiven values or a neighbourly physical space (Hale, 2004). However, Rose (2001) shows how in fact 'community' was actively constructed *through* Third Way discourse and policies. It became the site upon which individuals were exhorted to 'responsibly' manage their own biographies (as workers, consumers, parents). While using the rhetoric of empowering citizens, the Third Way actually displaced the problem of government from the state to individuals themselves: governance becomes fully internalised. This trend has only intensified with the subsequent rhetoric of Big Society from David Cameron's Conservatives since 2010 (Foster *et al.*, 2014).

Taken together, these perspectives also provide a critical angle on the culture governor and everyday maker described by Bang (2003). Gramsci (1971: 5–23) identified 'organic intellectuals' – ultimately grounded in one of the 'fundamental classes' of capitalism – as a bridge between theoretical analyses of social and economic change, and the diffusion of such ideas into everyday consciousness. The culture governors (and to a lesser extent the expert citizens) identified by Bang can be seen as a new breed of organic intellectual, operating (consciously or not) on behalf of the interests of a mutating capitalism. Their task is to promote the new theories of governance and the more fundamental sociological claims that underpin it, and then to mobilise citizens to 'get in line' with them. Such a reading of Gramsci indicates where he grants considerable agency to the ruling group. However, an alternative would be to interpret the condition of late or reflexive modernity as one of what Gramsci (1971: 210–18) called 'organic crises'. This is a period in which the dominant narratives that order the world no longer have any purchase upon people's experiences. In this state of relative turmoil, Gramsci (1971: 276) famously remarked that, 'the old is dying and the new cannot be born' and thus, 'a great variety of morbid symptoms appear' in the social world. The highly fluid, detraditionalised conditions of reflexive modernity and the decline of stable ideologies could be seen as expressing such a crisis. In this context, the rather haphazard, even chaotic worldviews of everyday makers embody the 'morbid symptoms' depicted by Gramsci. This would suggest that far from being the hope of a new bottom-up model of governance, the everyday maker is a transitional figure, still waiting to be articulated into something more politically coherent.

Again, the Foucauldian notion of power as productive is a useful supplement to Gramsci. If, as governmentality theorists claim, contemporary power operates through our autonomy and choices, then the 'do it here, do it my way' everyday maker is perhaps the ultimate expression of power flowing through individual conduct. In addition, rather than seeing power as reducible to Gramsci's fundamental classes, Foucauldians can show how culture governors are themselves constructed within a complex matrix of discourses and interests. While the refusal of Foucauldians to specify who or what ultimately has power can be frustrating, it has the merit of avoiding conspiracy theories: it acknowledges that the 'rulers' are themselves as much discursively constructed and bounded as the 'ruled'.

Conclusion: The state, governance and the society–politics relation

The analytical problem that runs throughout this book is what we have called the society–politics relation. Chapter 1 mapped out this problem and argued for an approach that keeps in view both the irreducibly political and the inescapably social. The former acknowledges power, politics, struggle, agency and contingency. The latter recognises that these political elements do not just occur in a vacuum: they are enabled and constrained by structured social institutions, practices, norms and ideologies. These are prior to and extend beyond the 'purely' political activities of individuals and groups. It was argued that holding onto a sense of both the social and the political enables us, through substantive case studies, to examine their complex interplay, and also enhances the possibilities for critique. This chapter has begun our investigation of substantive areas of political analysis 'from above': the nature of the state and governance and its changing relationship to the wider society. We have considered functionalist, Marxist, Gramscian and Foucauldian traditions of theorising the state, as well as contemporary theoretical perspectives on the nature of governance in late modernity. These were applied to two contemporary examples: the Third Way project as a political response to rapid social change, and work on the changing nature of the governor–citizen relation and the new identities it produces. The case studies and evaluation of them has illustrated the different ways in which social theory can relate to empirical political practices: as constitutive of them (in the case of the Third Way); as an interpretive device that enables the identification of new actors and practices (such as culture governors and everyday makers); and by offering a variety of critical perspectives upon those practices, often drawing on much older traditions of social theory and analysis.

In view of this, and returning to our overall problematic, what does social theory's understandings of the state and governance reveal about the society–politics relation discussed in Chapter 1? In the functionalist approach, as well as Marxism, looming social and economic forces are prioritised at the expense of political agency. Similarly, the social theory underpinning the governance literature, as well as the Third Way, implies that politics must simply adapt to social transformations such as economic and cultural globalisation. The state is still seen as important, and remains active, but it reflects rather than leads wider social forces. Marxist theory brings a critical sense of power and politics into such narratives, with its emphasis on enduring class relations and the struggle over a new phase of capitalism. But even this shares with functionalist accounts a sense that political activity is, in the Marxist language, 'epiphenomenal' to the tectonic plates of social and economic development. Such sociologically reductionist approaches neglect how those crucial 'social forces' might themselves be the outcome of political activity.

In the Foucauldian tradition, by contrast, all social relations and identities are seen as effects of power. In this politico-centric account, every society is characterised by its own particular problems of governing. What sociological theories regard as prior social relations are themselves the outcomes of governing strategies and acts of power. This approach not only pushes back against sociological reductionism, but collapses the social–political distinction by subsuming the social into the political: *everything is politics*. On this reading, the modernising social policies of centre-left governments, or new subjects such as the everyday maker or expert citizen, need to be understood in the context of new rationalities of government and technologies of rule. However, this politico-centrism underplays the social character and effects of institutions, practices and norms. In so doing, it diminishes our understanding of new political formations such as those captured by Bang. Political strategies, ideas and identities do not just emerge from thin air or the 'will to power' of elite political actors. They are formed upon – and shaped by – a definite social and cultural terrain. Social theories of individualisation, for example, capture concrete social trends which present a whole host of challenges for policymaking, ideology and political mobilisation. Similarly, the aspirations and capacities of both governors and citizens are shaped by prior institutions and structures. These might be in the form of enduring ideological legacies of left and right, which subvert claims to Third Way transcendence. Or they could involve persistent, structured inequalities: these will empower some actors to be expert citizens, or to pursue a politics of identity, while excluding others. The inescapable fact of the social remains.

The neo-Gramscian tradition shows some promise in keeping a sense of both the social and the political. To be sure, as a Marxist, Gramsci saw politics as ultimately grounded in the development of capitalism and the objectives of its fundamental classes. Yet Gramsci was the first Marxist thinker to highlight the importance of prior social norms, institutions and practices – embodied in what he termed civil society – as the site upon which political common sense is fought over. However, in this struggle, he granted a key role to political agency: through his account of the state and its organs ('political society'), his Machiavellian focus on the strategies of elite actors, and the key role he grants to organic intellectuals. This balanced approach is useful in critically theorising a modern governing project such as the Third Way. It recognises that governance occurs on a shifting social terrain and must respond to social and economic developments. However, governors exercise agency in constructing new types of worker or political subject. By the same token, the possibility of opposition lies in providing alternative visions of political subjectivity in the face of social change. This neatly highlights the importance of maintaining an analytical distinction between the social and the political – in order to analyse their interplay – as we argued for in Chapter 1. The task is to identify those areas of social change which are relatively entrenched and non-malleable, and those which are more fluid and subject to political intervention. For Gramscians, it is precisely achieving this resonance between political programmes and the shifting social world in which the 'art of politics' lies. For example, we might accept that something approximating 'globalisation' is occurring. However, we might simultaneously reject the fatalistic reading of neoliberal globalisation as being inevitable, and seek political spaces for a more regulated, social democratic form of global governance (see e.g. Held, 2004).

The story of this chapter has been a gradual *blurring* of the state–society distinction. We have seen a transition from traditional conceptions of government as acting 'over' society, to ideas about governance. In the latter, the sheer complexity of contemporary societies involves the diversification and devolution of rule, to the extent that rule itself becomes embedded in the activities and choices of individuals in civil society. The increasing emphasis by social theorists on individualisation and subjectivity, as well as evidence emerging from empirical studies, challenges traditional analytical categories. A subject such as the everyday maker exists at the very interface of debates over the social–political relation: she can be seen to embody empowering new possibilities for a politics of individual expression 'from below', or as being highly vulnerable to domination and manipulation 'from above'. Theories of the state and governance have grappled towards an account of the dilemmas posed by such new types of political subjectivity. But – as we shall see in the next chapter – social theory has plenty more to say about the nature of agency in late modernity, and its political implications.

3

Politics From Below: Political Identity and Participation

Introduction

The previous chapter showed how social theory's preoccupation with macro social change lends itself to analysis of major institutions such as the state. In this chapter, we shift our focus to the nature of the political Self and political identity. Macro social theory can seem far removed from individual subjectivity and its political possibilities. Despite this, it has had a great deal to say about the fate of the individual in modern societies. This is the part of the sociological imagination that C. Wright Mills (1959: 14) identified as being concerned with 'the personal troubles of milieu', in addition to 'the public issues of social structure'. Indeed, in recent decades questions of individual identity have become central to the discipline.

There is, then, a rich tradition of social theories of the Self to draw on. In refining down our selection, the distinction made in the Introduction between 'social' and 'sociological' theory is important. A major aspect of sociological theory is its attempt to develop a comprehensive, formalised account of agency. This is largely abstracted from concrete social and political context, instead trying to develop theoretical models that capture universal dimensions of human action (e.g. Archer, 1995, 2000; Bourdieu, 1990; Giddens, 1984). Here we are concerned less with these models than the implications of macro social theory for how agency – and in particularly political agency – is understood. In other words, how have accounts of large-scale social change affected the way social theory understands individual experience and its political consequences?

It is this concern with political agency in its much wider, macro social context that also guides us in our choice of theorists. In particular, we do not here draw on the micro-sociological tradition, with its focus on everyday interactions and meaning-making (see e.g. Roberts, 2006; Scott, 2009). This is certainly not to say that micro-sociology is not political. Indeed, the political potential of micro-sociology – especially in the context of culturally complex and diverse late modern societies – is underexplored (for exceptions see May, 2013; Smith, 1988). However, here we sustain our focus on predominantly macro social theory, as providing an account of the changing canvas upon which identities are politically constructed and contested. From among the various competing theories of this type, a reasonably consistent story emerges concerning the trajectory of individual experience. This is of a long-term shift from a society of more homogeneous, ascribed and stable selves to one of fragmented, complex and fluid identities – over which the individual is increasingly their own author. However, the underlying causes, character and political consequences of this shift are vigorously contested.

The relationship between the inescapably social and the irreducibly political is complex when it comes to theorising identity. With the exception of Marxism, the agent of classical political theory and mainstream political science tends to be abstracted from social relations and historical context. Actors are characterised in terms of a 'human nature' which, while occasionally altruistic as in Rousseau, is more often calculating and self-interested as in Hobbes or Machiavelli (Plamenatz, 1963). We begin, then, by outlining the contribution of classical sociological theory to developing a more rounded, socialised view of the agent, with particular reference to the political impact of economic and class relations, social norms and values. However, eventually the agent came to be presented as a 'puppet' in the face of social forces: the dynamics of political interaction – and prospects for creative political agency – were marginalised. But we then see how a number of factors – intellectual, empirical and ideological – combined to reassert the autonomy of individuals in constructing their political identities. The benefits of this restatement of the irreducibly political are noted. However, we conclude our discussion with a call for the need to reintegrate a sense of the inescapably social into our understanding of political identities.

To illustrate these theoretical issues, we turn in our case study to contemporary empirical research into 'political consumerism'. This refers to the increasingly widespread and sophisticated ways that citizens are politically mobilising their consumer activities and identities, for example through ethical consumption and associated lifestyle changes. Our case studies again illustrate the different senses in which social theory relates to empirical political research and practice: identifying/explaining; critiquing and constituting. Echoing work on new modes of governance explored in Chapter 2, researchers have drawn on social theories of reflexive modernity and individualisation to identify and explain the emergence of political consumerist actors, practices and attitudes. But the political character of political consumerism – and indeed whether it can be deemed 'political' at all – is fiercely debated. Within such debates there is again recourse to more traditional social theories of identity – discussed in the first half of the chapter – as a resource for contemporary critique. However, the final theory-empirical relation we identified – of social theory being constitutive of its empirical object – is more ambiguous here than in it was in our governance case study in Chapter 2: social theory is not imported into political consumerist practice in the same explicit way. Nevertheless, it does become difficult to disentangle social theories that identify, explain and critique political consumption from practices of political consumption themselves. But before moving on to our case studies, we begin with a detailed examination of how social theory has, over time, shifted its account of identity within rapidly developing modern societies.

Classical social theory and the Self

The socialised, integrated Self

The most important contribution of classical sociological theory to understanding political identity was its argument that the individual only makes sense in the context of social relations. In their very different ways, both Marx and Durkheim shared this view, and reacted against what they saw as the misguided, atomised conception of the individual that had dominated nineteenth-century thought.

Marx and the ensemble of social relations

It might seem curious to turn to Marx for insights into identity and politics, as he is frequently accused of neglecting both. Indeed, contemporary theories of the political subject typically position themselves against Marx's structural determinism, manifest in his preoccupation with the role of social classes in the context of inexorable laws of economic development (Laclau and Mouffe, 1985). While much of this criticism is justified, Marx nevertheless had a great deal to offer in terms of understanding political identity formation. Classical conceptions of the political Self had a universal, transhistorical character: they made little or no reference to social context, preferring theories of 'human nature'. There is considerable debate over the extent to which Marx himself held a theory of human nature (Ollman, 1971). But regardless of this, Marx offered one of the first and most influential accounts of the socialised individual.

Marx (1859: 4) famously insisted that, '[i]t is not the consciousness of men that determines their being, but, on the contrary, their social being that determines their consciousness'. For Marx (1845: 145), 'the human essence is no abstraction inherent in each single individual. In its reality it is the ensemble of the social relations'. With this view, Marx was offering a radical counterpoint to liberal, conservative and utopian political theory, as well as the utility maximisers of classical political economy. More specifically for Marx – and this was to be his most enduring insight – the 'social being' which determines consciousness is equated to social class, defined by one's relationship to the means of economic production. It is an individual's position within a (class-based) social structure which determines their worldview and political identity. One important consequence is that, on the Marxist reading, there is little point in discussing the individual psychology or 'character' of political actors. For example, despite contemporary 'banker bashing' following the Global Financial Crisis, Marxist theory implies that focusing on individual, 'greedy' capitalists might be a distraction from the structural issues. This is because the pursuit of immediate financial gain, and ensuring social and political arrangements to facilitate such gain, is simply rational behaviour for a capitalist: it is what it means to 'be' a capitalist in a capitalist economy and society (Marx, 1867).

Durkheim: homo duplex and group articulation

While Durkheim did not emphasise the role of social class, in seeking to establish the importance of sociology he shared Marx's rejection of atomised conceptions of the individual. Indeed, Durkheim (1893, 1897) went as far as to regard such conceptions as a threat to the stability and integration of developing industrial societies (Bowring, 2016; Marske, 1987). Just as Marx – with his conception of species being – implied that there is something natural about human sociability, Durkheim offered a model of human nature that explicitly points to this social dimension. In his account of *homo duplex*, Durkheim described the dual character of humans. On the one hand, we possess individualised, more atavistic personality traits. But no matter how much human diversity and complexity this generates, disparate individuals share in common a second core dimension: their capacity and need for social integration (Durkheim, 1912, 1914). Durkheim's (1912) anthropological work analysed the nature of religious rituals and practices in fulfilling this function. Durkheim was less interested in the specific content of such practices as in how religion *per se* had been able to fulfil the universal function of social integration. In modern, increasingly secular economies and societies, the need for this integrative function was still present but would need to be met by different institutions. A key task of sociology in general – and Durkheim's (1893, 1950) work in particular – would be to uncover the source of such integration in modern societies.

This overview has shown the contribution of two founding social theorists to understanding the individual as being a social product – and the particular way this manifested itself in the rapidly developing industrial societies of the nineteenth century. But, of itself, this does not tell us very much about the specific political character of these shifts: should we understand the impact of modernity upon political identity positively or negatively? Here we can introduce a broad distinction between social theories which point to problems of domination and the diminishing of identity and those that, while possibly sharing some of these fears, nevertheless see glimpses of the potential for human autonomy and liberation. We shall see later in this chapter that this distinction – and its ambiguities and limitations – remains a key feature of evaluating more contemporary debates about social change and political identity.

Self and political domination

Marx and alienation

In his so-called 'younger' works, Marx was preoccupied with the problems that capitalism posed for humans' lived experience. Although Marx (1845) portrayed humans as a 'blank slate', upon which the imprint of social relations would be stamped, in his more philosophical work he also presents a human nature which is diminished, or stifled, by the effects of capitalism. In his *Economic and Philosophic Manuscripts* (1844), Marx describes humans as being sociable, productive and having the capacity for detached, critical enjoyment of objects and experiences. Capitalism is the complete antithesis of this 'human essence' and, in Marx's language, humans become *alienated*. Marx (1844) understands alienation as occurring when an entity exists in a distorted relationship to something else. Under capitalism, humans become alienated in four key respects that diminish their fundamental humanity: from the process of production (because of the fragmentation of the 'production line' setting), from the product itself (because it becomes a commodity on the market place), from other humans (because of the division of labour and its polarising, class-based effects) and, ultimately, from their own *species being* – as a whole, fulfilled individual with the capacities we have described. So Marx presented an image of the essential completeness of the Self being undermined by capitalism: individuals are both dominated and unfulfilled. However, Marx is not depicting a conspiracy among capitalists to dominate the subjectivity of workers: it is the organisation of society itself which does the 'dominating'. This is illustrated by the crucial caveat that *the capitalists are just as alienated as the workers*. For all their relative power over workers, capitalists are nevertheless also subject to the dehumanising logic of capitalism (Ollman, 1971).

Durkheim and anomie

Durkheim, too, was deeply concerned about the fate of the individual in modern society. Despite his fundamental differences with Marx, he also observed a disjuncture between the individual and the social totality. Durkheim believed that societies were characterised by the means for their own stability, including the integration between the individual and the collective which would be ensured by a 'collective consciousness'. In his *The Division of Labour and Society* (1893), Durkheim noted that traditional, less complex societies were more easily bound together by overarching group norms. He characterised such societies as possessing a 'mechanical solidarity', in which the collective dominated over the individual. However, with a rapidly growing, urbanising population, an increasingly complex division of labour and diversifying social structure, the sense of overarching group identity was under threat. Consequently, Durkheim identified modern societies as being at risk of *anomie* – or 'normlessness'. Cut adrift from the moorings of integrative social norms, the consequences for individuals could be catastrophic. Indeed, Durkheim (1897) identified an absence of sufficient regulation and integration as being the driver of anomic forms of suicide in modern societies.

Both Marx and Durkheim, then, start from the premise of a socialised individual, and show the disruptive effects of a rapidly evolving industrial capitalism. What then follows are various negative consequences for individuals *vis-a-vis* their 'proper' relationship to the collective. In particular, each thinker has their own critique of the fragmentation of social life, and the isolated, self-directed behaviour it can engender. Marx was of course critical of dominant, bourgeois values and self-seeking behaviour in the market place, while Durkheim attacked what he saw as pathological forms of egoism and their anomic effects. Alienation and anomie are thus concepts which reveal some shared ground between Marx and Durkheim with regard to the journey of the individual in the modern world.

Rationalisation and disenchantment: Weber and the Frankfurt School

The founders of modern social theory were present at the birth of industrial societies, and their fears for individual experience reflect the immediacy of that time: the effects of urbanisation, the factory, naked exploitation and polarising social classes. In the first half of the twentieth century, such fears persisted, but new issues emerged as mass capitalism become embedded and more complex. In particular, critical theorists became preoccupied with how emerging mass culture was integral to producing passive citizens, productive workers and – increasingly – aspirational consumers. The Frankfurt School of critical theorists including Theodor Adorno, Max Horkheimer and Herbert Marcuse were émigrés to the United States from Nazi Germany. On arriving in the US – the classic modern consumer society of the 1950s – they were fascinated and horrified with capitalist mass culture and the passive subject it was producing (Jay, 1996; Kellner, 1989).

Like other (neo) Marxist thinkers, the Frankfurt School sought to explain how class consciousness and revolution had failed to materialise: understanding the operations of mass culture upon individual subjectivity was crucial to this. The Frankfurt School supplemented Marx's analysis of the dynamics of capitalism with the critical legacy of Max Weber (Arato, 1982). Weber had profound concerns about the nature of modern rationality and the individual and institutional forms of action it generated. Weber (1922c) recognised the benefits and efficiencies of calculating, instrumental forms of reason and their manifestation in capitalism's bureaucratic organisations, such as the state (see Chapter 2). But he simultaneously feared the human costs of this 'disenchantment' of the world – the elimination of 'magic' and the sense of the accidental in human affairs (Weber, 1918b: 155). In particular, Weber (1904–5) famously claimed that we were constructing an 'iron cage' of rationality that would come to enslave us.

The Frankfurt School tried to grasp a modern society that was still beset by anomie and alienation, but was now simultaneously glued together by a new, mass culture. Popular films, radio, television, novels and newspapers provided a readymade set of subject positions for people to identify with. While appearing to tell unique, individual stories, they reinforced powerful norms about gender, family, hard work, success and aspiration. In this sense, mass culture presented a 'pseudo-individuality' which actually homogenised the populace as workers and consumers (Adorno and Horkheimer, 1944). In this scenario, the possibilities for any kind of revolutionary class consciousness, or even basic social criticism, were bleak. Herbert Marcuse (1964) pursued these negative political implications in his account of the new 'One Dimensional Man'. With strong Weberian undertones, Marcuse pointed to how not just the distractions of mass consumption – but also the apparently progressive interventions of liberal welfare bureaucracies – were leading to a 'closure of the political universe' and a form of 'happy consciousness'. Under such conditions, the imagining of social and political alternatives became impossible.

Self and political freedom

Modern social theory, then, began with an assumption that individuals are the bearers of social relations. As societies became more complex, industrialised and under the sway of capitalist production and consumption, a range of problems emerged for the quality of individual experience and belonging. And from the point of view of those thinkers committed to critique and emancipation, the implications for collective political identities and agency seemed particularly bleak. However, in each of the gloomy analyses considered above, there was also consideration of how problems such as alienation, anomie and passive, false individualism might be overcome. What united the theorists' disparate diagnoses was the hope, ultimately, for repair, reconstitution and wholeness: that the human Self would be restored to a 'correct' relationship to the social totality.

Marx, communism and human flourishing

For Marx, there are two stages to the realisation of human identity. The first is the development of class consciousness from within the confines of capitalist conditions. This emerges through a critique of the present, and the growing sense of a future, better society. The determinist, orthodox Marxist position was that this consciousness would be generated by the structural tendencies and crises of capitalism itself. Thus, to overcome diminishing profitability, capitalists would inevitably put downward pressure upon wages, and intensify the labour process by, for example, extending the working day (Marx, 1867). This in turn increases the degree of exploitation and alienation among workers: it is ultimately the shared, brute fact of their material conditions that will galvanise workers around revolutionary politics (Marx and Engels, 1848).

The second phase, which speaks more profoundly to what Marx understood by identity, is the realisation of human potential under communism. Marx's reflections on what communism would look like are notoriously in short supply, fragmented and (somewhat necessarily!) speculative. However, beyond doubt is that he envisaged a society in which the dehumanising effects of capitalism would be overcome, and fully human attributes would be cultivated and flourish (Marx, 1844, 1875). But unlike Marx's analysis of class consciousness under capitalism, where the imperatives come from the failing social structure, his account of life under communism seems to foreground assumptions about human nature that we noted previously (Jaeggi, 2014). Structural forces do remain crucial: Marx (1844, 1875) points to the abolition of the division of labour and the money form, the overcoming of scarcity and the gradual diminishing of classes. But these are a platform for the (re)emergence of a human subject who is sociable, productive, intellectually curious and skilled across a range of tasks. This is most famously captured in Marx's (1846: 160) vision of communism in which it would be possible:

> for me to do one thing today and another tomorrow, to hunt in the morning, fish in the afternoon, rear cattle in the evening, criticise after dinner, just as I have a mind, without ever becoming hunter, fisherman, shepherd or critic.

Thus, the image is of restoration of the alienated and damaged human Self to a condition of fullness.

This idealised account of what the 'natural' human condition is – or could be – was echoed in the more optimistic moments of Frankfurt School analysis, a century after Marx. However, where Marx could only envisage such liberation of the Self in a future communist society, Marcuse comes to see self-liberation as a *precondition* of the revolutionary project. In his earlier *Eros and Civilisation* (1956), Marcuse critically engages with Freudian psychoanalysis, which he uses to describe how fundamental human impulses are co-opted and repressed under capitalism. *One Dimensional Man* (1964) is subsequently a pessimistic account of the shutting down of human potential. However, inspired by the student protests and New Left movements of which he was a figurehead in the 1960s, in his later *Essay on Liberation* (1969) Marcuse identifies the revolutionary role of a range of groups beyond just class actors (e.g. students, feminists and marginalised ethnic groups); he sees these as engaged in a 'Great

Refusal' of the existing order. Crucially, Marcuse identifies the cultivation of a radical new subjectivity – a 'new sensibility' – as central to social and political change. This is not guaranteed in advance by the structural contradictions or injustices of the present order, but is the object of politics itself: personal identity and the quest for personal liberation become inextricably linked to wider social and political transformation.

Durkheim: organic solidarity and secondary associations

Marx saw real autonomy as only possible in an entirely new, communist society. Durkheim, in keeping with his reformist outlook, sought to overcome anomie and other pathologies within a still broadly capitalist economy and liberal democracy. However, like Marx, Durkheim's structural proposals resonate with his assumptions about the nature of human identity. For Durkheim, all human societies have basic integrative functions: it is when these become out of kilter that problems arise for individuals and society as a whole. In his landmark study of *Suicide*, Durkheim (1897) characterised societies in terms of their degree of social integration and regulation: too much or too little of either created conditions that could lead to pathological symptoms, of which a high suicide rate was an example. As we saw above, in modern, individualist societies there was a risk of anomie – and the corresponding anomic form of suicide, resulting from a breakdown of the social norms which make individual behaviour meaningful. Like Marx, Durkheim (1893, 1950) was critical of laissez-faire liberalism which encouraged individualism at the expense of social integration. He also did not seek a return to conservative notions of tradition and community for reintegrating individuals (Durkheim, 1898). However, unlike Marx, Durkheim believed that all societies – including industrial capitalism – possessed the means of their own integration. The task of modern sociology was to discover this integrative basis and make it explicit, in contrast to social and political theories which presented rapid flux and change as social dissolution (Durkheim, 1893).

For Durkheim (1893), the key was the division of labour and complexity. To most observers, the increasing specialisation and differentiation of modern societies (in the economy, culture, forms of knowledge, family and kinship relations) seemed to be the root cause of social fragmentation. This was true of conservatives who lamented the disruption to traditional hierarchies and communities. But it was also the view of Marx, who saw the division of labour as central to alienation and sought to transcend it with communism. Durkheim, however, argued that on the contrary, specialisation through the division of labour actually provided the basis for a new form of 'organic' integration and social solidarity. It was *precisely* the fact that society was more differentiated, specialised and complex than ever before that generated a new form of interdependence and interconnectedness (Durkheim, 1893). The task was to understand, harness and regulate this latent new form of social cooperation. Durkheim (1950) went on to argue that, specifically, the state has a role to play in integrating individuals into collective forms of life. While the state was too remote from everyday individual experience to do this directly, it should co-ordinate the activities of the burgeoning 'secondary associations' of a growing modern civil society. In particular, Durkheim had in mind the professional associations and guilds that, in addition to reflecting people's working lives, also had more expansive functions around education, culture and leisure. Such organisations were ideally suited for integrating increasingly diverse, autonomy-seeking individuals: they faced and enhanced people's everyday experiences on the one hand, but also the over-arching, integrative institutions of the state on the other. While not quite on the 'new world' scale of Marx's vision, the goal is a more integrated, ordered and functional society, less likely to be at risk of anomie and other pathologies.

Summary

In contrast to political theory and philosophy's abstract accounts of human nature, classical social theory offered a socialised conception of the individual. As the late nineteenth and twentieth centuries unfolded, social theorists chronicled the impact of rapid economic and social development upon individual identity. Their analysis was typically bleak: they were variously concerned about exploitation, isolation, the decline of shared values and the general diminishing of human capacities. In seeking to remedy this, none of them looked nostalgically to an imagined past of happier individuals and shared values, but rather to how the sense of human fullness they sought could be reconstructed in a better, future society. While we have noted underlying conceptions of human nature in these analyses, the socialised conception of the individual remains consistent: for the fragmented, broken human Self to be 'fixed', social structures must be overturned (Marx, Frankfurt School) or repaired (Durkheim). Here we see again the potentially depoliticising aspects of an overly socialised analysis. While political consciousness and action are necessary to improve human experience, the more complete human subject ultimately aimed for seems to lack political capacity and identity. With regard to Marx, the question often posed is that if politics (and by extension what we today call political identity or subjectivity) disappeared along with the class struggle, what would be left to argue about? And in Durkheim's case, there seems to be little space for the tensions, contradictions and messiness of a political personality: politics is smoothly and benignly channelled in the relations between the 'social brain' of the state, and the intermediary institutions of civil society.

From stable Selves to fluid identities

Social theory from the 1960s has described – and perhaps contributed to – an unravelling of the classic image of a unified Self. This shift has occurred through the continued rapid development of the industrial societies first captured by nineteenth-century theorists. In particular, this has involved an increasingly globalised economy and culture, central to which are new information technologies and a mass media. New political movements and forms of political practice – to which questions of identity are central – have also arisen alongside these changes. But also important has been the opening out of social theory itself to a number of alternative theoretical currents, such as the work of Michel Foucault and the contribution of psychoanalysis. Our task is to understand the complex relationship between these empirical, political and theoretical developments, in generating new conceptions and practices of political identity. Of course, these connections were also important during early industrial capitalism, but there seems to be something about late or postmodern society which has made them even more interrelated and complex. Later, we shall examine the crucial social theory of individualisation – elaborated in the works of Ulrich Beck, Anthony Giddens and Zygmunt Bauman – as crystallising these varied empirical, political and theoretical dimensions.

Empirical transformations: work, culture, politics

The changing world of work

Virtually all accounts of how social transformation has impacted upon the Self begin with the now familiar story of the development and mutation of capitalism. We noted in Chapter 2 how economic globalisation and the rise of the knowledge economy have affected the state. In terms of political identities, those same developments are the backdrop to the decline of collective political attachments and the fracturing of individual political worldviews and practices. Nineteenth- and twentieth-century social theory, derived from the Marxist focus on production, assumed that work was central to identity. Work was the key determinant of class location, shared experiences and solidarities. Most importantly, it was the position from which one formed a worldview about the wider economy, society and polity: work was the lens through which one understood the nature of the market economy, the role of the state, patterns of inequality and rewards and a host of individual political questions (e.g. Goldthorpe *et al.*, 1968, 1969).

If we accept that work is central to identity, then it follows that changes in the nature of work will result in changes in the nature of that identity. So the move to a post-Fordist production regime had significant consequences. Post-Fordism involved increasing specialisation; more flexible and part-time working, with workers regularly changing jobs; the mass entry of women into the paid workforce; the rise of white collar and service sector jobs at the expense of heavy manufacturing; and a wider climate of increased individual competition (see Amin, 1994). The consequences, while characterised in different ways by theorists, all point towards the fragmentation and individualisation of identity. Manufacturing industry had been the key site of trade unionism, working-class community and labour politics, grounded in a shared, relatively homogeneous and sustained experience of the production process. As that process became more specialised and disjointed, as Ray Pahl (1995) demonstrates, the experiences and narratives of workers became increasingly privatised, with little shared vocabulary beyond that of individual success. Richard Sennett (1998) goes further, developing a critique of modern workplaces as key drivers of the 'corrosion of character', while Arlie Hochschild (2012) identifies the damaging self-management and emotional labour that individual service workers must perform. The irony is that individuals are working longer, with work being more central to their lives, than at any time since the Second World War. But they have simultaneously lost the means of collectively experiencing and reflecting on work and its political implications.

New technologies and cultural globalisation

Closely bound up with fragmenting economic processes are radical changes in technology and culture, which have a similar effect upon identity. We saw in Chapter 2 that for social theorists such as Giddens, it is the cultural aspects of globalisation that have the most significant sociological effects. Specifically, the proliferation of information intensifies social reflexivity, where the basis of action is the constant monitoring and processing of that information (Giddens, 1990). This opens up detraditionalisation and individualisation: challenges to established ideas and practices mean that individuals are 'cut adrift' from the certainties of earlier modernity (Bauman, 2001; Heelas *et al.*, 1996). We shall return to the theory and implications of individualisation below. Here we should note that, although Giddens is drawing a broad theoretical sketch of key features of late modernity, there are empirical reference points to his claims. Giddens himself invokes technology, by dating cultural globalisation to the first successful satellite broadcast in the late 1960s (1994: 80). Since that time we have witnessed the rise of the internet and, more recently, user-generated web 2.0 practices and social media. This has intensified information flows and reflexivity to levels that even Giddens would not have originally anticipated in the early 1990s. Such practices are allied to the longer-term trend of cultural exchange – opened up through travel, migration and multiculturalism – to generate the hybridity and cosmopolitanism that many theorists see as informing contemporary identities (Beck, 2006).

Mass media and consumption

Changes to the mode of production, and processes such as detraditionalisation, provide the deep background conditions for shifts in identity formation. The canvas on which these are most visibly played out brings together economic, cultural and technological dimensions: the global mass media and mass consumerism. Even the earlier critics most attuned to cultural questions, such as the Frankfurt School, could not have envisaged the extent to which society would become mediated and consumption oriented. The growth of the media has been staggering, from early newspaper and radio, through terrestrial then satellite television, to the internet and mobile technology platforms. These developments have produced disciplines such as media studies, as well as preoccupying cultural studies and sociology. They have *en route* given rise to claims that we live in the 'society of the spectacle' (Debord, 1967) or, more controversially, that society as such has imploded into an endless play of free-floating images (Baudrillard, 1980). Despite these developments, the issues originally identified by the Frankfurt School (e.g. Adorno and Horkheimer, 1944; Benjamin, 1936) still get to the heart of the implications of the mediascape for contemporary identity formation: does it represent homogenisation, pacification and the imposition of identities, or possibilities for active identity construction and the subversion of power? Wherever we stand on that question, there is no doubt that the sheer proliferation of media forms – and the ever shifting ways that individuals engage with them – contributes to the fragmentation of stable identities, and provides resources for media consumers to construct their sense of Self.

The media is itself the major vehicle for the second crucial site of identity formation: mass consumption. In the nineteenth century capitalism described by Marx, consumption was secondary to the productive process. This wasn't just because of a bias in Marx's analysis: there simply wasn't as much consumption by volume in earlier capitalism. The relative spread of affluence and easily available credit, the development of the retail sector, markets for cheap imports and latterly the emergence of online shopping, have all contributed to the rise of the consumer society. In conjunction with lifestyle advertising, the ethos of contemporary capitalism is that identity can be bought, just like any commodity (Bauman, 2007). As with debates over the media, whether this represents a narrowing of choice – and indeed a form of social control – or a creative and expressive act on the part of consumers, is contested and explored in detail in our case study on political consumerism. But also as with media, there can be no doubt that consumption provides another key site through which identity shifts from being stable and ascribed, to fragmented and constructed.

Political shifts and identity: '1968' and neoliberalism

Our overview of empirical shifts concludes with two key political developments since the late 1960s: the New Left countercultural politics embodied in the protests of 1968, and the New Right, neoliberal revolution of the mid-1970s onwards. The latter was associated first of all with Margaret Thatcher in the UK and Ronald Reagan in in the US, before achieving a global reach. While the New Left and New Right were ostensibly antithetical political propositions, they had more in common than either would care to admit in terms of pushing political identities in a more individualistic direction.

The student, worker, civil rights and countercultural protests of 1968 embodied a new form and content for progressive politics. Part of their impulse was dissatisfaction with the organisational forms, ethos and narrow policy agenda of established socialist and communist parties. Implicitly echoing the detraditionalisation thesis, and explicitly drawing on thinkers such as Marcuse (1964), this was allied to a wider critique of bureaucratic domination. Even institutions that had originally been hard won by progressives, such as the welfare state and public service bureaucracies, were now being criticised as sites of domination and control. At the same time, the predominantly white, male and heterosexual orientation of established political movements was being challenged by the fact of social complexity, and demands from women and ethnic minorities for active political participation and voice (see Bhambra and Demir, 2009). A host of new issues such as nuclear disarmament, an increasingly internationalist sensibility and environmental awareness were also gaining traction. The sense was that established parties and ways of doing politics could not deliver on these agendas, which required new forms of thinking and organising. This was manifest in the rise of the so-called 'new social movements' that mobilised in civil society (see Nash, 2010: 106–18). A shift away from the formal political sphere to everyday practices (in thinking about the politics of, for example, personal relationships or ethical consumption) was embodied in the slogan that 'the personal is political': the starkest confirmation of the individualisation of political identity.

In the popular imagination, the New Right, neoliberalism and the political projects of Mrs Thatcher and Ronald Reagan could not be further from the imagery of 1968 (and are explored in detail in Chapter 4). Coming from the political right, the neoliberal creed was developed in the context of socially and culturally conservative political parties: these were the natural enemies of progressive forces, even of 'the 1960s' itself. However, beyond the 'traditional values' and 'law and order' discourses, the essence of neoliberalism from the 1970s was an economic, political and arguably cultural ethos that had interesting resonances with the spirit of '68, adding weight to the trajectory of individualisation (Wagner, 2002). The figure of *homo economicus,* the self-interested utility maximiser of neoliberal economics, may have been anathema to the leftists of '68. However, the political critique of overbearing forms of bureaucracy and entrenched interests, and in particular of the centralised state, was held by both movements (Boltanski and Chiapello, 1999). Yet perhaps more important was the shared underlying cultural resonance: restlessness with being 'told what to do' and a desire for self-actualisation (Bhambra and Demir, 2009). For the 68ers this took many forms: countercultural forms of living, experimental forms of relationship, art and self-sustainability; while for the neoliberals it essentially involved breaking down barriers to personal advancement, and defining oneself through consumption. So while we are describing two very different political impulses, they both tap into a critique of established institutions and the state, a desire

to do things differently and a philosophy of self-actualisation. It is not difficult to see how the ethos of 1968 fed into and was co-opted by the neoliberal
project (Boltanski and Chiapello, 1999; Wagner, 2002).

Theoretical currents: Foucault, psychoanalytic theory, individualisation

We began this chapter by noting that the story of identity theory has been a
gradual loosening of the idea of wholeness and stability, towards fragmentation and fluidity. We also noted that in telling this story, there are complex
relations between the theories, the empirical changes they are describing,
and their political context. We began by reviewing how early modern social
theory embodied a strongly socialised view of identity. This portrayed a relatively powerless subject in the face of rapidly developing social structures.
The sense was of domination of identities in the present, but that this could
be overcome through future social transformation. In reviewing subsequent
empirical shifts, we have seen that the changes which did occur called in
to question the very connection between individuals and social structures:
would social theorists welcome this as emancipatory, or be concerned that
power and domination over individuals was becoming more complex and
insidious? In this section we consider some of the theoretical currents that
further reinforce the sense that late modern individuals have been cut adrift
from traditional social structures. Such theories are relatively disparate, and
while some attempt to base their analysis on empirical developments, others
are more abstract in attempting to make apparently universal claims about
the nature of subjectivity. However, all have played their part in the unravelling of the more stable conceptions of identity that we have been describing.

Foucault and the subject

The work of Michel Foucault has been central to debates in social and political
theory over the nature of identity (McNay, 1994). We saw in Chapter 2 how
Foucault's later work on governmentality generated a radically new conception of state power and the very nature of politics. Crucially, power is seen as
productive, that is, it should not simply be understood in negative terms as
one agent repressing or denying another. Rather, power is seen as generative
of social life itself (Foucault, 1980, 1983). Power is not a 'thing' possessed
by certain agents, but a set of discourses (closely allied to forms of expertise)
and practices that make up what we come to understand as normal social life.
As an historian, Foucault was keen to show how societal understandings of
normalcy in areas such as mental health or sexual behaviour were culturally
and historically variable. Foucault's earlier work developed these insights in
terms of understanding the production of the modern Self. He was preoccupied

with historical accounts of the rise of surveillance and bodily domination, exemplified in institutions such as the asylum (Foucault, 1963) or prison (Foucault, 1975). He explored how the development of such institutions, along with the rise of expert knowledge, were crucial to defining what came to be seen as 'normal' or 'deviant' (e.g. Foucault, 1976).

However, Foucault became conscious of the limits to a focus on discipline and surveillance in making sense of the contemporary Self: clearly the logic of the prison or clinic does not pertain in all domains of societies in which agents, increasingly, seem to be able to exercise a considerable degree of autonomy. To address this, Foucault investigated what he called the 'technologies of the self'. These are the widely dispersed, everyday means by which individuals cultivate their desires, sense of appropriate behaviours and mechanisms of self-regulation. In Foucault's (1982: 225) words, such technologies:

> permit individuals to effect by their own means, or with the help of others, a certain number of operations on their own bodies and souls, thoughts, conduct, and way of being, so as to transform themselves in order to attain a certain state of happiness, purity, wisdom, perfection or immortality.

Crucially, the means of acting on the Self does not just come 'from within', as a matter of psychology, but operates in a complex relationship with wider societal discourses, bodies of knowledge, cultural artefacts and organisational forms. Foucault (1982, 1984) sought to trace the historical rise of technologies of the Self, from the ancient Greek period onwards. However, viewed through his lens, all manner of apparently mundane contemporary practices such as reading lifestyle magazines, watching television soap operas, going to the gym or going on a diet can be seen as part of a matrix of self-production and regulation (see e.g. Bratich *et al.*, 2003; Mayes, 2016; Rose, 1999).

The implications of Foucault's work for understanding political identity, and in particular the possibility of resistance, are contested (McNay, 1994). To be sure, Foucault is widely admired for how he exploded the Enlightenment idea of a stable Self that would become civilised and even empowered through the growth of knowledge and expertise. Foucault provides a toolkit for deconstructing apparently neutral claims about normal behaviour: the Self needs to be seen as at the intersection of a range of discourses that reflect a ceaseless, if somewhat mysterious, power struggle. This holds out the hope that individuals are not powerless in the face of discourses and regimes of truth. On the contrary, the fact that power is 'everywhere' means that it does not operate through a zero-sum relationship between the 'powerful' and 'powerless'. Instead, power is a *resource* that all actors struggle over as they try to cement, or refuse, definitions of what it is to be a 'normal' individual.

It is this possibility of refusal and redefinition that is typically highlighted as making a Foucauldian resistance strategy possible. Aware that claims to expertise and normalcy are in fact contingent expressions of power, agents can refuse and subvert them in sites of resistance, such as the school, home, workplace or clinic. Challenging such relations of authority was an objective of the movements of 1968 discussed above. Unlike Marxist French intellectuals such as Althusser, who dismissed 'May '68' as 'infantile leftism', Foucault saw evidence of precisely the forms of subversion and reimagining that his later work in particular would gesture towards (Lopes, 2014). More expansively, inspired particularly by emerging debates and practices around gay identities, Foucault (e.g. 1981) pointed to the creative ways in which modern actors could re-describe, reinvent and perform their selves against prevailing discourses and norms. This could be seen as a strategy of reappropriating the ubiquitous technologies of the Self for one's own political ends. These insights have been taken up in particular by feminist theorists seeking to avoid essentialist identity politics (Butler, 1990; Sawicki, 1991).

Critics are sceptical that Foucault offers a radicalisation of political identity. Few deny that Foucault's analysis of ubiquitous power relations, and the importance of discourse and bodily discipline, is suggestive and broadened the field of political contestation. However, here we can highlight two contrasting criticisms of Foucault's approach. The first is that, far from opening out spaces for creative political agency, Foucault remains overshadowed by structuralism: this manifests in the way he presents subjects as passive in the face of overbearing discourses, systems of expertise and dominating organisational forms (Dews, 1984). And if power is 'everywhere', how can it ever be critically analysed, reconfigured or transcended (McNay, 1994: 105)? Alternatively, others suggest that far from being too concerned with the social element of the power of discourses, systems and expertise, Foucault in fact offers a hyper-individualist theory that collapses the social into micro-agential practices (Elliot, 2008: 101). Reading power at this level precludes analysis of the structural enablers of and obstacles to identity formation, and their embeddedness in social relations. In addition, Foucault's focus on mastering technologies of the Self belies a preoccupation with an enduring, 'heroic' (and masculine) idea of the Self, who will transcend social conditions through acts of will alone (McNay, 1994: 149–54). While these criticisms are forceful, they also appear as incompatible: Foucault cannot simultaneously be a structural determinist and documenter of the heroic, transcendental individual. However, supporters could claim that this reflects Foucault's genius for combining the complex interplay between the historical/structural, and the everyday/micro, in his account of political subjectivity.

Psychoanalytic theory, post-structuralism and identity as 'lack'

Foucault, with his focus on the constitutive role of discourse and power relations, offered a radical challenge to classical notions of a stable, enduring Self with the capacity to achieve 'wholeness'. However, as both Foucault's political advocates and critics suggest, he still indicates the potential for a relatively stable Self to creatively and strategically define their identity. In addition,

Foucault's subject is still a historical and social product, and to this extent is reconcilable with the socialised conception of the individual in more traditional sociological theory. It took the influences of psychoanalytic theory, structuralism and post-structuralism to radically disrupt the sociological conception of the Self. There is not room here to fully detail the complex intellectual history and relationship between these traditions, and we shall explore them further when considering the nature of ideology and discourse in the next chapter. For our present purpose, we will take two crucial ideas: of identity being a relational concept and, most importantly, one that is based on failure, or 'lack'. This represents the direct opposite of the image of totality in classic conceptions of the Self.

The notion of identity as a relational concept comes from the structuralist tradition, associated with thinkers such as Ferdinand de Saussure (1916) and Roland Barthes (1957, 1964). Structuralism contends that language does not simply represent objects. Rather, words and ideas only make sense in the context of their relationship to other words and ideas, as part of a structural totality. Thus, 'mother' only makes sense because there is also the category of 'son', 'dark' because there is also 'light', and so on. The task of the analyst is not, therefore, to understand the relationship between the object and the word, but rather the structural properties of systems of meaning (Ashenden, 2005). This approach reached its fullest expression in terms of understanding political identity in the work of French Marxist Louis Althusser (e.g. 1971).

The basic idea of identity being a relational, rather than an essential category, has achieved widespread acceptance in social and political analysis. However, the extreme determinism of structuralism fell out of favour relatively quickly, under challenge from a number of directions. The most explicit of these was the post-structuralist critique associated with Jacques Derrida (1966, 1967). Derrida and other post-structuralists accepted and had been influenced by much of the structuralist approach. However, they posed searching questions as to the social and historical construction of systems and structures themselves, the nature of human agency within such systems and, in particular, the role of contingency, power and politics. How could a space for creative human agency, and political contestation, be reinserted into the structuralist model? And could this be achieved without returning to classical, essentialist models of a preformed, ahistorical Self? The ingenious and, ultimately, highly productive solution to this conundrum in terms of political analysis was to conceive of the Self as being premised upon 'lack'. This subverted the classical idea of the integrated, whole Self, instead defining identity precisely in terms of its *inability* to achieve fullness (Derrida, 1966, 1967). Derrida and other post-structuralists argue that this condition of lack is itself a feature of any 'structure' or 'system'.

This counterintuitive idea is captured in the notion of the 'constitutive outside' (Staten, 1984). Derrida accepted the structuralist premise that objects only acquired meaning relationally. However, this position was then developed on psychoanalytic lines with the argument that not only is object B the necessary precondition of object A's identity (i.e. we only understand A in relation to B), but it is also, by virtue of its existence, a permanent *obstacle* to A ever achieving a 'full' identity. B is simultaneously the precondition of, but also obstacle to, A's identity. Identity is thus characterised not by completion or fullness, but by failure and lack (Torfing, 2005). This draws on Jacques Lacan's reading of Freud. In Lacan's (1949) famous account of the 'mirror phase', an infant gains a sense of its Self by seeing its own reflection, which it grasps as part of a wider symbolic order. We are consequently forever *seeking* the completion of our identity in this symbolic order, but such completion is, as we have seen, a logical impossibility. The subject is constituted through this very lack. This formulation, though highly abstract and speculative, opened the way to a whole new array of political concepts in the post-structuralist understanding of identity. Some of these will be discussed in the next chapter when considering discourse theory. For now, we should note how theory has travelled to the opposite extreme of the original, socialised conception of the stable Self. What characterises the Self here is its very impossibility, and yet the ceaseless, always doomed, quest for a 'full' identity becomes the stuff of politics.

Individualisation as sociological process

Foucauldian and, increasingly, post-structuralist and psychoanalytic approaches, have been extremely influential within social theory. However, the dominant approach to understanding the late modern Self and its political implications is within the sociological mainstream, in the form of the individualisation thesis. This is most closely associated with the work of Zygmunt Bauman, Ulrich Beck and Anthony Giddens. To be sure, these thinkers have variously been influenced by post-structuralism, psychoanalysis and the so-called 'cultural turn', as well as (in Giddens' case) micro-sociology, which all highlight everyday meaning-making. But the individualisation thesis can also be seen as a refusal of some of these theoretical traditions. This is because it tries to engage the classic sociological imagination by linking micro and macro sociological elements. Individualisation theory explains contemporary identities in terms of structural processes, bound up with the institutional development of modernity: the social thus continues to loom large. The concerns of our three key thinkers overlap to a considerable extent, but with important different emphases. Here, we shall characterise Giddens as focusing on the late modern, creative and reflexive Self; Beck as drawing our attention to the institutional context of that Self, in a world of risk; and Bauman as preoccupied more with the ethical implications of an individualised society.

Giddens, reflexivity and the 'clever people' of high modernity

The foundation for Giddens' account of late modern identities was his earlier work in formal sociological theory (see Kolarz, 2016). With his seminal theory of structuration (1984), Giddens attempted a solution to the classic

structure-agency problem that privileged agents as active, creative and knowledgeable, rather than the passive figures portrayed by structuralism. Giddens
re-theorised structures as having what we might call a 'virtual' existence: they
only exist at the moment they are drawn upon ('instantiated') by actors when
they, for example, make use of 'stocks of knowledge' as the basis of action.
Giddens went on to place the creativity of agents at the heart of his substantive theories of late modernity. Central to this is the category of reflexivity: the processing of information and self-monitoring of action as the basis
of conduct, which is then further reflected on and acted upon *ad infinitum*.
While Giddens argues that humans have always been reflective in this way,
there is something about modernity – and in particular the current 'late' or
'high' modernity – which accelerates and intensifies this condition (Giddens,
1990). It is here that the sociological dimension enters the equation. As we
saw in Chapter 2, when discussing reflexive modernity and the state, Giddens
(1994) focuses on cultural globalisation and the proliferation of information.
Essentially, the art of living in late modernity is the capacity to manage and
act upon the multiple sources of information that are available (Giddens,
1991). Giddens identifies a number of related processes that are set in train.
The explosion of information – about ways of living, or claims to expertise –
inevitably puts pressure upon the traditional ideas, institutions and practices
that have always been under threat in modernity: a process of detraditionalisation. The result is accelerating individualisation – where individuals are
increasingly cut adrift – or set free – from modern institutions, ideas and
practices (Giddens, 1994, 1998).

Despite pointing to the significance of background structural processes,
Giddens' main focus remains the creative, knowledgeable subject, its relations
with others and its potential for self-actualisation (Giddens, 1991). Giddens
sees the absolute levels of wealth and technological development of late modernity as unprecedented. These offer the potential for a focus on human self-
development at the emotional and cultural level, beyond previous struggles
over material goods. Critics on both the traditional left and right bemoan the
dislocatory effects of globalisation. However, Giddens (1994: 192) suggests
such a rapidly changing and open-ended social landscape creates the environment for a developmental, 'autotelic self' to thrive: we can learn to master and
reinvent ourselves under such dynamic conditions. As Giddens' thinking about
the state and politics evolved (see Chapter 2), he argued that social policy and
the welfare state should become an enabler of this type of development, rather
than just a top-down regulator of conduct and provider of benefits and services. In characterising the broader political implications of individualisation,
Giddens highlights the rise of 'life politics'. Life politics is focused on questions
of identity and wellbeing, increasingly displacing older forms of 'emancipatory
politics' that sought basic (typically collective) freedoms and access to economic goods (Giddens, 1991, 1994, 1998).

Beck, institutionalised individualisation and risk

With his emphasis on individual identity and self-mastery, Giddens is accused by critics of ignoring the late capitalist economic conditions which call for 'self-creating' subjects (King, 1999), or even of being an apologist for the neoliberal ideology which justifies them (Cammack, 2004). While sharing many of Giddens' core assumptions about late modernity, Ulrich Beck puts still greater emphasis on the structural and institutional dynamics of individualisation. Beck always stresses how individualisation is not the same thing as atomised individual*ism* (e.g. Beck, 1997: 94), but is the defining structural process of reflexive modernity, or what he sometimes calls the second modernity (Beck and Lau, 2005).

Beck's ideas on individualisation initially formed the lesser known part of his highly influential *Risk Society* (1986) thesis. He has subsequently explored individualisation and its political implications in more detail (Beck, 1997; Beck and Beck-Gernsheim, 2002), but it is useful to see his account in the context of the *Risk* argument. This details how modernity entailed moving from confronting external hazards (e.g. famine, earthquakes) to human-made risks, which are the outcome of modernity itself. Writing in the 1980s, Beck particularly had in mind industrial pollution and risks attached to nuclear power and weapons. More recently he addressed contemporary global risks such as terrorism and the financial system (Beck, 2009). What distinguishes all such risks is that optimum solutions are unknowable in advance, the consequences of engaging with them are potentially catastrophic and, paradoxically, while they are human-made, it is only further human interventions which will solve them. This requires high quality decision-making; but a further challenge lies in the fact that our faith in decision-making has become undermined. This is because the institutional and cultural certainties of the first modernity have been shaken, having turned their critical gaze upon themselves (Beck, 1986, 1997). It is at this point that risk interfaces with individualisation. With regard to individuals and institutions, Beck and Beck-Gernsheim (2002) note a paradox of the collectivist, productivist institutions of the first modernity, such as the welfare state. These institutions were an expression of social collectivism, and yet assumed *individuals* as their primary unit, for example as voters, workers with legal rights, or recipients of welfare entitlements. This contributed to the unravelling of such institutions as collective units, as they became increasingly focused on the individual. The result is that, far from late modern individuals floating free of institutional and regulatory constraints, they are as immersed in them as ever. But the difference between the more identity-repressing institutions of the first modernity and those of the present is that today's institutions *compel* individuals to manage their own lives, or move to a 'do-it-yourself' or 'risk' biography (Beck and Beck-Gernsheim, 2002: 24). The way that individuals must now confront complex, open-ended dilemmas in their own lives is analogous to how social institutions must engage with the macro risks of the second modernity.

Beck (1999) has called upon the social sciences to drop what he calls redundant, 'zombie categories' in the face of individualisation, such as class, the nuclear family and the nation state. This has led to criticisms that he neglects ongoing structural issues such as entrenched patterns of inequality and disadvantage (Atkinson, 2007). However, again, Beck does take pains to keep in view the structural dynamics of individualisation, and in particular its implications for inequality (Beck, 2007). Beck and Beck-Gernsheim (2002: xxii) note that a profound political problem of late modernity is that individuals are being compelled to 'seek biographical solutions to systemic contradictions' that they cannot exercise control over in isolation. In addition, they suggest that far from individualisation diminishing inequalities, they are in fact intensified: inequalities are pushed down to the level of the individual, but now without mitigating collective ties and support mechanisms. A further paradox is that the necessity of managing one's own biography is a *collective* experience, and one that a more traditional conception of class can't do justice to (Beck and Beck-Gernsheim, 2002: xxiii–xxiv).

In terms of where individualisation leaves political identity and participation, Beck presents a picture that is both optimistic and pessimistic. On the one hand, he is concerned about the gap that individualisation leaves between highly complex global problems – or risks – and the life-political concerns of individuals (Beck, 1986, 1997). The language of mainstream political institutions and actors is still that of simple modernity, and does not resonate with late modern individuals. However, Beck rejects claims that individualised agents are apolitical. A consistent theme through his work is the rise of 'sub-political actors' beneath the formal organisations of the first modernity (Beck, 1986, 1997, 2009; Holzer and Sorensen, 2003). These echo Giddens' account of life politics, but are noticeably more collectivist in character, reflecting Beck's own background in environmental issues. Sub-political actors include new social movements and citizens groups, as well as media and other civil society actors. Beck suggests that while it is precisely the rise of these actors that has undermined the 'simple' politics of the first modernity, they must be institutionally integrated into the political mainstream. Such actors are the vehicle by which more participatory, dialogic forms of political engagement can become the norm (Beck, 1997). More philosophically, Beck stresses that individualised political actors – seeking to navigate complex global risks and their everyday manifestations – are demonstrating a new sensibility. Their practices suggest that, far from being inimical to the idea of a public good, addressing questions of one's own identity, everyday choices and conduct is co-dependent upon such a conception: '[t]hinking of oneself and living for others, once considered a contradiction in terms, is revealed as an internal connection' (Beck and Beck-Gernsheim, 2002: 28).

Bauman, consumerism and the end of the public

The ethical dilemmas of individualisation are pursued further by Zygmunt Bauman, whose work contains more ambivalence and critique than Giddens or Beck. The character of Bauman's project is interesting. On the one hand, he indicates that we are more fully down the path of radical individualisation in everyday life, and societal dissolution, than Beck or Giddens suggest. In this sense Bauman is typically regarded as a theorist of the postmodern, rather than the reflexively or late modern. But, at the same time, Bauman brings to bear traditional critical tools of humanist leftist critique, and appears to mourn the loss of a more traditional sense of community and solidarity.

In his earlier *Postmodern Ethics* (1993), Bauman explored the ethical resources available in a world of extreme fragmentation and individualisation, in which shared, public language and meanings were breaking down. He draws on the work of Emmanuel Levinas, suggesting that all we have recourse to as a shared ethic is unconditional care for the plight of the Other. In the *Individualized Society* (2001) Bauman turns to a more recognisably sociological and political critique of individualisation and its consequences. He identifies how practices of individualisation have become elided with the politics and rhetoric of neoliberalism. The result is that we have lost all sight of structural causes and social problems, which are instead narrated as individual failings. The related political problem is that collective solidarities and movements lack a vocabulary or reference point and are difficult to mobilise. Indeed, in his *Liquid Modernity* (2000: 69–71), Bauman notes that today collective political action – either by the state, political parties or other social movements – has been crowded out by the encroachment of private language and private concerns. In a one-sided corruption of the sociological imagination described by C. Wright Mills (1959), there are no 'public issues', just an infinite variety of 'private problems': the means of translating between them has disintegrated. Consequently, Bauman argues that grasping individualisation in its sociological dimension is the central task of contemporary sociology, for political as well as intellectual reasons.

The key category Bauman deploys to make critical sense of the individualised society is consumerism, surprisingly neglected by both Giddens and Beck. In *Liquid Modernity* (2000) and a series of related titles, Bauman replaces the contested modern/postmodern imaginary with that of a shift from the 'solid' to the 'liquid' across social life. He puts consumerism and the valorisation of choice at the centre of this, describing it as the organising principle of society, a theme he elaborates in *Consuming Life* (2007). While Bauman is concerned by the dislocatory effects of consumerism upon all social agents, he highlights the unequal material contexts and power relations through which consumer identities are pursued and experienced. He also notes, in a rebuke to the self-actualising emphasis of Giddens, that for every individual who tears up a relationship to pursue their 'life project', there will be those not given a choice in the matter, such as children following the divorce of their parents, 'who hardly ever view the breakdown of marriage as a manifestation of their own freedom' (Bauman, 2000: 90).

Bauman directly applied his account of consumerism to a major socio-political event in 2011, when widespread looting and rioting, facilitated by social media, erupted across towns and cities in England. The familiar narratives in response to the riots focused on criminal irresponsibility, social breakdown, structural disadvantage or the powerless attempting to 'fight back'. By contrast, Bauman (2012: 11) identified both the looting and destruction of shops as deep seated and predictable, 'a mutiny of defective and disqualified consumers, people offended and humiliated by the display of riches to which they had been denied access'. At the same time, this was not a concerted political rejection of consumerism, for the vocabulary for such a critique has disappeared. On the contrary, 'they did not rebel against consumerism – but made a (misguided and doomed) attempt to join, if only for a fleeting moment, the ranks of consumers from which they have been excluded' (Bauman, 2012:12). Indeed, the rioters' desire to grab at an imagined collective experience, seek instant gratification and the thrill of the 'spectacle' were all classic imitations of the consumer experience itself. Bauman's bleak analysis of the centrality of consumer identity leads us to our empirical case study for this chapter, but one that reads consumerism and its social basis in a politically very different way.

Summary

We have charted the theoretical and empirical background to accounts of identity – and their political implications – as a journey. It began in the nineteenth century with a strongly socialised conception of the individual, which was itself a reaction against abstract visions of human nature. In the socialised conception, there was little room for the active construction or play of identity. The journey concluded with accounts of an individualised society, in which the ongoing forging of identity is perhaps the central feature of the late modern condition. The contemporary preoccupation with active agency has come about through analysis of rapid social change, the effects of neoliberal politics and some complex developments within theory itself. Through all this, there has been a persistent ambivalence: does the apparently inexorable march towards individualisation represent autonomy and freedom, or ongoing domination and control in the face of structural relations of power?

Case study: Political consumerism

Defining and debating political consumerism

Work on what has come to be known as 'political consumerism' (PC) captures much of what is at stake in theoretical debates around political identity. It also encapsulates our wider problematic of the society–politics relation. PC is the name given to the ways that citizens use their choices – as consumers in the market sphere – to further a political objective:

> It represents actions by people who make choices among producers and products with the goal of changing objectionable institutional or market practices. Their choices are based on attitudes and values regarding issues of justice, fairness or noneconomic issues that concern personal and family well-being and ethical or political assessment of favorable and unfavorable business and government practice…They may act individually or collectively. Their market choices reflect an understanding of material products as embedded in a complex social and normative context. (Micheletti, 2003: 2–3)

Most commonly, PC takes the form of boycotts of certain goods on ethical or political grounds (e.g. of clothing made under sweatshop conditions), or of so-called 'buycotts' that involve the positive purchasing or endorsement of certain brands or products (e.g. fair trade or recyclable goods). PC also embraces more expansive political practices, aimed at raising consciousness about or changing the practices of market actors (producers and consumers). This increasingly involves 'culture jamming': the attempt to subvert or re-describe the brand images and PR messages of corporate actors.

What makes PC political?

PC gets to the heart of the politics of active choice in contemporary societies: the space of consumption is regarded as a site of choice, and (for better or worse) identity construction. However, many are now exploring that space in political ways not previously associated with it. As activist Jonah Peretti (2004: 127) notes, '[c]onsumption becomes political when consumers assess products through the eyes of citizens'. At the same time, debates over (political) consumption reflect the profound ambivalence that exists over the politics of identity. On the one hand, there has been a long tradition in social theory criticising consumption in capitalist societies, from Marx's (1867: 63–77) account of commodity fetishism, through the Frankfurt School's observations on the culture industry to Bauman's (2012) portrayal of 'failed consumers' in the English riots of 2011. However, much contemporary analysis of PC urges critical social theorists and political scientists to suspend their hostility to the ideology and practice of consumption and choice. Instead, they should take seriously the possibility that PC represents a qualitatively new form of politics, centred on personal identity and ethics. In terms of our broader analysis of the society–politics relation, PC is a good example of the politicisation of areas of social life – namely the economic sphere and aspects of popular culture – beyond the more traditional 'high' political arena of political science. Indeed, researchers on PC, while typically political scientists, have deliberately drawn on social theories of late modernity to capture this expansion of the political field and identities.

The social context of PC

Just as 'regular' consumption is nothing new, analysts of PC acknowledge that there are numerous historical examples of political activity around consumption, even if those involved were not so self-consciously 'political consumers' as contemporary activists (Micheletti, 2003; Micheletti and Stolle, 2008). Today, though, the individualising conditions of late modernity are particularly ripe for a politics of active choice. Thus, a striking feature of work on PC is the explicit way that sociological concepts of economic and cultural globalisation, reflexivity and individualisation are invoked as its backdrop. Specifically, it is the interconnectedness brought about by globalisation – under the spotlight of a global media – that can generate consciousness about the political nature of consumer goods: who produces them, where, under what conditions, what are the effects on the local economy, the environment, the health of those who consume them? At the same time, an individualised citizenry, increasingly preoccupied with what Giddens (1994) labels 'life political' concerns, are more attuned to the origins of products and the wider impact of their purchasing choices. This latter aspect is often flagged in the literature alongside related concepts such as 'sub-politics', 'serial identities' and 'self-authorship' (Micheletti, 2003). Such terms are sometimes used in the context of trying to reconceptualise political participation more broadly, for example in terms of a new 'self-service democracy' (Eriksson and Vogt, 2013).

These accounts present PC as bound up with deep, long-term trends of individualisation as charted by social theorists. But while individualisation points towards an increasing politics of choice in various aspects of our lives (e.g. control of our bodies or sexual preferences), PC is focused on the market sphere of consumption. As such, we need to also keep in mind the particular dynamics of this sphere, which are sometimes underplayed in individualisation theory. Specifically, this means keeping in view the context of mass, 'hyper', consumer capitalism which dominates our contemporary understanding of 'choice' (Rice, 2013). This itself is framed by a neoliberal political ideology that privileges the consumer as sovereign, and describes and endorses the apparent decline in the efficacy of the state (see Stolle and Micheletti, 2013: 207–9).

Positive and negative political readings of PC

It is these twin developments – the rise of the market and decline of the state – which have created the space for PC, and this can be characterised both negatively and positively. The negative view is that the ubiquity of the market means political actors have nowhere else to go. In Chapter 2 we considered the hollowing out of the state and associated representative institutions, coupled with the power of transnational corporate actors within economic globalisation. One outcome of this is that many potentially politically minded citizens, even if they still trust the state and formal politics, no longer believe that it is equipped to confront the power of market actors. PC shows that, increasingly, citizens are bypassing the state and formal politics and directly targeting the operations of the market. This reflects impatience with a state that cannot and/or will not intervene robustly in the market sphere (Micheletti, 2003). A still bleaker analysis is in keeping with the original Frankfurt School critique of consumer society. This argues that the colonisation by the market of other areas of social life – as feared by Habermas (1987) – is near complete. Consequently, there is no longer any 'outside' to market activity (exemplified by consumerism), in which something separate known as 'politics' can take place (Arnould, 2007). On this view, if politics is to exist at all, it *has* to operate on the ubiquitous terrain of consumption.

The more politically optimistic reading of PC is that the very techniques and tools which are integral to mass consumerism simultaneously provide the resources to challenge it. Thus the internet – and other technologies which are indispensable to marketing and selling goods – is also the means of communication for networked global activists (Bennett, 2004). On this account, 'savvy', 'pushy' consumers – whose restlessness led to dissatisfaction with the state and traditional politics – could potentially become motivated to challenge the very system of consumerism (Thorson, 2012). Contemporary capitalism operates effortlessly through culture, using increasingly sophisticated, subtle and individualised strategies and messages. However, PC indicates that these can be challenged, subverted and even redirected against cultural capitalism itself.

Structure of the case study

In the discussion of PC practices that follows, our case study research is drawn primarily from Scandinavia and the US. In the former, work on PC has been pioneered by Michele Micheletti and colleagues since the early 2000s (Stolle and Micheletti, 2013). From the US there are two key staging posts in the development of academic research and debate over PC: these are in the form of editions of the *Annals of the American Academy of Political and Social Sciences* devoted to PC, in 2007 and then 2012. These dates are significant as they pre- and post-date the Global Financial Crisis, the possible effects of which are clearly relevant when considering the politicisation of identities in the market sphere. Our examples begin with the core, established PC activities of the boycotting and buycotting of products. We then look at more expansive, proactive practices of culture jamming: these seek to raise awareness about the political dimensions of consumption, and to subvert its architecture of, for example, advertising and branding. Here we see how the contemporary social-theoretical backdrop of globalisation, social reflexivity and individualisation – mediated by new technologies – is drawn on to identify and explain the rise of PC.

Building on this, we consider still more expansive research into the practices of PC activists. This seeks evidence of new subjectivities and worldviews, which might even herald a new form of politics and society. Here the role of social theory in relation to the research becomes more complex. A normative dimension is opened up, and social theory becomes a resource not just for contextualising new PC practices, but also evaluating their political character and trajectory. This aspect is explored systematically in our subsequent section, reading PC through the social theories of identity discussed in the first part of the chapter. Implicit in these discussions is the complex question of how far social theory might itself be constitutive of PC, and the identities and aspirations of some of its practitioners. Finally, we shall conclude the chapter again by reflecting on what it reveals about our ongoing problematic of the society–politics relation.

Enacting political consumerism

Boycotts and buycotts

If PC is a space where citizens directly engage the market in a political way, what forms does this take? The most widely recognised activities are boycotting and buycotting (Copeland, 2014). Boycotting involves deliberately refusing to purchase a particular product – or the products of a particular organisation – in protest at practices involved in its production (e.g. child labour) or what it symbolises (e.g. the corporate 'takeover' of local businesses and neighbourhoods). Famous examples of large-scale boycotts include of South African exports during the apartheid era, or of the multinational corporation Nestlé because of concerns about the impact of its powdered milk products upon infant care in Africa.

The less-widely discussed but increasingly common counterpart to boycotting is the buycott. Here, consumers make a positive choice to purchase a particular product, or products of a specific organisation or region, in active support of the practices and/or values associated with it. Dalton (2014: 55) cites survey data suggesting that buycotting may now be even more common than boycotting. Although regarded as more contemporary, buycotting also has plenty of historical precedents, for example mobilising consumers to buy 'patriotically' in order to support a national economy. However, what marks out contemporary buycotting is the proliferation of causes that are supported. Crucially, buycotting is seen to express a wider lifestyle and identity on the part of the consumer. Individualised and disparate choices in the marketplace are made to demonstrate commitment to causes, and/or affiliation with a particular value community or movement. Widespread examples include the purchase of fair trade products – such as coffee where a guaranteed income is protected for indigenous growers – environmentally friendly brands and organic and locally grown produce.

A key criticism of boy/buycotting is that individual purchase decisions in the marketplace – even if aggregated up to a large scale – will count for little unless accompanied by a clear message that gives the activity political meaning. The campaign needs to actually change the behaviour of any targeted organisations and lodge itself in the wider public consciousness (Stolle and Micheletti, 2013: 219–22). A good PR campaign is necessary not just to encourage consumers to participate but also to bring the practices/organisation in question under the spotlight. However, major corporations are very adept at controlling their brand image. Marketers, advertisers and PR executives – many of whom will be trained in the social sciences and humanities – understand that it is on precisely the cultural, individualised terrain of late modernity identified by social theorists that they are selling a lifestyle as much as products (Bennett and Lagos, 2007). In this sense, companies are themselves engaged in a relentless culture war to capture the attention and shape the affiliations and aspirations of consumers. The Frankfurt School theorists had intimations of this in the mid-twentieth century, but perhaps even they could not have envisaged the pervasiveness of branding in contemporary capitalism, particularly given the rise of new information technologies. Given this, a more aggressive form of political consumerism seeks to challenge and subvert the messages that companies propagate.

Subverting the market: culture jamming

The tactics used to subvert marketing messages are often referred to as culture jamming (Stolle and Micheletti, 2013: 172). Culture jamming is a form of political communication and intervention. It is designed to challenge mediatised mass consumption, typically by using its own strategies and tools against it. Culture jamming can take the form of, for example, defacing or reworking branded logos or advertisements to convey alternative messages, as with the Canadian anti-consumerist magazine *Adbusters*. It can also involve producing satirical advertisements, political or news outputs in print or on film, often with sophisticated production values. More participatory activities can also use 'actors' to infiltrate and subvert everyday commercial settings, or engage citizens in carnival-type ways to reclaim public spaces (e.g. the *Reclaim the Streets* movement).

An infamous example of culture jamming in the political consumerism literature is the 'Nike email incident' of 2001 (Peretti, 2004; Stolle and Micheletti, 2013: 179–203). Sportswear manufacturers Nike were offering a product where customers could go online to have a personalised message stitched into a limited edition trainer. Jonah Peretti, one of many who were opposed to Nike's employment practices in developing countries, ordered a pair of trainers with the word 'sweatshop' emblazoned on them. When Nike refused, the subsequent email exchanges between Peretti and Nike's customer services department became a global internet phenomenon, reaching an estimated 11.4 million people. The case became a *cause célèbre* in the mainstream news, among activist groups and to previously uninterested individuals. Subsequent close analysis of the massive correspondence received by Peretti indicated that the incident, 'created a virtual community for like-minded people who connect the anti-sweatshop cause with their consumer values' (Micheletti and Stolle, 2008: 762–63; see also Stolle and Micheletti, 2013: 181–92).

The Nike email is a clear illustration of the power of a new type of technologically mediated, cultural intervention to challenge corporate ideology and garner wider public engagement. In illustrating the specifically late modern character of such practices, the tone and content of both the Nike campaign and the Peretti email are significant: both were presented explicitly in the language of 'choice' and 'identity'. The Nike 'personal iD' campaign – rather like its famous slogan of 'Just Do It' – was pitched directly in terms of individual empowerment through personalised choice. Peretti focused on precisely this aspect. As he recollects; '[my] goal was to re-direct Nike's publicity machine against itself, by using the same on-line service that Nike was offering to associate itself with personal freedom, to raise awareness about the limited freedom enjoyed by Nike sweatshop workers' (Peretti, 2004: 128). This intent is captured in the email exchange, in which Peretti (2004: 129) sarcastically says, 'I was thrilled to be able to build my own shoes, and my personal iD was offered as a small token of appreciation for the sweatshop workers, poised to help me realize my vision'.

Discursive political consumerism: consuming for a new society?

The Nike email and subsequent, similar examples offer illustrative flashpoints of political consumerism as a field of conflict. In this arena, individualised, often technologically savvy political consumers come face to face with the corporations who are trying to tap into their behaviours, lifestyles and aspirations. However, sceptics might argue that these incidents – in keeping with mass consumerism itself – are transient, disposable and leave little collective imprint or lasting impact. Such critics seek evidence that PC is able to sustain a political campaign, generate collective action and actually change political consciousness. Micheletti and Stolle (2008), sympathetic analysts of PC, argue that there is the capacity for a more expansive 'discursive shift' as a result of PC activities (see also Stolle and Micheletti, 2013: 170–5). Empirical work in this area tests this claim, by examining more closely the characteristics of people who engage in PC and their networks. Most importantly, there is a focus on whether political consumers develop a stronger or wider political consciousness among themselves or others as a result of their activities. Micheletti (2003) suggests that PC does indeed generate new ties and social relations between participants. However, she goes on to make the stronger claim that PC doesn't just broker or reflect existing forms of social capital, but actually creates a platform for people to develop it in new ways. By this Micheletti (2003: 156) means not just the extension of networks, but the development and refinement of values, ideas and practical social and political skills. The result is that political consumers are far from being the rather limited and one-dimensional actors that critics imply. They are able to develop skills and attributes of a similar breadth and depth to traditional activists in civil society, perhaps also adding novel additions of their own (Micheletti, 2003: 17).

Further empirical work has sought to test different dimensions of these claims. In Denmark, Andersen and Tobiasen (2004) found that PC does not represent either a decline of civic trust in the face of individualisation, or a new type of post-materialist political identity and practice. Instead, while strongly linked to grassroots activism, PC is a *supplement* to more established forms of participation. Thus, in this study, PC is positively linked to voting in elections, party membership and trust in established institutions and politicians. Indeed, contrary to the view of PC reflecting alienation from politics, Andersen and Tobiasen (2004: 213–14) found that, 'political consumers actually regard all forms of political participation as *more* efficient than those who are not political consumers'. Political consumers were also found to have a 'sense of global solidarity and ... knowledge about global institutions' (Andersen and Tobiasen, 2004: 216).

The relationship between old and new modes of participation has been examined specifically in relation to new technologies and media, seen as so integral to lifestyle politics and PC. Monitoring the relationship between online activities and political participation, de Vreese (2007) found that, among young people, being engaged in a range of online activities was positively related to online political participation. More specifically, online rather than traditional news consumption was a stronger predictor for online political participation, as was online rather than offline social networks. De Vreese concludes that this adds up to a visible, emerging form of 'digital citizenship', where online activities, media consumption and networks provide a platform for online political engagement. To this extent, online activity mirrors well-established findings about the prerequisites for political participation in civil society. But what of the relationship between the online and 'offline' worlds? Are digital citizens – for all their online political activity – withdrawing from real-world political activism? Shah *et al.* (2007) conclude that both traditional and online news consumption can promote 'political talk' and greater social and political consciousness, which is itself a basis for PC. However, they note how the situation is complicated by pressures in the other direction, such as the depoliticising effects of habitual entertainment viewing.

Interestingly, some of the most empirically well-supported claims about the consciousness raising potential of PC have come at a time when early optimism over its political potential has faded. The 2012 *Annals* reflected on PC after the financial crash of 2008. Drawing on macro survey data from the US, Willis and Schor (2012: 180) confirm intimations from earlier in the decade, suggesting that conscious consumption should continue to be seen as among, 'a broader repertoire of actions that address a multiplicity of institutions'. Going further, they argue that the data in fact shows PC as a *means* to further activism: rather than 'crowding out' activism, PC 'crowds in' other forms of participation. Gotlieb and Wells (2012) support this with survey data on younger political consumers which shows that, if they are able to act alongside others, this can lead to the skills and competencies necessary for participation in more traditional forms of civic and political action.

The most radical claim made on behalf of PC is that it enables individuals to entirely renegotiate their identities, and even prefigure a vision of an alternative society. Nelson *et al.* (2007) researched the community around the 'Freecycle' movement, through which participants use online tools to make their unwanted belongings available to others. More broadly, they also examined those who have sought to entirely downshift their material existence, typically in terms of reduced consumption, working hours and income. They found that some individuals may be motivated to downshift out of value commitments, such as to live a more environmentally friendly lifestyle. However, others may see it as a solution to individual troubles such as the stress and related problems of work–life balance, or being on the 'work to consume' treadmill. But regardless of these initial motivations, having downshifted, there was a widespread and notable increase in forms of civic and political participation among individuals. Nelson *et al.* conclude that such individuals might even be said to have downshifted their consumption but 'upshifted' their civic engagement. Atkinson (2012) goes still further. Based on in-depth interviews with a range of socially conscious consumers, she concludes that their activities have become the vehicle for a renegotiation of identity – based on authenticity and social embeddedness – which is empowering and self-actualising. This involves certain sacrifices (e.g. loss of consumer choice), but even these come to be framed as being pleasurable. The overall experience is again presented as a platform for more altruistic and collectively oriented values and behaviours. As Atkinson (2012: 192) concludes:

> Socially conscious consumption taps into and encourages a kind of enlightened self-interest whereby concern for the Self, as expressed through consumption, facilitates concern for the collective.

At this juncture, the possibility emerges of social theory not just identifying and critically evaluating PC but also being constitutive of it and associated pre-figurative practices. It was noted above that the marketing and advertising industries opposed by PC often themselves rely on social scientific training. By the same token, post-materialist culture jammers and downshifters will have often received a university education, frequently in the humanities and social sciences (Stolle and Micheletti, 2013: 70–1, 182–4). It is plausible to suggest that some such activists will have reflexively absorbed social-theoretical models of identity formation and social and political transformation. But the only observable test of this would be further empirical work into how they narrate their own experiences. Alternatively, we might argue something similar to Giddens' claims around the reflexivity of sociological knowledge. On this view, in our information saturated age, theoretical knowledge will invariably inform the background cultural conditions and repertoires of lay political actors, whether they are conscious of it or not.

Reading political consumerism through social theory

In outlining some of the major social-theoretical accounts of identity, and in particular their political implications, we saw a definite empirical and theoretical trend. This was from classic nineteenth-century images of the socially produced individual – subject to both exploitation and redemption in the context of a social whole – to the fragmented and fluid, highly individualised late modern Self. This was accompanied by an increased emphasis on agency and the role of active choice. Let's now examine what contemporary PC tells us about this story, by considering in more detail its relationship to the theoretical perspectives we considered.

PC as embodying individualisation

The major analysts of PC explicitly used sociological theories of individualisation. This was evident in key texts on PC from the early 2000s, but it remains the case in the 2010s. In listing 'core themes' in the 2012 edition of the *Annals*, the editors rank as point number one: '[r]ise of individualization: people freeing themselves of institutions' (Shah *et al.*, 2012: 13). This is despite the Global Financial Crisis having called into question claims previously made around individualisation and apparently unbounded choice (Touraine, 2014). However, in other respects it is not surprising that assumptions about individualisation have become entrenched in the PC literature. The character and implications of PC will certainly remain contested, but it is clear that large numbers of individuals are reading their consumer choices in a political way. In so doing, they are expressing a political identity that seems to very closely resemble the life–political concerns described by sociologists such as Giddens, or the post-materialist values tracked by political scientists such as Ronald Inglehart over a longer period (Ingleheart and Welzel, 2005).

PC is thus not just about classic issues of material inequality and the distribution of resources – although these do feature strongly. It is also about the environment, the possibilities for both global solidarity and localism and, perhaps most importantly, an ethos or sense that through politicised consumption one is able to 'do the right thing'. PC also seems to confirm many of the insights of another key theorist of individualisation, Ulrich Beck. Awareness of the complex, human-made global problems that surround production/consumption reflect his characterisation of the nature of risk in late modernity. In addition, PC also captures Beck's account of the rise of sub-political actors beyond the state and traditional political parties. Risks come under the spotlight of global media; this in turn mobilises citizen agency beyond a state which is ineffective in the face of corporate power and global risks (Beck, 1986, 1997, 2009).

Traditional identity theories as critique of PC

There is, then, much about PC that seems to validate the individualisation thesis account of political identity. However, applying other, more traditional social-theoretical perspectives discussed in this chapter can point to very different conclusions. Three critical areas stand out: that PC underplays the significance of an enduring – perhaps intensifying – capitalist context and its associated problems; that, relatedly, PC creates a site of control rather than autonomy; and finally, that the particular form of individualisation PC represents is a depoliticising, pathological atomisation rather than a new cosmopolitan individualism.

With regard to capitalist context, it is not difficult to envisage a Marxist critique of PC. The features of capitalism that Marx saw as obstacles to being fully human remain intact, and are perhaps even exemplified by PC. On the Marxist account, PC represents at best a capitulation to the power of multinational capitalism – where, as predicted, the content of politics itself becomes literally commodified – and at worst colludes in its expansion. More specifically, Marx saw acts of production and work as defining identity, not consumption. For all that we have become a consumer society, questions of production – and attendant matters of exploitation and social class that arise from it – have not disappeared. Crucially, these are seen as prior to and indeed framing consumer identities and activities: (political) consumerism is a class-based activity just like everything else. For Marx (1844), what we might call identity failure was embodied in the condition of alienation. In particular, Marx (1867: 63–77) pointed to 'commodity fetishism' as the paradigm case of how we enter into a distorted relationship with the objects of our labour under capitalism. So, on this reading, consumerism is the worst imaginable area of social life upon which to build a political project: to engage with consumption in the market place is an alienating experience, regardless of any imagined 'ethical' dimension attached to it.

A second criticism we can draw from traditional identity theories focuses on assumptions about autonomy and choice. PC is presented as a means to achieve political objectives, in a way that resonates with people's desire to choose and construct their own identities. However, two strands of critique invert this idea. The first is the original Frankfurt School position that consumer products contribute towards a 'pseudo-individuality', amenable to the expansion of mass-consumer markets (Adorno and Horkheimer, 1944). On this reading, it doesn't matter whether the content of PC is ostensibly 'political' or 'progressive' – its overriding function is to create fragmented and individualised subjects. Marcuse (1964) put the case even more strongly, observing the production of 'false needs' which perpetuate commodification, and a 'happy consciousness' through which individuals were distracted from the manifest miseries of capitalism. Again, it could be argued that PC extends this idea even further than the Frankfurt School theorists could have imagined, by actually *enlisting* apparently altruistic or ethical citizen projects as part of an individualising capitalism (Boltanski and Chiapello, 1999).

The second critical perspective which challenges PC as representing autonomy is Foucauldian. Foucault (e.g. 1982, 2007, 2008) specifically showed how modernity's preoccupation with 'freedom' was actually central to the operations of power and discipline. PC can be seen as embodying this tendency, illustrating key areas pointed to by Foucault and his followers. Through this reading, PC is a field which constructs a certain type of subjectivity as being amenable to power. Foucauldians identify a contemporary 'ethico-politics', in which conduct is governed on the terrain of our values and choices (Rose, 1999). PC is thus the vehicle for a particular type of responsible individual to 'self-assemble' through their choices. More specifically, and again drawing on classic Foucauldian themes, PC grants a central role to *expertise*. For example, disentangling the mechanics – let alone the ethics – of complex, interdependent global supply chains, or the nature of global warming, places a premium on expert knowledge: experts are required to define and adjudicate over what constitutes ethical consumer behaviour under complex conditions. Political consumers are themselves often bewildered by the range of expert and scientific claims available. At the same time, as corporations, countervailing pressure groups and academic researchers all seek to understand the changing consumer behaviour that PC represents, vast amounts of data about consumers is captured and deployed. This is a major contributor to the expanding field of surveillance, a longstanding motif of Foucauldian analysis (e.g. Foucault, 1975).

A final major criticism of PC from traditional identity theories concerns the threat of social atomisation. For its advocates, PC could embody how social and political collectivism might be reimagined under conditions of individualisation and reflexivity. However, for critics this is either delusional or, worse, a smokescreen for the death of community and collective political identities. The key theorist of the relationship between social norms and political collectivities was Durkheim. We saw that while Durkheim (1893) recognised that economic and social complexity was inevitable, he argued that increasing interdependence would generate a new basis for social solidarity. To its advocates, PC represents precisely this new complexity and interdependence through, for example, the fact of global supply chains. It also contains the requisite Durkheimian collective awareness, through the global cosmopolitan consciousness of political consumers. However, for Durkheim (1950), the crucial additional element for modern solidarity was that it needed an *institutional* basis. In particular, Durkheim envisaged a key role for the state and what he referred to as secondary associations (see Chapter 2). The problem with PC from a Durkheimian view is that even if the ties between activists are meaningful and integrative – and some of the empirical evidence we reviewed suggests that they could be – they have no institutional basis to make them enduring and effective. Indeed, PC could be seen as an after-the-fact response to the decline of the types of institutions (e.g. the state, civil society associations) that Durkheim saw as crucial to social solidarity. As Sam Binkley (2008: 619) notes, in a Bauman-inspired analysis of anti-consumerism:

> Anti-consumerist practices, asserting ever more effusively the sovereignty of the consumer as supreme self-chooser, radicalize rather than reverse the disembeddedness resulting from a commodified life, reinscribing in verbose terms the freedom and autonomy of the choosing consumer.

The limits of PC's collectivist claims are also a problem on a Marxist analysis. Here, PC fails to make explicit the class-based solidarities that are the prerequisite of a mature political consciousness. The sterner critique is that PC simply represents the lifestyle choices of predominantly affluent individuals. This aspect was intimated by Weber, in an area of his work that is in fact taken as a rebuke to Marxists. Weber (1922d) predicted the increasing importance of *status* issues in forming social groups, in addition to class, and that consumption would be central to this. In particular, he argued that status would become a more important marker in periods of relative economic affluence and stability. This was because, in such periods, class differences diminished, but the human need to differentiate and draw boundaries did not. Drawing on these elements of Marx and Weber, PC could be read as promoting status differences around niche aspects of consumption (e.g. supporting local retailers or organic produce), at a time of relative affluence when traditional class markers are less visible. If we accept this as a plausible hypothesis, then the fate of PC following the Global Financial Crisis and diminished consumer spending becomes a crucial test. Weber (1922d: 54) argued that such times of, 'technological and economic convulsions and upheavals pose a threat to [status differentiation] and thrust the "class situation" into the foreground'. If this is correct, political consumerism – as a form of lifestyle or status activity – is likely to decline in the face of a global economic downturn and sharpening class divisions. Put more starkly, are consumers still willing to buy often more expensive ethical products when they have less money in their pocket?

Conclusion: Political identity, participation and the society–politics relation

We began this chapter by noting that, at first sight, macro social theory might be an unexpected place to look for insights into political identity, which has often been read in terms of 'human nature'. This is evident in the classical political theory tradition, the dominant economic model of the rational actor, and also in contemporary, increasingly prevalent attempts to use neuroscience to explain political behaviour. So in summing up debates over political identity in terms of the society–politics relation, we begin by re-emphasising the importance of the socialised conception of the individual. However, the overly socialised model has its own limits. These were brought into focus by empirical and theoretical developments, all of which pointed towards a more fragmented and fluid understanding of identity. This has been productive, but we shall argue that it should not herald an implicit return to atomised, human nature conceptions, or an unquestioning embrace of neuroscience and psychology. The social must be kept in view if the role of politics in generating identities is to be properly understood.

The inescapably social Self

The inescapably social was a key aspect of the identity theories we considered. Marx arguably had his own theory of human nature. Nevertheless, he insisted that individuals represent the 'ensemble of the social relations' (Marx, 1845: 145), and elaborated this in terms of social class determining political identity. Durkheim wanted to establish the primacy of sociological explanations for human behaviour. He comes close to a theory of human nature in his (1914) model of *homo duplex,* but this was really a vehicle to show that the social, integrative aspect of humans is core to their being. It was on the basis of this that he developed his more substantive political proposals (Durkheim, 1950). In the twentieth century, as social structures became more complex, theories of identity formation broadened their focus. Thus, the Frankfurt School supplemented their Marxism with Weber's account of rationalisation, as well as aspects of psychoanalysis. They used this to analyse a new popular culture, emerging technologies and bureaucratic organisations in post-war America, and how these combined to produce 'one dimensional' subjects (Adorno and Horkheimer, 1944; Marcuse, 1964). Despite Foucault's many differences with the Frankfurt School, his accounts of the institutional technologies which construct and discipline normal/deviant subjects resonate with their analysis. The contemporary individualisation thesis returns to a structuralist reading of modernity: this is at odds with the 'individual' focus implied by its title. Its leading theorists view the 'freedom' and 'play' of contemporary identities in

the context of a longer-term social logic of modernity: this is towards complexity, differentiation and institutional and individual reflexivity (Beck and
Beck-Gernsheim, 2002; Giddens, 1990, 1991). Further structural processes
of technological development and cultural globalisation have intensified this
long-term dynamic.

What are the strengths and limits of foregrounding the social in our understanding of political identity? The most fundamental contribution of the socialised conception was to challenge atomistic and human-nature based accounts.
Social theorists stressed how political dispositions and beliefs are not just a
function of 'character': they have a social context ranging from sites of primary
socialisation such as the family; through ideologies, civil society and even up
to a wider logic of modernity itself. Our case study showed how the contested
field of consumption is one such site in contemporary societies. While relatively
uncontroversial today, the socialised view did depart from classical accounts
that invoked human nature, often through one-sided and therefore highly
political assumptions. Consequently, Marx (1846) attacked the atomised, asocial liberal conception of the individual as an ideological vehicle for capitalism,
while Durkheim (1898) saw it as an error that misread the underlying basis of
social integration. The critique of liberalism's image of the individual continued
into the twentieth century. We have seen this in the Frankfurt School account
of one-dimensionality and pseudo-individualism, and Foucault's (2007, 2008)
analysis of how the 'autonomous' subject of liberalism is in fact crucial to
power and governmentality.

We have also seen how the social can be a vehicle not just for the repression or domination of identity but also for its mobilisation and politicisation.
Marx and Weber explored how human identity was challenged by the effects
of capitalism and bureaucratic rationality respectively, and these aspects were
drawn together by the Frankfurt School. Foucault (1963, 1975, 1976) mapped
in detail the institutional sites and societal discourses that constructed mental
and bodily discipline. Each of these aspects give rise to criticisms that social
theory is preoccupied with overbearing structures, marginalising how agents
author their own identities. However, a sense of the inescapably social is also
crucial to understanding how political identity is constructed in positive ways.
Marx predicted that the operations of the capitalist structure would generate
revolutionary consciousness (Marx and Engels, 1848). Durkheim (1893, 1950)
detailed how societal norms and institutions would offer individuals and society an identity that was more than the sum of its parts. In more recent accounts
of individualisation, it is the social terrain provided by globalisation, detraditionalisation and new technologies upon which the reflexive and cosmopolitan
individual has the potential to flourish (Giddens, 1994; Beck, 2006). In each of
these instances, the social is not anathema to autonomous political identity; it
is the means of its realisation.

This dual character of the social, in relation to the repression or mobilisation of identity, was again captured in our PC example. For those sceptical of

PC as a progressive political practice, it is at best incapable of challenging deep capitalist structures, and at worst an ideological smokescreen: the 'choosing' subject of PC in fact legitimises enduring, exploitative capitalist relations. But others see PC as having the potential to subvert the very consumerist structures that gave rise to it. This ranges from basic practices such as boycotts, through more proactive resistance such as culture jamming, all the way up to developing a new social consciousness and prefiguring a more localised, environmentally sustainable, less consumption (and work)-centric society.

The irreducibly political Self

Despite the importance of the socialised conception of identity, without a sense of the irreducibly political it can indeed be monolithic and lacking in dynamism. Marx's ideas have undoubtedly led to representations of political identity as merely a reflex of the economic structure, with individuals condemned to fulfil a particular class-based political role. A similar tendency is evident in the Frankfurt School and Foucault: bureaucratic rationality and expertise is substituted for class, but still fulfil a determining function. This stifling aspect even extends to where a full, flourishing identity is supposed to be achieved. Marx offers a utopian (although he recoiled from the term) vision of individual experience in communist society. But it is striking that there is no discussion of the *political* identity of this individual, or of politics *per se*. This reflects the wider question of whether politics as such is held to 'disappear' under communism. Such a state of affairs would be impossible and undesirable to those who see political contestation not just as constitutive of society, but also integral to freedom and fulfilment (e.g. Mouffe, 2005). Durkheim is credited with highlighting the role of social norms and values, and we might reasonably understand these as a positive resource for identity construction. However, Durkheim's master category is integration *per se*. There is little sense in his work of different political varieties of – or struggles over – integration, nor of the different political identities possible within overarching, functional structures. For example, it is difficult to apply Durkheim's framework to a contemporary practice such as PC, given that the market is not an object of political activity in his model of institutional relations.

Interestingly, individualisation theories – which supposedly foreground active choice – are also subject to criticisms of depoliticising identity. Beck's (2006) global cosmopolitans, or Giddens' (1994) autotelic selves, are criticised as modernist fantasies of an agent 'beyond' the old political categories (Mestrovic, 1998): the range of political identities within earlier periods are neglected. Social theory is littered with ideal-typical accounts of 'traditional' societies in which the human capacity for political – or any kind of – reflexivity is understated. This ranges from Durkheim's account of life under homogeneous, mechanical solidarity up to the contemporary distinction between early and reflexive modernity.

For authors such as Beck (1986, 1997), 'the first modernity' or 'simple modernity' ran from the Enlightenment up to the 1960s. But this period included centuries of social and political upheaval and transformation, culminating in the
intensely political 1960s itself. The danger of such stylised accounts is that it is as
if the art of political self-reinvention did not appear until the particular cultural
globalisation of recent decades, embodied in practices such as PC.

In keeping with our overall argument, then, the irreducibly political elements
of identity need to be kept in view, and are evident in various guises in the theories
and case studies we have considered. Thus, despite his determinism, Marx does
leave spaces for politics to raise consciousness. Even if the proletariat's interests
are objective as Marx believed, political mobilisation towards them cannot just
be a reflex of structure: politics has to intervene. As for the communist future,
it could be argued that the development of a 'real' political identity *begins* with
the onset of communism, free from the distortions that capitalism places upon
political thought and action. Marxists increasingly came to grapple with questions of the relative autonomy of politics (Jessop, 1990; Poulantzas, 1978); the
extent to which socialist identity had to be constructed; and the potential for
coalitions beyond those of class (Laclau and Mouffe, 1985). As we shall explore
in the next chapter, questions of ideology and discourse are central to this, with
Antonio Gramsci being a crucial figure. But we have already seen above how,
from the Frankfurt School, Marcuse (1969) saw the possibility for broader social
coalitions, cultivating a 'new sensibility' and uniting around a 'Great Refusal'.

This theme of cultivating individual political identity highlights the irreducibly political aspects of other of our theories, often involving a turn towards
more psychological explanations. Of the classics, Weber (1922b) argued that
it was only charismatic leadership – embodied in an individual invested with
particular qualities – which could break out of bureaucratic deadlock. In theorising what might motivate the 'new sensibility', Marcuse (1956) engaged
with Freudian theory to explain the repression of 'libidinal impulses' that
could be converted to political action. But it was post-structuralism and
psychoanalytic theories which restated the irreducibly political aspects of
identity most forcefully. Thus, Foucault's (1981, 1984) project examined the
construction and disciplining of individual subjects, but also the possibilities
for such subjects to redefine and empower themselves. On this view, identity
is arguably the site of political struggle *par excellence*.

This is made explicit in the post-structuralist social and political theory
inspired by the psychoanalytical work of Jacques Lacan (1949). In such
approaches, identity is based upon *lack*. This is explored more fully in the
context of discourse theory in the next chapter. Here we should note that for
Lacanian post-structuralists it is the permanent – but always unsuccessful –
quest to 'complete' identities which is irreducibly political: there is no political
'closure' to be found as in, say, Marx or arguably Durkheim. On this view, the
figure of the choosing, capitalist consumer at the centre of our PC example
can never be totally commodified. Consumers will inevitably experience lack
and disappointment, because of the impossibility of fully realising whichever

aspirational, consumer subject position they seek. This could, of course, be read as the perfect, restless and insatiable psychological disposition to sustain consumer capitalism. But it could also be seen as the platform for dissatisfaction becoming conscious critique, of the type that PC seeks to cultivate.

The implicit relationship between post-structuralist/psychoanalytic social theories and the individualisation thesis in sociology are interesting. All broadly accept the substantive arguments about new technologies, globalisation and a more individualised terrain. For post-structuralists – following Derrida – this simply intensifies the condition of 'undecidability': the constant making of choices, without universal principles as a guide, and to which there is never any closure (Torfing, 1999: 62–6). The type of democratic subject that needs to be cultivated is thus one who embraces uncertainty and open-endedness (Laclau and Mouffe, 1985; Mouffe, 1993, 2000). Interestingly, this also potentially dovetails with a certain type of consumerist mindset and practice, suggesting that consumerism could be inflected towards democracy, rather than being seen as anathema to it. Of the individualisation theorists, the post-structuralist approach resonates with the work of Bauman (2000, 2001), who addresses the ethical dimensions of the choosing, 'liquid' Self. There is also similarity with Giddens' (1990) characterisation of reflexivity as the constant monitoring of information, or Beck's (2006) call for an open, cosmopolitan outlook. However, in both Beck and Giddens, *contra* post-structuralism and psychoanalysis, there remains the modernist possibility of a transparent, rational and complete Self who can master their late modern environment (see Mestrovic, 1998). There are hints of this quest for mastery of complexity in the figure of the ethical consumer, weighing up the vast information required to adjudicate between 'good' and 'bad' consumption (see Stolle and Micheletti, 2013: 248–55).

Summary

The argument of this book is that the inescapably social and irreducibly political should be treated as important and analytically distinct, so that their interplay can be examined in empirical contexts. We have also drawn attention to the specific senses in which social theory can relate to political research and practice. Social theories of political identity – and empirical work on new forms of participation such as political consumerism – exemplify each of these overarching themes.

Although they may themselves be underpinned by implicit assumptions about human nature, sociological theories have offered a more rounded picture of identity, one that takes full account of its (changing) social context. However, today it is behavioural economic, psychological and neuroscientific accounts of identity that dominate (Davis, 2011). As such, the fundamental insights of classic and contemporary social theorists should not be taken for granted, and often need to be reasserted. But social theory has run up against its own limitations where it has treated identity – and especially political identity – as an effect or function of determining social structures. There are irreducibly political aspects to the constitution of the social landscape, the identities formed upon it and the choices that agents make. Crucially, we have seen that the social can be both repressive and enabling of political identities, which in turn can reproduce or challenge social structures and practices (such as consumerism). The theories and empirical work on identity we have discussed are at their most sophisticated and effective where they are grappling with the interplay between these social and political aspects: does Marx really allow for politics in the present, or in an imagined future? Can the repressive technological apparatus also provide the means of empowering individuals against it? Can consumer choices be regarded as political?

Our political consumerism case study highlighted the different senses in which social theory can inform concrete political research and practice: as a resource for identifying and explaining political phenomena; as a means of critique; and sometimes even directly informing or constituting political thought and practice. With regard to the first of these, the backdrop of a technologically mediated form of reflexive modernity, characterised by increasing individualisation, was particularly important. Individualisation was consistently invoked by researchers as the context which enables politicised consumption. This social theory helps to identify and explain such novel forms of political practice, and expands the definition of what might constitute political activity in late modernity. More complex was the extent to which social theory might be directly implicated in political consumerism. There is no doubt that social-theoretical knowledge informs the work of the advertisers and marketers who are targeted by consumer activists. As for the activists themselves, we noted that those who move through political consumption to a more developed political consciousness and social vision conform to post-materialist worldviews. In addition, such activists may reflexively engage with the very social-theoretical concepts that academics use to explain their subjectivity. But we concluded that this aspect is itself a further empirical question. What is beyond doubt is that the remaining sense of theory's relationship to its political object – as a resource for academic and political debate and critique – is fully intact in political consumerism. Some seeking social change are sceptical of political consumerism, seeing it as depoliticising and an effect of commodification. Others see in it opportunities for new forms of political subjectivity and action. These echo dilemmas within theories of social change and political identity since the nineteenth century: we were able to return to these as a resource for evaluating twenty-first-century political practices and subjectivities.

Throughout historical and contemporary discussions on the construction, character and implications of political identities, a crucial related aspect has been the social function of ideology and discourse. To avoid relying on theories of human nature, and to make sociological sense of political identity, we need to understand the role of ideas, language and culture. These are central to repressing, mobilising and contesting political identities – and the field of politics itself. It is to these elements that we now turn.

4

Politics All Around: Culture, Ideology and Discourse

Introduction

The previous two chapters considered the role of social theory in analysing politics 'from above' in the form of the state and governance, and 'from below' in the political identities and behaviours of individual citizens. In each case a crucial ingredient was the role of the *ideational*: ideas, norms, values, culture. We saw in Chapter 2 how these provide a framework of meaning through which the state is legitimised in the eyes of citizens, or through which state actors themselves come to understand their operating environment (for example as being globalised). In Chapter 3 we witnessed the central role of norms and values in providing citizens with a sense of their political subjectivity, and mobilising them towards political action. In the present chapter we elaborate on these aspects by focusing in detail on how social theorists have understood the political role of culture and, in particular, of ideology and discourse.

Following this introduction, we examine key theorists who reflect a move from a socialised towards a politico-centric account of the role of ideas. Throughout, the relationship between ideology and the operations of a capitalist economy and society are a central issue. Consequently, for our illustrative study we focus on the development of neoliberalism. This represents the paradigm of capitalist development from the 1970s to the present, and has become one of the most entrenched and widespread ideologies in history. It has also assumed centre stage in political debates following the Global Financial Crisis of 2008. This case study will again illustrate the different senses in which social theory can relate to its empirical, political object: as a descriptor, critic and even constitutively. However, we shall see that what is interesting about this particular example is the different way it embodies these categories. This is because social theory has been almost universally critical of neoliberalism. As with previous chapters, we will then then reflect on how our key theorists shed light

103

on our case study, before concluding by discussing what these debates reveal about theorising the society–politics relation.

Definitions

Each of the three terms that head this chapter – culture, ideology and discourse – are notoriously contested and (perhaps ideologically!) loaded. While definitional issues will certainly be implicit throughout, our focus will be on how these categories are deployed in thinking about the society–politics relation. However, we should outline some broad definitional contours at this point. 'Culture' is one of the most contested terms in the human sciences. There is a consensus to the extent that it is broadly concerned with meaning-making, or the symbolic and ideational aspects of social life (Williams, 1981). But its drivers, scope and causal weight varies significantly between, for example, political science (where it remains relatively marginal), through sociology (where it is crucial but often imagined as a domain within a wider category of the social), to the newer discipline of cultural studies (where it is coextensive with both the social and the political. See also Nash, 2010: 30–5).

What follows will be more concerned with the treatment of ideology and discourse. 'Ideology' is typically treated as something more specific than culture, although of course it operates on the cultural terrain. Ideology tends to be regarded as having a more or less organised and systematic (but by no means necessarily coherent) quality, as being related to power and interests, and typically aimed at either legitimising or subverting social arrangements. In so doing, it can involve legitimising appeals such as, for example, 'human nature', 'the good society', or 'justice' (see e.g. Freeden, 1996; Goodwin, 2014). Specific ideolog*ies* are the relatively organised and enduring manifestations of these types of appeals, including familiar projects such as liberalism, conservatism or socialism (see e.g. Heywood, 2012). However, many other, more nebulous phenomena in social life can be designated (often pejoratively) as 'ideolog*ical*' such as, for example, 'consumerism' or 'individualism'.

It was in part because theorists became dissatisfied with narrower definitions of ideology, and aware of the ideological dimensions of social life more broadly, that 'discourse' became the increasingly favoured term in social and political analysis (see Howarth, 2000; Torfing, 1999). Sometimes discourse and ideology are used interchangeably, but this tends to overlook significant conceptual and political distinctions (Purvis and Hunt, 1993). Discourse is a more comprehensive category than ideology that, in its scope, actually returns us to something more approximate to culture. As Torfing (1999: 300) summarises, '[i]t does not merely designate a linguistic region within the social, but is rather co-extensive with the social'. Discourse is thus variously taken to include, for example, texts, utterances – and practices – in a variety of settings. It can describe phenomena that would straightforwardly be regarded as political (e.g. a discourse of 'human rights') as well as those that – at face value – might not (e.g. a discourse of 'workplace wellbeing'). However, analysts typically attempt to show how such discourses are, indeed, profoundly political. To be described as a 'discourse theorist' tends to have post-structuralist and/or postmodern connotations, but not exclusively so, and discourse analysis is a well-established methodology across the social sciences (see e.g. Gee and Handford, 2012).

These broad distinctions in defining culture, ideology and discourse are worth keeping in mind in what follows, but they are not the main focus of the chapter. Instead, they will be treated as the building blocks which help us to chart how social theorists have treated the ideational dimension of politics, prior to our case study of neoliberalism.

Theorising culture, ideology and discourse

We begin our critical survey of key theorists with strongly socialised conceptions of ideology. With their origins in the classical sociological theory of Marx and Durkheim, such approaches move away from traditional philosophical and political-theoretical notions of ideas as things in themselves, and locate them in their social context. However, just as Marx and Durkheim fundamentally disagreed over the basic character of modern, industrial societies, so they generated very different approaches to understanding the role of culture and ideology. Here we characterise these in terms of, firstly, a Durkheimian tradition of focusing on the functional, integrative role of culture and – in particular – political rituals. We then turn to a Marxist framework that broadly understands the ideational as a vehicle of social control: both reflecting and masking the exploitative class character of capitalism. These approaches developed over the full course of the twentieth century and encompass key social theorists such as Talcott Parsons and Jeffrey Alexander on the functionalist wing, and Louis Althusser and Antonio Gramsci in the Marxist tradition.

Gramsci in particular was a crucial figure in considering the relationship between social forces, ideas and politics. He supplemented Marxism with a range of concepts that took the causal power of ideology and political action seriously, rather than relegating them to an effect of economics. Gramsci thus begins to take us away from the totally socialised conception of ideology, pushing us towards more politico-centric accounts. These involve the rise of post-structuralism and the move away from ideology towards discourse. To illustrate this we turn again to Michel Foucault whose project, like Gramsci's, can be seen as encapsulating a creative tension within the society–politics relation. We shall see how, on the one hand, Foucault's investigations into the production of power and truth draw on quite formal linguistic analysis, as well as focusing on agential strategies, to offer an account of ideas that seems fully 'politicised'. However, Foucault and his followers are also preoccupied with the material apparatus and institutional sites for reproducing norms, values and subjectivities, in a way that keeps in view an account of the social. But our final key thinkers – Ernesto Laclau and Chantal Mouffe – do away with such a conception altogether, and move to a comprehensive post-structuralist theory of discourse. Offering a fully politico-centric account of the role of ideas, for Laclau and Mouffe everything, including 'society' itself, is discursively constructed. Laclau and Mouffe locate themselves in the Marxist tradition but claim to have transcended it with their 'post-Marxism'. They thus enable us to ask has what been gained and lost by moving from those earlier, socialised accounts of ideology to a politico-centric theory of discourse.

Durkheim and cultural integration

Standard secondary accounts of Emile Durkheim's project say little about what he might offer to the study of ideology. However, Durkheim's analysis of the role of norms and values is a crucial reference point for thinking about ideology as a social phenomenon, as opposed to being confined to an abstract world of ideas.

At the centre of Durkheim's sociology was a classic problem of order: how do societies cohere and function? Durkheim's core assumption was that societies possess a 'collective consciousness'. This is a form of societal awareness that is greater than the sum of its individual parts, and crucial to social integration. Social norms and values are the concrete embodiment of this collective consciousness. For Durkheim, it is not so much the specific *content* of norms that matter but, rather, that they perform an integrative function. Importantly, Durkheim (1893) outlined how such normative integration could occur in different types of society, in particular as they moved from being 'traditional' to 'modern' via rapid processes of industrialisation and urbanisation. Religion was a key integrating institution in Durkheim's analysis of traditional societies. It served the purpose – analogous to many subsequent accounts of ideology – of providing a cognitive route map for individuals to make sense of themselves and the world. More expansively, religion integrated the society as a whole around shared symbols and practices. In his anthropological work on Australian Aborigines – presented in *The Elementary Forms of Religious Life* (1912) – Durkheim drew attention to two fundamental dynamics of integration. Durkheim pointed, on the one hand, to the importance of symbols and rituals which positively *bind* the community through, for example, acts of worship or totemism that 'rally' members of the group together. Alternatively, symbolic representations are sometimes concerned with forming boundaries. These establish *oppositions* between, for example, the 'sacred' and 'profane', in ways which indicate desirable or deviant behaviour. On this basis, punishment of deviance is legitimated, in a way which further reinforces the solidarity of the wider group against its other.

Clearly, such practices were most explicit in relatively homogeneous, traditional societies where religion dominated. Durkheim understood that integrative religious practices would dissolve or become harder to sustain in increasingly

complex and individualised modern societies. However, he was relatively optimistic about the prospects for integration under modern conditions. Durkheim
(1893) envisaged the emergence of a new 'organic' form of social solidarity, based
on recognition of the *interdependence* that arises from modern differentiation
and complexity. However, such organic solidarity would not – contrary to what
its name perhaps implies – just happen of its own accord. We saw in Chapter 2
how Durkheim (1950) granted a leading role to the state and the 'secondary
associations' of civil society in promoting modern forms of integration. With
specific reference to the symbolic aspects of social life we are considering here,
Durkheim predicted that knowledge about self and society would increasingly
be formalised and provided by science. However, what he termed the *elementary*
integrating functions would endure into modern industrial societies. Durkheim
insisted that symbolic integration would retain its 'sacred' group character: eventually, new forms of religious-type practice, appropriate to modern conditions,
would emerge (Durkheim, 1912; Giddens, 1971: ch. 8).

With his emphasis on the integrative aspects of symbolic rituals, Durkheim
provides a platform for thinking of what we call ideologies as normal, even
necessary, aspects of social life. On this view, ideologies should not be studied 'in themselves', but rather in terms of their social origin and function of
integrating individuals and groups. However, Durkheim is not a theorist of
ideologies, and there are clear limits to his approach for understanding the role
of ideologies in modern societies. Most notably, a Durkheimian approach to
the *function* of ideologies is relatively unconcerned with the particular form
and *content* they took over the course of the subsequent twentieth century.
Nevertheless, later (neo-)functionalist theorists gradually adapted Durkheim's
approach to make sense of the integrative functions of modern polities.

Parsons, neo-functionalism and political rituals

Talcott Parsons' mid-twentieth century American sociology attempted a formal synthesis of the major theoretical traditions. However, it was Durkheim's
problem of order and integration – and in particular its ideational elements
(the role of norms and values) – that loomed largest. The way that ideational
issues dominated Parsons' work is encapsulated in his famous 'AGIL' model
of the social system, developed across his writings (e.g. Parsons, 1949, 1951,
1969). This acronym states that societies are characterised by the need for
'Adaptation' to the environment, typically through the production and use of
material goods (the role of the economy), while 'Goal attainment' is the capacity to steer the society towards particular objectives (the role of the political
system). But it is 'Integration' that reveals the significance of a socially cohering
set of norms (e.g. through religion). As with Durkheim, it is not the content
of the integrative element that matters (e.g. protestant, catholic, socialist, liberal), but that it exists at all, is robust and consistent. This normative element

is further elaborated in the fourth category, 'Latency'. This denotes 'pattern maintenance' which secures the transmission of societal norms and values in everyday life, across social groups and even generations. It is performed by cultural institutions such as school or church (see also Craib, 1992).

Again, as with Durkheim, Parsons stresses the importance of culture as the site of integrating norms and values. What others might refer to as 'ideology' is simply one possible expression of the necessary integrative elements of any given society. Subsequent political sociologists have applied this functionalist theory to specific political practices (see Baringhorst, 2004). Two features of this more recent work are noteworthy. The first is a departure from Durkheim's belief that ritualistic, symbolic integration would in future be sustained through a reconstituted religion, that is, at the level of 'the sacred'. Instead, researchers began to explore the more varied ritualistic practices that could serve an integrative function in wider, 'profane' social life. In particular, there was a focus on the quite formalised and ritualistic practices of high politics. The second aspect was a new focus on moments of social and political *crisis*. Durkheim's original approach – and then especially that of Parsons – had been criticised for being static: integration seemed to work well under relatively benign conditions, but what happens at moments of social conflict or dislocation, when the cohering values don't seem to function any more?

The most famous neo-Durkheimian exploration of these modern themes is Shils and Young's (1953) account of the Queen's coronation in Britain. This presented the rituals and media coverage of the event as an affirmation of the sacred character of community, highlighting the idea of the nation, of the great institutions of state, and of the relationship of the people to the monarchy. A stable monarchical regime like 1950s Britain was a relatively easy case study with which to affirm neo-Durkheimian integrative themes. It was extended by Robert Bellah's (1967) account of US society and its public institutions which, he argued, were underpinned by a 'civil religion'. Bellah offered a similar analysis of the integrative role of presidential inauguration ceremonies to Shils and Young's account of the British monarch. The former in particular draws attention to how, at potentially stressful moments for the political and social system, order is not just maintained but actually *reinforced* through familiar national rituals which transcend partisan divides. This might occur, for example, with a smooth handover to a new president following a particularly bruising or divisive election.

This theme was further developed in the US context by Sidney Verba (1965), adding the crucial role of the modern mass media. Verba took the case of the Kennedy assassination – a moment of trauma in the American national psyche. He argued that TV coverage converted the crisis into a sense of shared rituals and integrative emotional expression, with families experiencing the events together on a mass scale that had not been previously possible. The media acted as a crucial 'cooling valve', turning a systemic crisis into a moment where collective bonds were reinforced. The neo-functionalist work of Jeffrey Alexander subsequently tried to move away from the sense that the system 'automatically' stabilises in such moments (Hicks and Lechner, 2005). He offered an account of the American 'Watergate' political scandal of the 1970s, in which President Richard Nixon's administration was linked to a break-in at Democratic Headquarters in Washington. In charting how this episode developed into a full-blown systemic crisis, Alexander pays careful attention to longer-term system strains and the conflictual role of specific actors. However, ultimately, Alexander (1988) offers the familiar integrative account, pointing to the ritualistic healing power of the Watergate Senate hearings and impeachment proceedings against President Nixon. This is seen as affirming the shared norms and 'rules of the game', returning us to familiar Durkheimian themes, albeit in a modern context.

Marx and ideology as illusion

We saw in Chapter 3 that Marx's key contribution to understanding political identity was a fully socialised conception of the individual, in the context of historically formed social structures. This was in contrast to atomised accounts, which were overly reliant on a fixed, one-sided reading of 'human nature'. Marx's contribution to understanding ideology is analogous to that he made towards identity: he insisted on situating 'ideas' – which had tended to be seen as abstract things in themselves – in their concrete historical and social context.

Prior to Marx, there was an ambition to understand 'ideologies' in terms of systems of ideas. However, this was simply in terms of mapping categories of concepts in the manner of, for example, Antoine Destutt de Tracy's early nineteenth-century classifications (Kennedy, 1978). Marx's materialist ontology radically subverted this view of the nature and function of the idea. For Marx, human life is first and foremost physical, derived from the fundamental act of human labour. This leads to his focus on the economic base of society and, in particular, the role of social classes. Other elements of social life exist at the level of the social 'superstructure' and are secondary to – indeed determined by – dynamics at the level of the economic base (Marx, 1859). Crucially, this is as true for what are often imagined to be abstract, mental entities such as 'ideas' and, on the larger scale 'culture' itself. Today, the observation that ideas are historical and social products – or at least that their historical and social context needs to be taken seriously – is relatively uncontroversial. However, in Marx's time such an argument represented a profound challenge to established ways of conceptualising ideas. But the feature which really made this insight most recognisably 'Marxist' was an added claim: that to refer to ideas as social products was by no means politically neutral. For Marx, what characterises social relations is the unequal and exploitative relationship between classes. The social institutions of the superstructure are all shot through with the traces of this relationship, and the same is true of ideas. Ideas are social products, the social is predicated on class domination and subordination, and therefore ideas reflect this relationship. Thus, just as the ruling class occupy key positions in the state and the institutions of civil society, they also dominate the production of ideas. As Marx (1846: 172) put it, in one of his most famous phrases, 'the ideas of the ruling class are in every epoch the ruling ideas'.

It is often said of Marx in his 'crude' form that ideas as such lose their interest as objects of study: they are relegated to being vessels for a ruling class power that we know about in advance. For Marxists, to become embroiled in trying to determine the 'meaning' of ideas in themselves, as much philosophy has tried to do, is a distraction or indulgence. As Marx (1845: 144) expressed in his *Theses on Feuerbach*, '[t]he dispute over the reality or non-reality of thinking which is isolated from practice is a purely *scholastic* question'. What needs to be understood is the character of the economic base and, perhaps, the mechanisms through which it comes to determine ideas in the superstructure. While it is true that Marx seems to marginalise the content of ideas, the realm of ideas *per se* is nevertheless crucial in his theory. Ideas become the vehicle for either obscuring or justifying the injustices of capitalism. They render the entire system – and the dominant position of the ruling class within it – as necessary and natural. Ideas, as we saw in the last chapter, are also key to forming the identities of and *motivating* agents – from all classes – to 'perform' their role within the wider system. This prioritising of the wider, often latent social function of ideas over their specific content is very similar to Durkheim's account of rituals and norms. But the key difference, of course, is that in Marx's account ideas, norms (and any associated rituals) are literally *obscuring* an underlying reality of class domination and exploitation. In Marx's (1846: 154) words, 'in all ideology men and their circumstances appear upside-down as in a *camera obscura*'.

For Marx, it seems as if there is an inbuilt mechanism within capitalism, through which certain ideas necessarily emerge to 'paper over' real contradictions and sustain the wider system. However, this image begs a critical – and enduring question – about the relationship of the ruling class themselves to ideology. In the structuralist, machine-like reading, members of the ruling class may be as subject to ideological 'indoctrination' as anyone else: they just fortunately (for them!) happen to be the material beneficiaries of it. However, on a more agentially focused – and therefore *politicised* – reading of Marx, the ruling class and their allies consciously and proactively manipulate cultural forms to entrench their domination. Put starkly – although Marx would have recoiled from such an interpretation – there is a 'conspiracy' among the ruling classes to secure their advantages by ideological as well as materially coercive (economic, political) means. This action is necessary to ensure that ruling class ideas are, indeed, the ruling ideas.

These themes were later empirically debated in the context of a 'ruling class' in Britain. In the *Dominant Ideology Thesis* (1980), Nicholas Abercrombie *et al.* offered a novel conclusion. They argued that to the extent to which there was a dominant ideology, its key function was to actually integrate and bind members of the ruling class, rather than to subjugate or dupe the proletariat. Institutions such as elite education, religion and family provide ruling-class actors with a sense of the legitimacy and purpose of their own dominant position.

Marx's class-centric account of ideology raises fundamental issues about the possibility of truth, and its relationship to political action. A distinctive aspect of Marx's contribution is his negative reading of ideology as a *distortion* of social reality. Marx contrasted ideology – which obscured and reinforced the nature of capitalism – with science, which uncovered the reality of the social world (Thompson, 1990: 33–44). Specifically, by science, he meant his own dialectical materialist conception of history. However, while Marx insisted on the objective reality of a social world which science could reveal, his account of ideology opens the door to a surprisingly perspectivist, or even relativist, vision. Marx's broader account of history posits the proletariat as the 'universal class', representing the true general interest and future of humanity (Marx, 1846; Marx and Engels, 1848). For Marx, the bourgeoisie produce ideology which distorts the reality of exploitation and domination. However, the proletariat – when politically 'mature' and presumably encouraged by Marxian science – would expose that distortion and generate true knowledge about the social world. Marx (1845: 144) argued that, '[m]an must prove the truth, that is, the reality and power, the this-sidedness of his thinking in practice'. It may be the case that Marx saw the truth about society and history as an external fact, revealed by Marxist science and which the proletariat would eventually discover and embody. However, Marx still recognises that truth is socially produced, in that it has a direct relationship to specific social groups within a class structure. Put simply, different types of social actor produce different types of knowledge. Today, again, this is a largely uncontroversial observation among both Marxists and non-Marxists. But in Marx's time it was a radical new insight, the implications of which were to unfold in the work of subsequent theorists of ideology, most notably Karl Mannheim.

Mannheim and ideology as group product

In his classic *Ideology and Utopia* (1936), Karl Mannheim – although not a Marxist – develops Marx's insight that knowledge and ideas are relative to class location. Mannheim argues that *all* knowledge (including Marxism) is socially produced by groups who work within a particular 'climate' of ideas. Famously, Mannheim distinguishes between 'ideologies' and 'utopias'. Like Marx, he suggests that ideologies are incongruent with reality and, indeed, designed to protect or conceal the nature of that reality. In this respect, ideologies necessarily support the status quo. However, 'utopias', while also not reflecting reality, make appeals to the *future* or an imagined preferable set of social arrangements. If such blueprints were to be implemented, they would constitute the overthrow of the existing order. In addition to making this status quo preserving/challenging distinction, Mannheim also distinguishes between what he describes as 'particular' and 'total' ideologies. The former emerge directly from the interests of a particular group, and are used to promote their interests through deception. The latter, more expansive category refers to the worldview of an entire society or epoch. A total ideology transcends group interests, with even powerful groups being subject to it as a mental reference point. A belief in the divine, or later of the explanatory power of reason, would qualify as such 'total' conceptions. Mannheim argues that it is impossible for an individual to escape or transcend a total ideology, except by 'migration' to another society or culture which has alternative total visions.

Given how Mannheim highlighted the link between all knowledge and group interests, as well as the near impossibility of stepping 'outside' total conceptions of the world, his conclusion – and hope for the future – is somewhat surprising. Mannheim (1936) suggests that in modern societies, intellectuals could form a 'classless' group, producing objective, non-ideological accounts of the world. Such a view underpinned the mid-twentieth-century vision of technocratic, non-ideological specialists, delivering incremental change through social planning and state intervention.

The idea of classless intellectuals has led to Mannheim being seen as inconsistent and unrealistic: if all knowledge is a group product, then why not that of intellectuals? His apparent distaste for ideology and the technocratic implications of his vision for incremental change have also led to him being labelled as politically conservative. Even Mannheim's most important contribution, the novel distinction between ideology and utopia, is queried. This is on the grounds that many status quo preserving ideologies in reality tend to contain utopian elements – in the form of a vision of the good society – as a means of reinforcement (Goodwin, 2014: 23–9). Thus, idealised images of an imagined national past, or the ideal citizen of the future, could be integral to elaborating ideologies of the present. However, Krishan Kumar (2006) argues that there is a dynamic element to the interplay between ideology and utopia. Mannheim had a practical understanding of utopias, in the sense that he felt they could be made reality by political actors. But, once actualised, what were once utopian visions may themselves become entrenched as status quo preserving ideologies. These in turn generate new countervailing utopian visions: an ongoing cycle of ideological stability and change.

Mannheim was a non-Marxist who steered some of Marx's insights on ideology towards a more 'neutral', mainstream sociology of knowledge (Thompson, 1990: 47–52). However, those within the Marxist tradition tried to develop a Marxist theory of ideology that reached what they saw as its logical conclusions. Here we focus on the two most significant of these theorists – Louis Althusser and Antonio Gramsci – who each offer a profoundly different vision of the ontological, social and political role of ideology in capitalist societies.

Althusser and ideology as structure

Louis Althusser was a Marxist who embodied the rise of structuralism in mid-twentieth-century France. Structuralism sought to explain all elements of a given structure as moments of a totality which, for Althusser, meant the capitalist system. Applying this to Marxism, Althusser rejected the philosophical humanism of the 'young Marx' who, for example, analysed alienation in the *Economic and Philosophic Manuscripts* of 1844 (see Chapter 2). Instead, Althusser (1965) insisted on the strictly 'scientific' character of Marx's later work in *Capital*. However, Althusser also wanted to avoid the crude base-superstructure determinism which scientific Marxism was prone to. He thus proposed the *relative autonomy* of the economic, political and ideological levels of society. In any given historical and social formation, one or other of these levels might become the most important in terms of securing the power of the ruling class and the integrity of the overall system (McLennan *et al.*, 1977: 78–82).

Notoriously, however, Althusser (1971: 8–10) insisted that the economic level would still determine 'in the last instance'. But the fact that Althusser granted relative autonomy to ideology was significant, reflecting the growing sense among Marxists that they would have to take the power of ideology seriously. How else were they to explain how capitalism had apparently stabilised around a mixed economy consensus, rather than degenerating into collapse and revolution as Marx had predicted it would? Althusser (1971: 14–22) identified an 'ideological state apparatus' that secured the reproduction of capitalism; this operated alongside the more visible 'repressive state apparatus' which relied on law and organised violence. The ideological state apparatus is expansive, including key sites of socialisation such as the church, family and education. The content of ideological messages generated through such institutions has varied historically and geographically. In liberal capitalist societies, they served to create the illusion of the autonomous, calculating individual.

Althusser saw the task of scientific Marxism as unmasking this 'illusion'. This was for the obvious political reason that Marxists wanted to encourage alienated and exploited individuals to understand the reality of their plight, as a platform for revolution. However, just as important for Althusser was that liberal, bourgeois ideology was preventing a truly scientific understanding of the relation between agents and social structures: it was an ontological misrepresentation as much as a political one, or an 'ideology of ideology' (Althusser, 1971: 36–44). It is here that Althusser's strong structuralism comes through, marginalising human agency and endorsing the so-called 'death of the Subject'. Althusser (1968) argues that individualist ideology masks the reality that we are the mere 'bearers' – *Träger* – of ideological structures. Such structures provide subject positions (e.g. citizen, worker, consumer) which interpellate (or 'hail') us and confer our identity (Althusser, 1971: 44–51). On this view, agents are empty vessels, 'topped up' by ideology. Althusser thus presents the most ideologically determinist model of the human subject, within which agents are mere puppets of overbearing structures. This is ironic, given that he set out to avoid determinism by arguing for the relative autonomy of economy, politics and ideology.

Gramsci and the ideological war of position

Antonio Gramsci was a leader of the Italian Communist Party and imprisoned by the fascist regime in 1926, resulting in his famous *Prison Notebooks*. Although writing decades before Althusser, he also sought an account of ideology that acknowledged the relative autonomy of politics and ideas, while remaining true to the basic Marxist framework. But Gramsci's relationship to Althusser is complex, with the latter variously praised by commentators for having 'systematised' Gramsci, or criticised for crushing the flexibility of Gramsci's concepts with his functionalist tendencies (see e.g. Hall *et al.*, 1977: 56–65). This illustrates how Gramsci's fragmented writings can become something of a canvas upon which a variety of – often incompatible – theories and strategies can be projected (Anderson, 1976: 5–7; Davidson, 2008). Gramsci has proved a rich and enduring resource for understanding culture, ideology and political strategy in modern societies, both within and beyond Marxism. However, despite Gramsci's maverick reputation and the credit he receives for reinvigorating Marxism, in the *Prison Notebooks* his adherence to Marxist orthodoxy is striking. He remains attached to the base-superstructure model, the idea of 'fundamental classes' of the bourgeoisie and proletariat, and – at least implicitly – a stagist account of historical development that would culminate in communism. Nevertheless, Gramsci introduced a set of tools that revolutionised the field of critical ideology studies.

Gramsci's own experience as a political leader taught him that the development of revolutionary consciousness was not guaranteed. This was certainly true of social groups such as the peasantry – who were deeply immersed in religion and tradition – but it also applied to the proletariat itself (Joll, 1977: 36–45). The fact that people consented to capitalism had to be taken seriously, and the mechanisms for that support understood. This led Gramsci to a concern with what we today call political identities, as discussed in Chapter 3. In particular, he wanted to grasp ideology in terms of how it appealed to people's everyday experiences; their life lived as it is, rather than with reference to abstract political doctrine. It was on the terrain of culture that this battle for hearts and minds was increasingly fought. This occurred through traditional values, institutions and practices as it always had. But increasingly in modern societies, ideological struggle took place in an expanding civil society, between economy and state. This encompassed education, family, associational movements, developing forms of media, and cultural activities (Gramsci, 1971: e.g. 12, *56n*; Simon, 1991: 68–72). With the importance of ideological politics established, and this broad site of struggle identified, a host of entities came to be seen as ideologically significant on a Gramscian reading. These included public rituals (echoing Durkheim and others), civic spaces, architecture and the incorporation of custom and tradition into everyday life. Gramsci famously compared civil society to the network of fortifications seen in trench warfare, over which the strategy is to fight a 'war of position'. This involves gradually colonising as much of the terrain as possible, sometimes making visible gains forward, but also knowing when to concede ground to your opponents or 'dig in' for the long haul (Gramsci, 1971: 229–39). This is a long-term battle, perhaps played out over generations. But the goal is to achieve hegemony – defining the 'common sense' of an epoch or age.

Gramsci's vision of the role of ideology in the pursuit of hegemony had profound implications for political strategy. Moving away from a narrow, fixed sense of social classes who entered the political field fully formed, Gramsci instead identified *historic blocs*: coalitions of classes or interests that are constructed and mobilised at a particular time (Morton, 2007: 95–9). In theorising the construction of political identities towards hegemony, Gramsci kept in view both the power of ideas in themselves, and the need to articulate them with the current social and historical reality. This is illustrated by his account of the role of intellectuals, and the need for active 'intellectual and moral reform' (Gramsci, 1971: 132–3). Gramsci distinguished between 'traditional' and 'organic' intellectuals – but both are crucial to his overall vision of knowledge production and political practice (Olsaretti, 2014). The former, typified by the 'ivory tower' academic, are concerned with clarifying and developing ideas in themselves. Organic intellectuals, by contrast, are allied to the interests of specific social classes. They seek ways of linking an overarching political vision or philosophy with the experiences and interests of agents in civil society (Gramsci, 1971: 5–14). In so doing, they contribute towards the necessary intellectual and moral leadership required for constructing a new type of social and political actor – what Gramsci referred to as a 'collective man' – as the basis for a longer-term political project (Gramsci, 1971: 323–43).

Gramsci thus kept in view thick sociological context by recognising the force of tradition, custom and practice, while at the same time appreciating the intrinsic power of ideas and new conceptions of the world. Ideology is no longer to be unfavourably contrasted with science but is the raw material of politics itself. Politics is the art of mediating between the worlds of lived experience and abstract ideas, or the 'is' and the 'ought'. We have seen that Gramsci claimed that such ideological work involves a subtle, long-term war of position in civil society. Organic intellectuals are in the forefront of this struggle over which vision of the world will achieve hegemony. Gramsci's ultimate attachment to Marxian reductionism lay in his insistence that organic intellectuals will reflect the interests of one of the 'fundamental classes' by which, like Marx, he meant bourgeoisie and proletariat. Nevertheless, Gramsci became the key reference point in the development of critical cultural, ideology and discourse studies (Hall, 1987). He is also an ongoing inspiration for modern day activists engaged in the cultural war of position that he identified: an interactive 'Gramsci Monument experience' was even installed in New York's Bronx in 2013 (Hirschhorn, 2015).

Foucault: between ideology and discourse?

When social and political theory's shift of focus from ideology to discourse is mapped, Michel Foucault is usually the first thinker invoked. However, while Foucault is often characterised as having rejected or bypassed the concept of ideology (McNay, 1994: 107–10; Vighi and Feldner, 2007), his work overall can perhaps be seen as a bridge; one that foregrounds discourse but – at least implicitly – retains key elements of the ideology analyses we have traced, as well as potentially enriching them (Purvis and Hunt, 1993: 487–91). Foucault exemplifies a central concern of our discussion: is the social at least relatively independent of the play of discourse? In Chapter 3 we saw that, while Foucault wanted to understand the discursive conditions which make subjectivity possible, he also described the material apparatus which discipline bodies and minds. Foucault sought to understand the historical construction of what comes to be regarded as 'normal' and 'deviant'. He was particularly concerned with the role of power and expertise in shaping (and being shaped by) these definitions. His career is typically presented as having two distinct phases: a (structuralist) period of 'archaeological' work, and a (post-structuralist) period of 'genealogical' writings (Howarth, 2000: 49–50; Torfing, 1999: 90–1). We can use this distinction to trace what Foucault offers in terms of the rise of theories of discourse, and the status of the social within this.

Foucault's archaeological writings were informed by mid-twentieth-century structuralism. They revolve in particular around his *The Order of Things* (1966) and *The Archaeology of Knowledge* (1969). His wider objective was to reject theories of history that were either overly agential (e.g. in the 'Great Men' tradition); or invoked determinist external laws of progress (e.g. 'Whig' history); and/or were reductionist (e.g. as with Marxism and the economy). In his earlier works, Foucault was instead concerned with mapping the discursive, structural conditions which enabled particular 'truths' to become spoken and established. For example, how is it that some accounts of the world become accepted as scientific truths, and that certain institutional sites and individuals are recognised as the authorities for reproducing them? In this, Foucault was primarily concerned – in quite a formalised way characteristic of structuralism – with the systemic preconditions of discourse as such, rather than the content or politics of specific discourses (Dreyfus and Rabinow, 1982: ch. 3; McNay, 1994: 52–6). He wanted to discover the rules governing discourse formation, and consequently there was something rather formalistic and descriptive about this early project.

Despite this apparent formalism, Foucault's archaeological investigations were not just a logical exercise: he was equally concerned with the concrete historical and institutional context within which discourses were produced, as evidenced, for example, in his *The Birth of the Clinic: An Archaeology of Medical Perception* (1963). Nevertheless, Foucault's focus on discursive structures as being consti-tutive of subjects, practices and institutions represented a significant departure from previous theories of ideology. As we have seen, such approaches – from Marx onwards – tended to foreground ideology by either defining it negatively, in the sense of it being a distortion or misrepresentation of an objective reality, and/or contrasting it with superior scientific accounts of the world. However, in Foucault's archaeological frame, 'ideologies' and 'scientific' narratives can have shared discursive underpinnings: neither are outside power/knowledge relations or regimes of truth (Howarth, 2000: 60; McNay, 1994: 107).

Foucault's desire to describe the concrete historical conditions and implica-tions of discourse opened out the genealogical stage of his work: this encom-passed projects such as *Discipline and Punish* (1975) and *History of Sexuality Vol I* (1976). The genealogical studies detailed the themes of power, discipline and, ultimately, resistance, with which he has come to be associated. Here, Foucault moves away from mapping the logics and systemic properties of discursive formations. Instead, he engages directly with how the exercise of power and domination – specifically via claims to expertise – is integral to the development of those very discursive formations, and the exclusion of others. In short, 'extra-discursive' factors are brought explicitly into play.

The shift to genealogy draws attention to the specific strategies and tactics of powerful actors at crucial moments. Foucault's focus moves from *epistemes* – the more formalised discursive systems which constitute and make certain practices possible – to *dispositifs* (Howarth, 2000: 77–9; McNay, 1994: 28). *Dispositifs* are variously characterised as apparatus, networks or grids. They consist not just of formalised discourses but also extra-discursive practices. This includes the full matrix of philosophical justifications, claims to knowledge and expertise and their relationship to power, technologies, bureaucratic systems and everyday practices. Crucially, this comprehensive grid is not just able to block or repress but also to *produce* and mobilise individual subjects, ways of being and assump-tions about 'normal' behaviour. This is the basis of Foucault's positive account of power as productive (McNay, 1994: 90–1; Nash, 2010: 20–3). Foucault's concern with the mechanisms for producing and governing subjectivities led him further towards material practices and techniques, captured in his later accounts of bio-power and governmentality (Foucault, 2007, 2008). Bio-power denotes the increasing preoccupation with acting on individual bodies – and entire popu-lations – in the name of both control and efficiency. Bio-power is manifest in gov-ernmentality, and we saw in Chapter 2 how this captures a fundamental shift in the nature of political rule. Power shifts from being exercised straightforwardly 'over' others by a sovereign. Instead, it becomes aimed at constituting and gov-erning individual subjects and all aspects of social life, mediated by the rise of scientific knowledge and claims to expertise (Dean, 2010).

Finally, in his genealogical work Foucault also explicitly confronts the role of the analyst (the genealogist) him/herself. He recognises that there is no 'outside' from which the theorist observes; that they are inevitably making an intervention into the discourses and power relations that they are analysing; and that their task should be to expose the contingency of those relations – that they could have been 'otherwise'. However, Foucault also stresses – and given his own theoretical framework he could not do otherwise – that such critical intellectual work operates from no privileged scientific or political position (Talshir, 2005: 219–20). The contrast with either Karl Mannheim's account of objective, technocratic intellectuals, or Marxian conceptions of the role of a critical science, is stark.

What does Foucault's vast project mean for the status of society within conceptions of ideology? His earlier archaeological work insisted on understanding the relationship – or 'articulation' – between discursive and extra-discursive elements. However, the archaeological approach is characterised by a more formalist analysis of discursive structures. With the turn to genealogy, Foucault moves towards material–social relations, practices and struggles. Taken as a whole, Foucault's project arguably holds the potential for a more fully developed theory of ideology: a sophisticated conception of the structural properties of discourse (archaeology), now allied to an extra-discursive conception of interests and institutional forms (genealogy). However, in his genealogical approach, Foucault by no means invokes a prior concept of society or social structure, in the manner of classical sociologists such as Marx and Durkheim. Instead, the concept of the *dispositif* carries echoes of Weber (O'Neill, 1986; see also Chapter 2). The *dispositif* depicts a field of action, struggle and contestation. To be sure, social norms, as well as institutional power, are key features of this field. But these are presented as the instruments of agents engaged in a power game, rather than pregiven structures (e.g. a dominant ideology) that determine – or even shape – the tactics and strategies of those actors.

Perhaps more than any other major theorist, Foucault walks the tightrope between grasping the discursive and extra-discursive dimensions of what others call ideology. He revealed the significance of what we now routinely refer to as discourse. But, at the same time, he comes to focus on how this is embodied in struggle and material practices across social life. We have indicated that Foucault offers a potential toolkit for a comprehensive account of ideology. However, it was the vehemence with which he was reacting against particular theoretical traditions that ruled out any attempt to develop a 'theory of ideology'. Specifically, reflecting his deconstruction of enlightenment reason, Foucault rejected the notion of undistorted truth as the other of ideology; reflecting his critique of universal liberal humanism, he rejected the vision of a fully formed human Subject who is to be 'freed' from ideology; and reflecting his refusal of Marxian determinism, he opposed the idea that economic relations mechanically 'produce' interests and their associated ideologies (Howarth, 2000: 79; Vighi and Feldner, 2007: 143). Despite this, Foucault's work does sustain a distinction between the discursive and the extra-discursive, which at least keeps the door open to a recognisably sociological analysis of discourse and ideology. But we shall see below that, taking Foucault's reaction against universalism, liberalism and Marxism to what they saw as their logical conclusions, subsequent post-structuralist, post-Marxist discourse theorists dismissed the category of 'society' altogether.

Laclau and Mouffe: post-structuralist discourse theory

It took a subsequent generation of theorists to extend Foucault's project into a comprehensive discourse theory of society and politics. There are various bodies of work that go under the label 'discourse theory', often theoretically very dense, and increasingly engaged with practical methodological issues (Gee and Handford, 2012; Marttila, 2015). It is beyond our scope to engage with the full range of these approaches. Instead, the seminal contribution of Ernesto Laclau and Chantal Mouffe (LM) will be taken as an exemplar for a number of reasons. The first is the significant influence of their work over a sustained period, most notably since the publication of their now classic *Hegemony and Socialist Strategy* (1985) and Laclau's *New Reflections on the Revolution of Our Time* (1990). Since then, LM have individually developed the political implications of their theoretical insights (e.g. Laclau, 1994, 2005, 2014; Mouffe, 1993, 2005, 2013). Secondly, LM are of interest because of the intriguing way in which they draw on post-structuralism, while also locating themselves in the Marxist tradition (albeit in a way that seeks to transcend it with a 'post-Marxism'). Thirdly, LM have a radical and original approach to the society–politics relation: we shall suggest that this involves subsuming the former into the latter and developing a politico-centric account of social life, mediated by discourse. We shall begin by outlining LM's philosophical position on the nature of the discursive and the extra-discursive. We then introduce their key theoretical concepts for understanding the constitutive role of discourse, ranging from individual identities to 'society' itself. Finally we will reflect on the political implications of this approach, particularly in terms of how it relates to the question of ideology and hegemony.

Discourse, the discursive and the extra-discursive

Underpinning LM's project is a claim about the discursively constituted nature of reality. They are critical of Foucault's lingering attachment to the discursive/ extra-discursive dichotomy, and seek to move to what we might call a total theory of discourse. This is premised on the argument that, 'every object is constituted as an object of discourse, insofar as no object is given outside every discursive condition of emergence' (LM, 1985: 107). However, this led to criticisms that LM deny the existence of 'reality', in the form of an external world of objects (Geras, 1987). LM (1985: 108–10; 1987) retort that their account of discourse has nothing to do with whether there is a world of objects 'out there': they take it as given that there is. However, the existence of objects in themselves is banal: such objects only acquire *meaning*, or are activated, through the intervention of discourse. Thus, the splitting open of the earth, or snow tumbling down a mountain, only become an 'earthquake' or 'avalanche' when they are named as such. Of course, this claim becomes more interesting when it is applied to human relations, where a wider range of discourses are available and contested. In a commonly used example, it is possible for a politically motivated individual detonating explosives in a public place to be designated a 'terrorist' or a 'freedom fighter', and these expressions will themselves be linked to other discourses such as colonial oppression, the right to armed struggle or the sanctity of life.

At first glance, there seems little to differentiate LM's claim about the primacy of discourse from previous forms of structuralism and linguistic analysis. However, building on elements of Foucault, LM insist that discourse is not just about linguistic relations and designation – the act of naming (Howarth, 2000 102–3). While linguistic interventions are of course crucial, LM also take discourse to encompass identities, the full range of social practices and institutions: all of these elements are produced by discourses, as well as involved in their formation, reproduction and contestation (LM, 1985: 107–9; Torfing, 1999: 90–4).

LM move most clearly towards post-structuralism in their treatment of specific discursive structures – and what lies 'beyond' them. In formalist structuralist analysis, discourses form a total structure, the elements of which are internal moments of the whole. However, because LM see all entities as acquiring meaning through discourse, which will involve multiple and contested interpretations, there will always be a *surplus of meaning* to any discourse or discursive structure. Put simply, the range of discursive interpretations available will always exceed or 'overflow' the capacity of a particular discourse or object to absorb them (LM, 1985: 105–14). The surplus of meaning constitutes the relatively unfixed 'horizon' or 'field' of the discursive as such, and is not reducible to specific discourses (Torfing, 1999: 91–3). This also opens up the idea of a 'constitutive outside', which we introduced with regard to identity in Chapter 3. There, we saw how Derrida, drawing on psychoanalysis, revealed that identities operate through the experience of lack in relation to an external, other identity. LM use this same framework in their account of discourse with regard to the surplus of meaning. They argue that such a surplus forms the constitutive outside to any particular discourse. Crucially, it is the permanent presence of this outside – of alternative meanings – which renders all discourses as contingent and unstable. Specific discourses are always subject to challenge by the infinite range of alternatives on their discursive outside (LM, 1985: 122–7; see also Howarth, 2000: 103).

To summarise, with their overarching category of the discursive, LM present what they claim is a radical new ontology which collapses the discursive/extra-discursive dualism, but without denying that external objects have an existence. Within this infinite discursive field, specific discursive structures exist. While these may present themselves as being total or complete, the fact of the surplus of meaning in social life means they are constantly subject to challenge from an external other, which is not captured by the discourse. With these fundamentals established, we can turn to the social and political implications of LM's project, via some of the more specific concepts they introduce.

Discourse and the (unstable) securing of political identity

The first point to highlight is what LM see as the *productive* character of discourse. Earlier we saw how for Foucault power in general, and discourse in particular, is enabling of social life. Similarly, for LM discursive structures provide the (malleable) frameworks of meaning that enable both 'society' and individual identities to be produced. Discourses are constitutive of the social world and identities. They also provide the raw materials of politics, in that they are a permanent site of contestation. As in structuralist accounts (e.g. Althusser), for LM discourses provide subject positions for agents to identify with. However, unlike in structuralism, the discursive structure and the subject positions themselves are precarious, subject to change and, indeed, are the key site of political activity (see Smith, 1998).

From here we might ask what provides the *dynamic* for all the political activity that LM claim occurs around discourse? The answer is that no matter how apparently all-encompassing and 'total' a particular discursive structure is, agents will ultimately experience antagonistic relations with what lies beyond it (Mouffe, 2005: 14–19). That 'beyond' is the surplus of meaning, which is experienced as lack: it is both the precondition of, and obstacle to, the realisation of the agent's present identity. For example, in today's workplace, the subject position of a 'modernising manager' is predicated upon the other of a regressive or unproductive set of workers: without these, there would be no need for modernising management. However, the recalcitrant workers are simultaneously the obstacle to the manager's vision of a perfectly integrated organisational culture: the manager's identity is blocked in this respect. Similarly, the presence of interfering managers could be the other against which a worker's sense of autonomy and professional ethics is defined. But again, simultaneously, the worker's vision is perceived to be blocked by the constant interference of those very managers.

LM thus paint a picture of social and political life in permanent, unstable flux. Given this, it is difficult to imagine how any political project or social institution could ever stabilise or endure over time. However, LM and allied theorists introduce concepts to account for the relative stability of identities and social structures. With regard to the apparently most entrenched institutions, norms and identities, the notion of *sedimented discourse* has been developed. The claim here is that such entities are just as contingent, politically instituted and precarious as every other discursive structure: they have simply become 'sedimented' through ongoing reinstitution over time (Smith, 1998: 172).

Within discursive structures, the concept of 'nodal points' is used to describe sites where meaning is at least partially fixed around a particular discursive trope (LM, 1985: 112–13; Torfing, 1999: 98–9). The image of the nodal point fits well with that of an infinite discursive field, or grid, within which for social life to happen at all there must be a degree of stability. However, the term is used quite loosely by researchers to apply to different levels of social reality. Thus, it might refer to a particular element within a discourse, for example the tropes of 'nation' or 'duty' within traditional conservatism. Alternatively, what seems to be a macro discourse might itself be part of something broader. For example, a comprehensive discourse such as 'liberalism' may be understood as a crucial nodal point within the wider discourse of 'Enlightenment', along with others such as 'reason' and 'progress'. Similarly, a vast and disparate set of practices such as 'the state' or 'family' can be seen as nodal points that are crucial to sustaining the classical sociological imaginary of 'society' itself.

If nodal points describe the partial fixation of meaning, LM introduce the more specific concepts of *logics of equivalence* and *logics of difference* to explain the mechanisms through which this is achieved (LM, 1985: 127–34). Given the flux and instability of meaning, the trick that a discourse needs to achieve is to conceal this, and present itself as sufficiently stable and 'natural' for agents to identify with. Logics of equivalence and difference indicate contrasting ways of managing the problem of the constitutive outside and antagonism: each is a different way of approaching the inevitable frontiers between different discourses and identities. A logic of equivalence draws dispersed elements (agents, ideas, practices, demands) into a discourse by reinforcing what they have in common (their 'equivalence', or sameness). This commonality is stressed *in opposition to* a particular other: it highlights an 'us and them' boundary such as 'workers vs owners' or 'hardworking people' vs 'scroungers'. Not only is the unity of the group *contra* its other established, but also that the other represents a *threat* to the identity of the group (e.g. by 'exploiting' them in the case of 'owners', or 'ripping them off' in the case of 'scroungers'). By contrast, a logic of difference integrates a plurality of elements by *underplaying* boundaries and showing how differences can be successfully and inclusively accommodated within the discourse. Classic formulations here include – in their varying ways – 'human rights', 'multiculturalism' or appeals to 'One Nation'. Another way of putting the distinction between the two strategies is that the logic of equivalence seeks to highlight and politicise the antagonistic boundaries that LM see as inevitable, whereas the logic of difference seeks to (create the appearance of) diminishing and depoliticising such boundaries. It does this by drawing as many elements as possible into an inclusive, overarching discursive formation (Howarth, 2000: 106–7; Torfing, 1999: 96–7).

Despite such devices for stabilising meaning, LM's ontology of precarious discursive structures means that at some point such stability will be disrupted and/or challenged: we are not destined to simply reproduce discourses. Laclau (1990: 39–60) expands on this moment of disruption with the concept of *dislocation*.

Dislocation occurs when the contingency of a discourse is revealed, that is, the fact that it could be otherwise becomes apparent. In terms of considering the status of the discursive/extra-discursive and society, it is striking that it is developments in an external, empirical world that apparently lead to the dislocation. Thus, Laclau (1990) and leading analysts such as Torfing (1999: 148–9, 301) refer to the dislocatory effects of external events or shocks that a rapidly mutating capitalism presents for established identities and practices, for example the impact of economic globalisation upon national cultures. Howarth (2000: 111) confirms this reading of dislocation by suggesting that, 'Laclau uses the concept to introduce an "extra-discursive" dynamism into his conception of society'.

The effect of dislocation is that a given discursive structure is no longer able to incorporate the surplus of meaning. Consequently, the structure can no longer provide (seemingly) stable and coherent subject positions for agents to identify with. At such moments, what post-structuralists refer to as the contingency and undecidability of the discursive structure is revealed: agents must make choices in terms of developing – and identifying with – new subject positions. In this period, political alternatives become most visible. Moments of political revolution are the most extreme example of such a dislocatory conjuncture, but smaller-scale examples are continually occurring as agents negotiate their identities (Glynos and Howarth, 2007: 110–12). To further illustrate how his conception of the agent is not passive, Laclau (1990: 60–1) makes a distinction between subject position and political subjectivity. The former is the more or less 'allotted' role within a discursive structure, familiar to structuralism. But the latter describes agency at those dislocated moments – such as a revolutionary situation – when the contingency of the structure is revealed, and agents are compelled to make decisions *about* rather than just *within* it (Howarth, 2000: 122; Miller, 2004).

The political implications of discourse: ideology and hegemony

We have outlined LM's philosophical account of the discursive, and some of the key terms they have developed for how it interfaces with political subjectivity. On this basis, we can now assess some of the broader political implications of the post-structuralist discourse-theoretical approach. First, we can consider how it relates to the issue of social theory and *ideology* we have discussed in this chapter. Do discourse theorists see a role for the concept of ideology, or does discourse entirely replace it? Critics and analysts of discourse theory continue to debate this issue (e.g. Macdonald, 2003: 27–51; Purvis and Hunt, 1993; Torfing, 1999: 113–18). However, somewhat ironically, post-structuralists seem to have reached a consensus over the character of ideology that has eluded more traditional ideology theorists: 'ideology' simply describes a discourse which attempts to 'totalise' and/or denies its own discursive contingency. This might be in the form of a reified, reductive conception of society and social change (e.g. strong claims made about globalisation), or an essentialised claim about identities (e.g. 'national character' or, at the extreme, 'racial supremacy').

For discourse theorists, then, ideology simply represents a particular type of discourse or discursive practice in the political field, one that denies its own contingency and attempts an artificial discursive closure (Torfing, 1999: 114, 302). Furthermore, in contrast to previous attempts to dismiss or transcend ideology, this is seen as simply one type of routine political practice – almost to the point of being banal. Asked to outline his approach to 'Ideology and post-Marxism' for the leading *Journal of Political Ideologies*, Laclau does not even mention the word 'ideology' until, in an afterword, he suggests that, 'This [discursive] closing operation is what I would still call *ideological* which, in my vocabulary, as should be clear, has not the slightest pejorative connotation' (Laclau, 2006: 114, see also Laclau, 1996).

This view of ideology as a specific, routine type of political practice relates to the more important post-structuralist discourse concept of *hegemony*. In previous theories of ideology, and in more popular usage, hegemony tends to describe an endpoint: a condition of dominance reached by a particular group of agents and/or idea or worldview (Howarth, 2004: 256). In social theory, hegemony is often taken as shorthand for the control of 'common sense'. In each of these cases, hegemony is treated critically, or as an aberration to be contrasted with more objective or transparent forms of knowledge. However, for LM (1985: 134–45) – building on Gramsci's sense of the term – hegemony is a perfectly normal political activity or practice: it is treated more as a verb than an adjective. In essence, hegemony is the attempt to do the work of ideology as defined above. Hegemony seeks to develop an expansive discourse, rendering the contingent as appearing necessary and inevitable. Thus, in explicitly arguing for an understanding of 'politics as hegemony', Mouffe (2005: 17) urges us to recognise, 'the hegemonic nature of every kind of social order and the fact that every society is the product of a series of practices attempting to establish order in a context of contingency'.

The work of hegemony involves perhaps the crucial political activity on the post-structuralist analysis: articulation. This is the knitting together of contingent discursive themes, ideas and identities in an attempt to persuasively stabilise meaning around the kinds of 'nodal points' discussed above. However, reflecting the post-structuralist insistence on contingent, unstable identities, the crucial feature of articulation is that the identities of the elements involved become altered as a result. In LM's (1985: 105) widely cited definition – which also returns us to our starting point of the character of discourse itself:

> we will call *articulation* any practice establishing a relation among elements such that their identity is modified as a result of the articulatory practice. The structured totality arising from the articulatory practice, we will call *discourse*.

The more expansive a discursive hegemonic practice, the wider the range of elements it will attempt to draw into its re-description of the world. This might mean, for example, attempting to integrate claims about the nature of 'society', 'economy', 'politics' and 'the individual' into an apparently seamless worldview (such as that of 'socialism' or 'neoliberalism'). However, given the contingency of interests, identities and discourses, hegemony is not something that can ever finally be achieved: it can only ever represent a precarious and temporary, even if deeply entrenched and widespread, stabilisation of identities and meanings. The possibility of alternatives is thus permanently kept alive.

Case study: The hegemony of neoliberalism

To illustrate how social theory engages with substantive questions of ideology and discourse, we are going to examine neoliberalism: the ideology of free markets, a small state and the primacy of the individual. In some respects, this is an impossible undertaking. Neoliberalism is prolific and entrenched, even described by Perry Anderson (2000: 13) as, 'the most successful ideology in world history'. It has become coextensive with the very idea of the social and political – a 'horizon' beyond which it is difficult to imagine – and thus perhaps the most significant object within contemporary social theory. This book is no exception: neoliberalism has been the 'ghost at the feast' across our chapters. While many (not unreasonably) believed that the Global Financial Crisis 2008 would herald neoliberalism's demise, its resilience and the apparent lack of alternatives merely confirm its hegemonic status. As Colin Crouch (2011: viii) notes, 'neoliberalism is emerging from the financial collapse more politically powerful than ever' and, as such, we have to fathom its 'strange non-death'.

Neoliberalism blurs – and maybe even dissolves – the lines we have drawn between identifying and explaining empirical practices, critiquing and consti-tuting them. The main reason for this is that social theory is almost universally hostile to 'neoliberalism'. Terry Flew (2014: 51) suggests that in this respect the term has become an, 'all-purpose denunciatory category', denoting 'forces that are large, dark, relentless and all-encompassing that constitute the underlying source of explanation of everything' (2014: 53). Social theorists have been integral to explaining the rise of neoliberalism as an expansive project, with implications far beyond its basic economic doctrines and political rhetoric. But from the outset, most analysts have simultaneously been engaged in critique, seeking weaknesses and alternatives.

It is through such critique that, ironically, social theory might even be said to be partly constitutive of the neoliberal project. By identifying the full sig-nificance of neoliberalism as ideology and practice, social theory has arguably contributed to its own self-understanding (if 'it' can be said to have such a thing). It has also played a role in elevating neoliberalism to its present status of a master signifier in academic, political, media and – to a certain extent – public discourse. Latterly, (despite its 'non-death') theorists have become weary of the ubiquity of the term neoliberalism, asking if it has ceased to be descrip-tively or critically useful (Clarke, 2008; Venugopal, 2015). As a result, there has been a turn towards a more detailed, intellectual history of the neoliberal project, drawing out its internal complexity and fault lines (see Davies, 2014; Gane, 2014a; Hardin, 2014). Such work is useful, but still tends to confirm broad consensus over neoliberalism's fundamental essence, which will inform our discussion here (see also Gilbert, 2013; Hall, 2011).

While neoliberalism has increasingly been characterised as a global phenomenon, our case study will focus primarily on the UK. Since the avant-garde of the Thatcher Governments (1979–90), through the variations of the New Labour administrations (1997–2010), up to the explicitly small-state and 'austerity' discourse of David Cameron's Conservative regime, the UK has seen perhaps the most significant and sustained neoliberal 'experiment'. In so doing it has also revealed the variety of party political and governing projects neoliberalism can accommodate. As the *Guardian* editorial (8 April 2013) remarked upon the death of Margaret Thatcher in 2013:

> British public life is still defined to an extraordinary degree by the argument between those who wish to continue or refine what she started and those who want to mitigate or turn it back. Just as in life she shaped the past 30 years, so in death she may well continue to shape the next 30.

It is thus no surprise that the UK is a key site of academic debate about the economic, political and sociocultural dimensions of neoliberalism as ideology and practice.

Defining neoliberalism

Neoliberalism draws on political and economic theories that revolve around the value of individual freedom. Its origins are traced as early as the 1930s, among German economists trying to find a middle way between free market capitalism, which was held to be responsible for the Great Depression, and state planning, which was viewed as potentially authoritarian (Bonefeld, 2012; Gane, 2014a). However, neoliberalism began to assume a more developed form in theory and practice following the Second World War, when it emerged as a clear reaction against the prevailing trend for economic and political planning (Gamble, 2009: 2–3). By the 1970s, when neoliberalism was in the political ascendancy in the US and Britain, a more unified set of themes emerged. These became associated with the political and economic theory of Frederick von Hayek and, eventually, the free market economics of Milton Friedman and the Chicago School (Stedman Jones, 2012). These strands continued to present neoliberalism as a reaction against collectivism and economic planning. This is premised upon a negative conception of individual freedom, defined as freedom from external interference. Individuals are seen as rational and self-interested, with the market economy the best means of guaranteeing their liberty. It is also the most efficient means of producing and distributing goods, and allowing for innovation. As a result, there is a default preference for private enterprise, and a hostility to state ownership and intervention: the state and its agencies should themselves as a far as possible be run on market principles. In particular, there is a strong critique of the post-war welfare state, which is seen as creating dependency and being a drag on the economy. There is also hostility towards taxation as a disincentive for private enterprise and individual effort, and a means of funding dubious state projects (see Gamble, 2007; Harvey, 2005: esp. 1–4).

Neoliberalism contains its own internal variations, as well as theoretical and political tensions and contradictions. Most notably, these revolve around the appropriate role of the state in securing freedom for the market economy (Gane, 2014a). As we shall see, the *active production* of neoliberal subjects and sensibilities has in fact been a key feature of the neoliberal project as it has developed. But despite its conceptual, geographical and historical variations, neoliberalism's key basic ingredients remain constant. Jeremy Gilbert (2013: 11) thus observes, 'the sheer regularity and similarity of the basic elements of "neoliberal" policy the world over'. He also notes how these are sustained and expanded through a proliferation of sites across contemporary culture (e.g. from reality TV to self-help literature) in a way that seems:

> so overwhelmingly consistent with the norms and objectives of classical neo-liberalism that the onus of proof must be on those who might wish to refute the assumption that they belong to a singular discursive formation, and that they are in fact expressions of a coherent ideology. (Gilbert, 2013: 12)

Below we shall use a two-stage typology to characterise the social and political development of neoliberalism since the mid-1970s. While overly neat, this offers a reasonable description of how neoliberalism has developed as ideology and practice, as well as how social theorists tend to narrate it. What we shall call Phase 1 neoliberalism refers to the politically aggressive dismantling of key aspects of the post-Second World War settlement. Following the success of this aspect, Phase 2 denotes the extension of neoliberalism across social life, in terms of institutions, policies, norms and identities, until it has reached a position of profound hegemony. Building on this mapping of the neoliberal project we will – as we have throughout the book – 'read' it through the social-theoretical perspectives discussed in the first part of the chapter. We will then explore in further detail what neoliberalism adds to our ongoing understanding of the relations between social theory and its empirical, political object.

Phase 1: dismantling the collectivist enemy

Like many ideologies, neoliberalism in practice began by defining itself in terms of what it was *against*, or a reaction to. Neoliberalism's anti-collectivist intellectual roots meant that those associated with it were always hostile not just to communism and state socialism but also the post-1945 welfare settlement. In the UK, when that settlement reached what seemed an irreversible crisis in the 1970s, the critique went onto the offensive with a readymade, radical alternative. The so-called Keynesian welfare consensus had underpinned society and economy from the time of post-war reconstruction (Kavanagh and Morris, 1994). Economically, it relied on using demand management (through taxation and spending) to stimulate the economy as necessary, aimed for full employment and assumed steady economic growth. This was underpinned by a political framework where the state mediated between capital and labour (represented by trade unions) over wage bargaining, therefore controlling inflation. The whole approach was underpinned by an egalitarian and collectivist ethos, evident in the expansion of public services and the provision of generous, universal welfare entitlements (pensions, unemployment benefits). These were funded out of steeply progressive taxation as a direct means of redistribution. This served not just an economic purpose but also reflected an *ideological* commitment to equality, or narrowing the gap between rich and poor.

The 1970s saw a range of crises that undermined this economic and social model, particularly in the UK (see Hay, 1999; Saunders, 2012). Especially notable was the external 'oil shock', when the oil producing (OPEC) nations dramatically increased prices. For the first time it became alarmingly clear how reliant Western economies were upon the security of oil. But ideologically more significant was the disintegration of the basis of the post-war consensus. Large parts of the British economy were in public ownership, increasingly inefficient and non-adaptive. In economic good times this could to some extent remain hidden, but in the face of increased international competition and crises such as the oil shock, it became dysfunctional. Trade unions represented workers accustomed to secure work and steadily increasing wages, ensuring their participation in an ever-expanding consumer economy. But this was undermined by the rise of stagflation: the simultaneous presence of rising unemployment *and* inflation, in defiance of orthodox economic theory. Facing diminishing profitability, employers sought to keep wages down. However, this was made difficult by the entrenched bargaining power of trade unions. Industrial conflict eventually exploded through widespread strikes and other forms of unrest. At the same time, faith in the main political parties to manage the situation declined. The traditional two-class, partisan voting model (the working class supporting Labour, and the middle class favouring Conservatives) began to break down (Salvik and Crewe, 1983), and there was a rise of new parties and extremist groups on left and right. 'Racial' tensions grew and there was a less tangible, but in retrospect well-documented, cultural disenchantment, malaise and anger. This was embodied, for example, in punk and the protest music of the time.

The convergence of these factors led political scientists to ask whether British government had become 'overloaded' and the country 'ungovernable' (King, 1975). The situation was ripe for a new ideology to emerge. Neoliberalism offered a longstanding critique of the limits of the collectivist model; a clear and radically different economic strategy; and a political theory and rhetoric based on the primacy of the individual, resonating with growing individual aspiration and dissatisfaction with the establishment. These were the conditions that ushered in the first, aggressive phase of neoliberal politics. This sought to dismantle the intellectual credibility, ethos, policies, institutions and political defenders of the post-war welfare settlement. It has been labelled by Paul Cammack (2004:152) as neoliberalism's 'initial shock phase that unsettles "anti-market" forces', while Jamie Peck (2010) has characterised such practices as 'roll back' neoliberalism.

In Britain, the aggressive intent of this phase of the project was embodied in the persona of Margaret Thatcher and her governments from 1979 (Jenkins, 1987). High levels of unemployment were tolerated as consonant with neoliberal economic doctrine. But in the early 1980s the application of this doctrine seemed to be failing (Gamble, 1983). In the midst of recession, there was widespread unrest in the inner cities. This was met with military-style policing and justified by a wider 'law and order' discourse (Hall, 1979). Such a discourse dovetailed with the beginnings of now commonplace, punitive rhetoric about the 'idle', 'unproductive' and 'scroungers' and the importing from the US of underclass theory, associated with American sociologist Charles Murray (1990). Manufacturing industry was run down and its associated communities (which were heavily unionised and linked with the Labour Party) were left unsupported. This was crystallised in the aggressive policing of the miners' strike of 1984–5 (see Beckett and Hencke, 2009). The conflict between the government and the then powerful National Union of Mineworkers came to be emblematic of the state restoring the 'right to manage' not just economic policy, but the nation itself, paving the way to anti-trade union legislation. In foreign policy, Thatcher's bellicose anti-communist stance was developed in alliance with the Reagan administration in the US (which was also at the forefront of neoliberal economic policies). As ideologically significant, this anti-communism was used to open up fears of an 'enemy within'. It was a means of discrediting as extremist – by spurious but often effective rhetorical association – the Labour Party, trade union and growing civil-society opposition such as the Campaign for Nuclear Disarmament.

Phase 2: building neoliberal hegemony

Phase 1 neoliberalism was an explicit reaction to the perceived (inevitable) failures of collectivist ideology, which it fought to dismantle intellectually and in practice. However, being a solution to a crisis is not enough to secure longer-term consent to, and entrenchment of, a political ideology. The more expansive element of neoliberalism sought to *positively construct* the institutions, norms and forms of subjectivity that would sustain the project into the future: Peck (2010) characterises this as neoliberalism's 'roll-out' aspect. The task was to replace the post-war consensus with a new, entirely different common sense based on neoliberal ideology.

We should note here that Phase 1 was not only about the negative task of defeating opposition; it had its own forward-looking aspects. Part of the appeal of Thatcherism, Ronald Reagan's 'It's morning again in America' rhetoric and neoliberalism more widely – was its ability to present a narrative that individuals wanted to identify with (Clarke, 2010). We thus need to account for this more 'constructive' aspect, even in Phase 1. Neoliberalism provides a simple toolkit of ideological assumptions which are readily translatable into a wide-ranging political narrative and programme. So, at the same time as demonising opponents and pointing to what was failing in Britain, Thatcherism presented appealing imaginaries – revolving around the neoliberal trope of 'freedom' – to different elements of a new electoral coalition (Hall, 1987; Hall and Jacques, 1983). At the leading edge of this was Thatcherism's fetishisation of the figure of the entrepreneur and alignment with the 'freeing' of the City of London and the rise of a dynamic and deregulated form of finance capitalism (Keat and Abercrombie, 1991). However, Thatcherism was simultaneously a populist project that did not want to appear elitist in a traditional sense: neoliberalism, after all, was also supposed to be an assault on aspects of the prevailing establishment (Marquand, 2004: 95–6). This populism was conveyed in the image of a 'share-owning democracy' (sometimes a 'property-owning democracy'). It was embodied in classic neoliberal policies such as the privatisation of state assets; the related opening out of share ownership to individual citizens; and the controversial policy of allowing tenants of rented council homes to buy their properties cheaply, thus becoming homeowners. Beyond these attempts to use economic policy to create aspirational subject positions, the wider popular culture of the 1980s was replete with imagery that reinforced the 'have it all' messages of consumer-based neoliberalism. These ranged from glossy family soap operas such as *Dallas* and *Dynasty* to the 'greed is good', 'lunch is for wimps' ethos of Gordon Gekko; the cult antihero of the hit movie *Wall Street* (see also Hall, 2011: 722–3).

In retrospect Thatcherism's particular attempts to draw neoliberal subject positions, as well as the way they were reinforced by the wider culture, seem dated and rather crude. But these were really just the first forays into extending the neoliberal project. With the major obstacles to neoliberalism defeated after the battles of the 1980s, Phase 2 saw its apparently inexorable march extended from the economy through politics and culture to become the common sense of the age. Politically, the fall of the Berlin Wall in 1989 and the collapse of Soviet Communism set the scene for the argument – made famously by Francis Fukuyama (1992) – that ideological alternatives had been exhausted: free market liberal democracy represented the 'end of history'. This period also saw the rise of neoliberalism's global dimensions, most notably in the form of the 'Washington Consensus'. Through this, key institutions of global economic governance – such as the International Monetary Fund (IMF) and the World

Bank – aggressively implemented neoliberal theory as a basis for lending and development criteria. This effectively forced receiving national governments to apply neoliberal measures domestically, such as deregulation and reduced public spending (Harvey, 2005; Lechner, 2009: Ch. 5).

Unsurprisingly, with the fall of the Soviet Union and the global rise of neoliberalism, communist and radical socialist groups in the West underwent an intellectual crisis and steep decline in support. But it was changes to the more mainstream parties of the social democratic centre-left that were most telling in understanding the extension of neoliberalism across society (see also Chapter 2). Led by Bill Clinton's New Democrats in the US and mimicked by Tony Blair's New Labour in the UK, centre-left parties rapidly discarded any residual opposition they held towards free market liberalism (Callinicos, 2001). More strikingly, they went some way beyond this and sought to position themselves as being at the forefront of an increasingly globalised form of capitalist economy. Centre-left politicians claimed to be the ones who would further modernise economy and society to meet the demands of the new age, while adapting what was understood by social justice in this context (Blair, 1998). For a period in the 1990s and 2000s, it seemed as if it was indeed possible for parties of the centre-left to govern in a way that embraced free market economics, while avoiding some of the harshest elements of neoliberal conflict and rhetoric of the 1980s.

The new centrist rhetoric sought to overcome the ideological binaries of the past (Fairclough, 2000). The language of class was replaced with that of 'community' and the pledge to govern 'for all our people' (Goes, 2004). The private/public division was replaced by 'partnership' and the promotion of private interests to carry out state functions. The education system and even the welfare state were to be treated as a vehicle for increasing economic competitiveness, acting as a springboard to propel individuals into the global knowledge economy (Giddens, 2000: 65–75). Further financial deregulation and low taxation would continue to be the key to economic dynamism. Few critical questions were asked, as continued economic growth seemed able to sustain both low taxes and investment in public services. In this economic and political context, it is again the subtle shift in cultural markers that illustrates much about the ideological work that was being done. In the more combative 1980s, the figure of the heroic entrepreneur was valorised, but also seen as selfish and aggressive, which could alienate moderate voters. In a subsequent climate where neoliberal assumptions were to be universalised, the figure of the 'caring capitalist' needed to acquire resonance. Among existing market actors, this took the form of the 'corporate social responsibility agenda', which pledged to account for the environmental and social impact of business (Farrell, 2012). But, more significantly, the figure of the 'social entrepreneur' took hold, since, as Giddens (2000:75) argues, 'the same drive and creativity are needed in the public sector, and in civil society, as in the economic sphere'. Sceptics, however, suggested that the discourse of creativity and dynamism was a cover for the extension of market relations and private interests across the public realm (Crouch, 2004: ch. 5; Marquand, 2004).

Despite the 'caring' rhetoric, unprecedented consumption and a focus on material goods were required for Phase 2 neoliberalism to be sustained. This was legitimised in quite unsubtle ways by, for example, Tony Blair's explicit wooing of celebrity and the super-rich. More insidiously, subject positions in popular culture seemed to co-opt impulses that had originally been sources of social opposition to neoliberalism. This is illustrated by the complex developments that took hold in feminist debates (Budgeon, 2011). In the 1990s and 2000s it became clear that a crucial figure to consumer capitalism was the young, educated and aspirational woman. That women should be able to progress in the economic sphere beyond the home had, of course, been a long-standing progressive objective. But that this goal should come to represent the leading edge of roll-out neoliberalism had not been anticipated (Rottenberg, 2014). The tension was symbolised in cultural reference points such as the hit TV show *Sex and the City*, depicting the glamorous and upwardly mobile lives of a group of women in New York. Crucially, their fictional experiences were often pointed to by female viewers as representing a form of gender empowerment. But the context of the show was a rampant consumer capitalism that was the unquestioned precondition of the characters' experience (see Gill and Scharff, 2011). This indicates how the ideological status of 'choice' has remained a crucial political battleground as neoliberalism has unfolded.

Reading neoliberalism through social theory

Functionalism: neoliberalism and system imbalance?

At first sight, functionalism seems to tell us little about the ideology of neoliberalism; indeed, the example may indicate the limits of the functionalist approach. We noted that a tendency in both Durkheim's account of the integrating features of culture, and in later functionalist work, was to neglect the content of norms or ideologies, focusing instead on their integrative functions *per se*. In this respect, functionalists would be uninterested in neoliberalism's political arguments about liberty, the primacy of the individual, the need for a minimal state and the spontaneous, coordinating role of markets. However, neoliberalism makes ontological claims about the nature of the social and the individual that would surely be intellectually objected to by functionalists. Specifically, the asocial neoliberal view of the rational, choosing subject is anathema to functionalism's account of the causal role of social structures, as well as the instincts of most other varieties of sociologist (see Gane, 2014b). More substantively, the neoliberal critique of state action and valorisation of the market runs contrary to functionalism's (more or less explicit) concern with social equilibrium and integration (see Mennell, 2014). Consider, for example, Parsons' (1949, 1951, 1969) AGIL scheme described above: this imagines a functional balance between different social, economic, political and cultural spheres in which – since Durkheim – the state has a key coordinating role. On this model, the aggressive colonisation of some spheres by the logic of one (i.e. the market in neoliberalism) is unbalancing and unhealthy (Habermas, 1987).

In addition, it is questionable to what extent functionalists would regard the extraordinary levels of social inequality generated by neoliberalism as being functional for the wider system, or sustainable in the longer term. Again, this is not because of an *a priori* value commitment to equality, but because of a pre-occupation with system stability. For example, a functionalist analysis might endorse an ideology such as 'the American dream' for its integrative poten-tial. However, when material inequality – which neoliberalism generates and largely takes as natural – makes the 'dream' unobtainable for the vast majority, there is a risk to system stability: citizens may lose faith in key political eco-nomic and political institutions (see Stiglitz, 2013). This could be manifest in the rise of unpredictable populisms (such as Donald Trump's 2016 presidential candidacy) or disengagement from civic life altogether.

However, neoliberalism could alternatively be seen as incredibly adaptive, integrative and functional. It certainly provided one means of overcoming eco-nomic and political crises in the 1970s, and it has offered an (albeit one-sided) route to 'development' for many nations, resonating with functionalist mod-ernisation theories of the 1960s (e.g. Rostow, 1960). Despite inequality and outbreaks of conflict, societies subject to neoliberal doctrine have proved to be remarkably internally peaceful in relative historical terms, even weather-ing the sustained turbulence since the Global Financial Crisis of 2008. So it seems that while there may be functionalist objections to neoliberalism, it is ultimately compatible with the overall framework. It remains unclear, though, how important functionalists regard the specific ideological content and mech-anisms of neoliberalism to be.

Marxism: economic vs cultural dimensions of neoliberalism

We saw in our discussion of Marxist approaches that ideology is only 'func-tional' to the extent that it patches up the contradictions of a doomed capitalist system. In performing this role, it distorts economic and social reality. Ideology presents capitalist relations as being natural, and the particular class inter-ests of the bourgeoisie as universal. However, we observed a tension between aspects of the Marxist analysis which imply that hegemonic ideology is some-how automatically generated by the capitalist 'system', and those which focus more concretely on the conscious activities of the ruling classes in manufac-turing and securing consent. Of course, the foundational insights of Marx, Gramsci and Althusser were developed in relation to nineteenth- and early twentieth-century capitalism. So how does the Marxist tradition understand the specific rise of neoliberal ideology since the 1970s?

On the materialist Marxist reading, Phase 1 neoliberalism can be seen as both a reflex response to a capitalist crisis, and naked class war. On this view, the crisis of the 1970s was straightforwardly one of profitability. The post-war capitalist settlement had reached its economic and political limits: an assault was required to reduce state intervention on behalf of labour, neuter trade unions and restore profitability (Harvey, 2005). Given this, it was no surprise that there was a return to some of the free market ideology of the nineteenth century, and its associated doctrines of the primacy of the individual and personal responsibility (Crouch, 2004).

Acknowledging that the facts of capitalist crises necessitated the emergence of a 'new' ideology – neoliberalism – to restore order and profitability, echoes the strand in Marxism that presents ideologies as a 'reflex', structural response to (economic) changes. However, the establishment of neoliberalism did not, of course, just 'happen', it was part of a hard-fought political offensive. As Crouch (2011: 6) notes, core neoliberal tenets of 'unchallenged property rights, low levels of regulation and low taxes remained extremely attractive to very wealthy people, who were always available to fund economic liberalism's intellectual projects and keep its protagonists going during the lean years'. A supplement to this analysis concerns the balance of class forces, and the relationship of the ruling class itself to neoliberal ideology. Neoliberalism legitimated the rise of a *particular* fraction of the ruling class – the new financial elite – displacing more traditional 'gentlemanly' city capitalists as well as manufacturers (Harvey, 2005; Scott, 1991). In this respect, Thatcherism's vision of entrepreneurship and modernisation represented both an economic need to restore profitability, and a political need to legitimise the newly ascendant fraction of the bourgeoisie, its worldview and behaviours.

Marxism's engagement with neoliberalism illuminates the core dilemmas in the Marxist account of ideology. Pointing to 'purely' economic phenomena (the need to restore profitability) is not sufficient, as an account of class agency – including tensions between ruling class factions – is also required. But we also need to explain neoliberalism's ability to entrench itself over the long term: its capacity to achieve a sufficient degree of consent, legitimise and reproduce itself. Thus, David Harvey's (2005: 39–63) influential account of neoliberalism dwells on its 'construction of consent'. Similarly, Leslie Sklair (2002: 105–15), a Marxist theorist of globalisation, echoes the Frankfurt School in describing a 'culture-ideology of consumerism', that creates and sustains global markets for goods. These concerns reflect Gramsci's focus on how hegemony is developed at the level of culture and civil society.

Such theoretical issues at the heart of Marxism were famously captured in exchanges between the sociologists Stuart Hall (1985b) and Bob Jessop *et al.* (1984, 1985) over the nature of Thatcherism in Britain. Was Thatcherism animated more by political economy and state strategy, or by a powerful new ideology – or discourse – that was able to stabilise a number of contradictory elements of the project? In essence, Jessop *et al.* (1984, 1985) saw Thatcherism as a classic ruling-class response to capitalist crises, in which the state restored the capitalist order. Specifically, this was through a 'two nations' strategy. This involved promoting the interests of an aspirational, service sector population concentrated in the south of England. This group was set directly against and 'outside' the public sector, those reliant on the state and manufacturing industry, concentrated in the North. While Hall (1985b) recognised much of this materialist analysis, following Gramsci he argued that it didn't give due weight to the expansive – hegemonic – ideological and discursive ambitions of the Thatcher project. Indeed, it was Hall (1979) who first described Thatcher*ism* and encouraged us to think of it as a 'project'.

Hall had grasped not only the destructive aspect of what we have called Phase 1 neoliberalism, but also its forward-looking 'Phase 2' aspects, and the crucial role of culture and ideology within this. He noted how Thatcherism was not just about reasserting governability and profitability via the political and state power of the Conservative Party. The task was to irreversibly reshape the institutions and culture of Britain along neoliberal lines including, crucially, the worldview of its citizens: 'Thatcherism presented people with a philosophy of life, of what the whole society was like' (Hall, 1985a: 18). Significantly, Hall pointed to how Thatcherism was not just an ideology 'in itself', but that it was being skilfully deployed in a way that resonated with longer-term structural – sociological – changes in British society. In achieving this, it was managing apparent ideological contradictions through a form of 'regressive modernisation' (Hall, 1987: 17–19). This gestured towards an aspirational future of consumer capitalism, but did so through simultaneous 'backward'-looking appeals to conservative tropes such as family, patriotism, duty and law and order. The political economy of the project was of course crucial. But Hall drew attention to the relative autonomy and importance of these ideological and discursive aspects. This reading of the long-term, *hegemonic* character of Thatcherism was confirmed by the way that the political centre-left had to adjust to it. In the British case, in a subsequent critique of New Labour, Hall (1998: 14) simply commented: 'Mrs Thatcher had a project. Blair's historic project is adjusting us to it.' (See also Hall, 2003; Harvey, 2005: 62–3.)

Foucauldians and 'advanced liberalism'

Foucauldian accounts of neoliberalism open up a very different focus to Marxist themes of capitalist restructuring, class power and hegemony (Flew, 2012). Earlier we presented Foucault as a bridging figure between ideational and material approaches to the study of ideology and discourse. We saw that, on the one hand, Foucault examined the formal, intellectual conditions that enabled some 'truths' to be uttered. But he also focused on the concrete strategies of powerful actors, and the material apparatuses through which discourses are realised and subjects constructed and disciplined. Foucauldian analyses of neoliberalism draw together these themes, and highlight how the genealogical method can capture the specific combinations, contradictions and varieties of an ideological formation. Crucial to this has been the relatively recent translation into English of a series of lectures Foucault gave at the Collège de France in 1978–9, translated under the title *The Birth of Biopolitics* (Foucault, 2008). These lectures occurred before the electoral successes of Thatcher and Reagan, and the formation of 'neoliberalism' in the wider political imagination. However, with remarkable prescience, Foucault outlined what were to become key tendencies of the neoliberal project over subsequent decades (Brown, 2015; Gane, 2014a).

Foucauldians do not understand neoliberalism primarily in the context of capitalism, as functionalists and Marxists (in their different ways) do. Rather, the ideas and practices that we designate as 'neoliberalism' are simply one assemblage of the ongoing historical project to imagine, construct and govern 'society' and human populations: this reflects Foucault's (2007) governmentality framework discussed in Chapter 2. Neoliberalism is understood in terms of the uneven historical development of liberalism more broadly, and specifically the 'advanced liberal government' which characterises contemporary societies. Mitchell Dean (2010: 194) defines this as being:

> composite, plural and multiform. It is reducible neither to philosophical principles nor to a political ideology. Of crucial importance is the way it operates through a multiplicity of these practices of liberty, i.e. practices concerned with structuring, shaping, predicting and making calculable the operation of our freedom, and working off and through diagrams of free subjects constituted by forms of governmental and political reasoning.

It is striking that in the index to Dean's (2010) seminal overview of Foucauldian governmentality studies – to which comprehending neoliberalism is central – there is no entry for either 'ideology' or 'discourse'. However, it is not always recognised how seriously Foucault and his followers treat understanding key texts and ideas in themselves. Thus, Foucault (2008) analysed in detail the emergence of different strands of neoliberal thought in relation to the wider intellectual history of liberalism. In tracing this lineage, Foucauldians are interested in how key discursive themes are 'displaced' over time, leading to complex configurations of neoliberalism in practice. For example, Dean (2010) notes the contested and changing status of 'freedom' in neoliberal thought. This has been treated as a 'natural' and 'spontaneous' master concept, which leads to the critique of the overbearing state. However, 'freedom' has also been seen by neoliberals as needing to have certain social conditions met in order to flourish, and indeed for these conditions to be constructed by an activist state. Understanding such intellectual tensions enables an account of the complexities and contradictions of neoliberalism in practice (Foster *et al.*, 2014). With regard to the Phase 1 neoliberalism discussed in our case study, the Foucauldian approach captures the famous tension between Thatcherism's bold anti-state and pro-freedom rhetoric on the one hand, and centralising, interventionist tendencies on the other (Gamble, 1988).

Foucauldians thus reject the notion that neoliberalism is a mere ideological reflection of economic relations, and instead locate it within the longer-term, shifting discourse and politics of liberalism. They also analyse additional discursive themes that have shaped advanced liberal government. Perhaps the most crucial is 'crisis' (Clarke, 2010: 381–6). For Foucauldians, the 'ungovernable' 1970s was not a crisis of capitalist economy and society as such, but of the longer-term liberal project. The post-war welfare settlement was a particular variant of liberalism, aimed at collectivising societies. But this became subject to critique not just by neoliberals, but also the New Left, countercultural and new social movements. These political voices challenged entrenched interests, bureaucratic domination (including by parties and governments of the left) and claims to professional expertise, and called for more participatory governance and opportunities for self-actualisation (Dean, 2010: 180). It is easy to see how this resonated with the harder-edged neoliberal critique of government and call for market-based freedom, as noted in Chapter 3 (see also Boltanski and Chiapello, 1999). On the Foucauldian view, then, the 'crisis' was not of capitalism, but of the mode of governing. The population still needed to be governed, but bureaucratic collectivisation no longer functioned. We are thus left with an alternative explanation of how 'the market' came to be presented as the organising principle for the state and, eventually, all spheres of social life (Brown, 2015). Rather than emphasising the need to restore profitability, ruling class power or the ideological zealotry key neoliberal actors, Foucauldians identify marketisation as an available, wide-ranging solution to challenges of *governance*.

As neoliberalism has developed, Foucauldians have increasingly focused on discourses surrounding the *responsibilisation* of individual citizens. This reflects the harsher rhetoric of Phase 1, Thatcherite neoliberalism and its hectoring of individuals and groups to 'take responsibility' for themselves and their families. But, more significantly, it captures the long roll-out of Phase 2. This constructs new subjectivities within which 'freedom' and 'choice' are again central, but now as a means of responsibilising citizens as part of a shifting governmentality (Foster *at al.*, 2014). Thus, consumerism and the self-management of one's career, relationships and body all designate a shift towards individual self-governance, and what Foucault (2008) identified as the active, entrepreneurial subject.

This account also indicates what Phase 2 neoliberalism meant under the guise of modernising social democratic government: 'community' and new forms of state-sponsored 'participation' are actually integral to constructing acceptable citizenship. So, where Marxists and other leftists might bemoan the corrosive effects of neoliberalism upon the community, for Foucauldians such as Nikolas Rose (2001) in particular, 'community' itself is central to advanced liberal government: a site where citizens can be responsibilised. In a further discursive tension within neoliberalism between 'freedom' and 'regulation', the agendas of responsibilisation and governance through community increasingly require the tracking and monitoring of supposedly 'autonomous' institutions and individuals. This is evident in the explosion of the quantification, audit and micro-management of public services. It is also manifest in increasingly invasive surveillance techniques, from the level of nations down to individual neighbourhoods and homes. This echoes Foucault's (1963, 1975) own earlier historical focus on disciplinary sites such as the clinic and the prison.

Post-structuralist discourse theory: (unstable) neoliberal hegemony

Foucauldian analyses are often subsumed under a broad heading of 'post-structuralism'. However, following our account of Foucault as bridging ideology and discourse, and the discursive/extra-discursive, it is possible to construct a more 'fully-fledged' post-structuralist discourse reading of neoliberalism. Such a reading rejects any lingering sense of an inevitable, unfolding logic of capitalism: this would include the simple two-stage model of Phase 1 and Phase 2 neoliberalism we have used here. This rejection is particularly important to our exemplar post-structuralist theorists, Laclau and Mouffe, given their explicitly post-Marxist break from stagist versions of history. Of course, Foucault was similarly determined to break from linear Marxist models of development. But post-structuralist discourse theorists might be sceptical about even Foucauldian categories such as advanced liberalism, or the assumption of a 'progression' from a socialised to a post-welfare form of governance. The suspicion would be that Foucauldians reify 'liberalism' in the way Marxists do 'capitalism'.

Consequently, in another departure from the Foucauldian account, post-structuralists are unlikely to dwell on the classic texts or intellectual history of neoliberal thinkers in themselves. They are instead interested in the discursive production and reception of the signifier 'neoliberalism', its implicit and explicit claims about the nature of the social and of identity, and how these are articulated with other discursive themes. In addition, post-structuralists do not seek to describe an overarching shift in the nature of economy (Marx) or governance (Foucault), but the discursive strategies that enable such a shift. Thus, Mouffe (2013: 73) argues that we need to understand the transition to contemporary neoliberalism in terms of, 'a process of discursive re-articulation of existing discourses and practices', and that grasping this, 'allows us to visualize this transition in terms of an hegemonic intervention'. In this respect, there is overlap with the Foucauldian focus on, for example, the discourse of 'crisis' that accompanied Phase 1, or how the objects of neoliberalism are brought into being so as to be made governable. However, rather than focusing on changing technical expertise or programmes of government, as Foucauldians do, a post-structuralist discourse reading is interested in the more strictly political aspects of such phenomena: how they relate to political ideologies, alliances, tactics and strategy. As David Howarth (2000: 132) argues with regard to analysing Thatcherism:

Determining how and what form Thatcherite discourse took, as well as its consequences for the structuring of social relations, requires careful empirical analysis of *the way in which social antagonisms were constructed and political frontiers drawn* during the period. (my emphasis)

This in turn opens up a more detailed account of discursive *mechanisms*. For example, analysing logics of equivalence and difference is particularly useful in examining the politics of neoliberal discourse. We saw that a logic of equivalence seeks to unite a range of different identities *against* a discursively constructed other or outside identity. This helps to describe key aspects of Phase 1 neoliberalism, and at different levels of analysis. Thus, at the macro level, the social imaginary of the 'postwar Keynesian welfare state' was situated as defunct and crisis-ridden, and needed replacing with alternative macro abstractions such as 'market', 'entrepreneurialism' and 'rule of law' (Glynos and Howarth, 2007: 173). More specifically, an equivalence was successfully drawn between collective actors who, on a materialist reading, may objectively have had *competing* economic interests and values. Thus, 'the City', 'entrepreneurs', 'the traditional family' and 'aspirational working class' were set against a long list of 'others', including 'producer interests', 'bureaucrats', 'welfare dependents' and 'loony lefties' (Smith, 1998: 164).

Of course, Thatcherite Phase 1 neoliberalism could not rely entirely on 'othering' and drawing logics of equivalence. The maxim that successful political ideologies need to contain an inclusive, forward-looking vision also informed the discourse. Thus, a logic of difference – subsuming different and/or competing identities under an imagined universalism – was also in operation. Most notably, this relied on articulating an older vision of 'patriotism' with the aspirational view of a wealthy, dynamic, modern market economy in which all who worked hard could participate. However, it was during Phase 2 neoliberalism that this aspect came to the fore. The more communitarian Third Way rhetoric of New Labour sought to distance itself from the 'divisive' politics of the past (although this in itself might be seen as drawing a logic of equivalence against an imagined other). It sought to include 'all our people' under the inclusive trope of 'community' and a 'modern Britain' in which 'citizenship' was also a related theme (Little, 2002; Mouffe, 2000: 108–12). But it should also be noted that – often in response to a perceived political failure to define 'enemies' – logics of equivalence were also drawn in Phase 2 by New Labour. Some of these lingered from Phase 1 (the 'unproductive', 'deviant'), while others were developed to meet more immediate, centre-left political imperatives. The most notable of the latter type was Blair's (1999) famous speech against 'the forces of conservatism' – on left and right – who opposed his modernising agenda. We should thus be alert to the interplay between logics of equivalence and difference.

A final distinctive aspect of a post-structuralist and post-Marxist discourse approach concerns the construction of neoliberalism as hegemony, its necessarily unstable nature and the possibility of alternatives. The orthodox Marxist reading sees neoliberal ideology as a 'reflex' of the economic base and class structure. This account underplays the political work of assembling the identities underpinning neoliberalism, and the discursive themes that unite them and sustain the project. Foucauldians, for their part, are certainly preoccupied with both subjectivity and discourse. However, their main focus is on how subjectivities are acted upon from above, or made to be self-regulating, as neoliberalism rolls out as a mode of governance. A post-structuralist discourse account moves away from these materialist concerns. It focuses instead on how discursive mechanisms such as logics of equivalence and difference, or the dynamics of identity experienced as lack, are articulated into a neoliberal narrative (Dean, 2009). It asks how such a narrative is able to present itself as natural and inevitable, garnering widespread support: the condition of hegemony. A post-structuralist approach also points to how neoliberalism's hegemonic appeal is able to shift between apparently different political regimes, such as the move from Thatcherism to Blairism, or Blairism to 'Cameronism' (see Byrne, 2013).

In the Hall–Jessop debate described above, Jessop *et al.* (1984, 1985) criticised Hall for overstating the hegemonic intent of Thatcherism, and for placing too much emphasis on its discursive aspects. However, by highlighting the (relative) instability of these elements, Hall indicated how they had the potential to be *rearticulated* away from neoliberalism. For neo-Gramscians such as Hall, the political task is to identify discursive themes which resonate with people's experiences of the contemporary world, but have been co-opted by neoliberalism. These include the desire for greater individual autonomy and self-actualisation. The objective is to elide these themes away from neoliberalism towards a democratic socialist political narrative (Leggett, 2005: ch. 8, 2009). This might highlight, for example, how state action and collective provision can in fact be the guarantor of such 'individualised' life projects. Post-Marxists such as Laclau and Mouffe also see a discursive political task. But for them it is a more deconstructive one, of exposing the precariousness of neoliberalism's own claims, and extending them. Neoliberal discourses of 'choice' and 'democracy' open up a chain of demands that can, discursively, be continually extended – perhaps in the direction of 'equality' (e.g. Mouffe, 2013: 74–5; Smith, 1998: 181). The *underlying* democratic, freedom-seeking impulse of neoliberalism might become a force for the radical destabilisation of entrenched interests, norms and values.

Social theory and its empirical object: The challenge of neoliberalism

At the outset of the book we identified three senses in which social theory interfaces with empirical political research and practice: by identifying and explaining, by critiquing and by constituting political practices themselves.

In our studies on both the state and new forms of participation (Chapters 2 and 3), we saw that the boundaries between these categories are always fluid. However, in the example of neoliberal ideology and politics they become particularly blurred, and merit a more detailed examination. The blurring is due to social theory's near universal critical stance towards neoliberalism (Flew, 2012). Such hostility would make it seem unlikely that social theory could be implicated in *constituting* neoliberalism: but there are some unexpected possibilities in this respect.

If we firstly take description and explanation, social theory has shown that neoliberalism extends well beyond the narrow economic and political doctrine it is often presented as, including by its own advocates. Thus, Marxist analysis bypasses neoliberalism's ideational content, and locates it within a wider historical, political economy. This emphasises the role of specific class interests and actors, and/or the wider requirements of the capitalist system. Foucauldians also offer an expansive historical explanation for neoliberalism. However, the Foucauldian genealogy does engage with neoliberalism's founding texts and ideas on their own terms, as well as broadening the analysis to include practices of self-governance and discipline under the guise of 'advanced liberalism'. The post-structuralist discourse perspective is less concerned with explaining the origins of neoliberalism, not least because it has philosophical problems with explanatory social science *per se*. However, it continues to expand our sense of neoliberalism's reach by arguing it exemplifies hegemonic politics. Discourse analysis also offers tools for understanding the mechanisms of constructing and transmitting neoliberal discourses throughout social life.

However, each of these explanatory accounts are already informed by critique, and lay the ground for its expansion. For Marxists, this consists in 'stripping away' neoliberals' claims as to how their project will benefit the whole society, or rubbishing those on the moderate left who might seek to accommodate neoliberal ideas (Callinicos, 2001). The Foucauldian analysis is not similarly aligned with a political project of its own. However, its account of advanced liberalism – and the self-governing practices of late modernity – certainly has political implications. Foucauldians pose a direct challenge to neoliberals – and others across the political spectrum – who use 'freedom' as an ideological principle. Contemporary ideas of freedom are shown to embody a particular set of power relations, and a new mode of governmentality (Rose, 1999). In the post-structuralist discourse approach, the contingent and unstable character of neoliberal discourse is further highlighted. Post-structuralists seek to deconstruct neoliberal discourse and open the way for new social imaginaries and subjectivities, (re)-informed by tropes such as 'equality' or 'democracy' (e.g. Dean, 2009; Mouffe, 2013).

What these perspectives share is a comprehensive critique of neoliberalism, a search for its vulnerabilities and a desire for an alternative politics. Given this, it might seem strange to talk of social theory being *constitutive*

of neoliberalism. However, social theory has arguably had significant empirical effects upon neoliberalism's development. The first is through influencing
the way the political left orients itself to neoliberal ideology, which in turn
affects the operating environment and trajectory of neoliberalism itself. For
example, Hall's account of Thatcherism articulated an emerging, wider critique of the traditional left for failing to recognise the new social terrain that
the neoliberals were both operating on and constructing (Hall and Jacques,
1989). This gradually changed the terms of debate on the left, with dramatic
consequences. Most notably, it opened the political space to engage with ideological markers such as 'freedom', 'choice' and 'identity', which it had historically been uncomfortable with. To Hall's orthodox Marxist and other more
traditional left critics, this kind of culturalist, Gramscian analysis offered at
best a ceding of territory to neoliberal ideology, and at worst a celebration of
the consumer society (Rustin, 1989). This criticism was directed even more
strongly at post-structuralist discourse theorists, with their central focus on
identity and spaces for new subjectivities (Wood, 1986). One argument is that
this creates an intellectual climate in which the left can relax about pursuing a
'me first', neoliberal politics. As Jodi Dean (2009: 3) disparagingly observes of
the American situation:

> The left had assumed and enjoyed the values of neoliberalism, firing its own
> salvos at the state and celebrating the imaginary freedoms of creativity and
> transformation offered by communicative capitalism.

Given this, we might deduce that orthodox Marxists have more in common
with Foucauldians than they do with other, culturally focused neo-Marxists
and post-structuralist discourse theorists: Foucauldians at least sustain a
focus on, for example, mechanisms of discipline, or processes or techniques of
economisation (Clarke, 2010: 385–6). However, the traditional left is equally
uncomfortable with the implied libertarianism of Foucault, where 'power' of
some sort is always going to 'dominate' and need subverting. The problem is
that this, too, resonates with neoliberal rhetoric, and problematises a leftist
vision of state intervention in the name of the collective good. Again, social
theory is here affecting its empirical, political object in unanticipated ways.

Such internecine argument on the left is familiar. But a more novel, albeit speculative possibility is the extent to which social theory may have actually embold-
ened neoliberal actors themselves. By giving strategically minded neoliberals and
their intellectual allies a more expansive sense of their own project, critical social
theorists may, ironically, have delivered the political right a helpful masterclass
in what hegemonic politics means. Traditionally, the UK Conservative Party
was characterised as being anti-intellectual. Conservatives assumed a natural fit
between their worldview and the common sense of the nation: there was no need
for theory. A noticeable feature of the Thatcher project was that – for all Mrs
Thatcher's own sense of 'mission' – it was the academic left and, most famously,

Hall again who identified the elements of a fully hegemonic neoliberal politics – of Thatcher*ism*. Looking to future generations of Thatcherites, Hall (1987: 21) suggested that, 'a new era will dawn and these new kinds of possessive men will be in charge of it. *They dream about real cultural power* (my emphasis)'. Three decades later it is indeed striking how, post-Thatcher, the hegemonic skill and intent of Conservative strategists seems to have gradually expanded – along with the social-theoretical critique of neoliberalism itself.

A striking example of this was David Cameron's 2010 electoral offer of a 'Big Society' (Conservative Party, 2010). This tapped into widespread disaffection with 'nanny statism', and an appetite for a more participatory, social politics associated with the third sector, civil society activists whose support Labour took for granted. It then elided these themes with the neoliberal critique of the state and a conservative emphasis on communities: the idea of 'society' was being rehabilitated and rearticulated in neoliberal terms. Big Society rhetoric waned in the face of economic austerity. However, Conservative Chancellor George Osborne was subsequently lauded as a strategic genius for his 2015 budget. In this, he audaciously co-opted and subverted many of the key themes of the New Labour era such as, for example, the minimum wage or the rhetoric of being on the side of 'hardworking families'. The leading left think-tank and campaign group *Compass* produced a report on what they labelled the 'Osborne Supremacy'. In this, they explicitly drew on Gramsci to argue that:

> from 2005 the Conservatives did their homework on New Labour and carefully built a comprehensive political and intellectual strategy with supporting structures … While leading conservative thinkers have not seriously engaged with the logic of [Gramsci's] work … they act as if they have done. (Spours, 2015: 4)

Hall (1987) seems to have been prescient that the neoliberals in the Conservative Party, 'dream about real cultural power'. They have learnt the meaning of hegemonic politics, and are apparently more adept at practicing it than the centre-left politicians whom social theorists hoped would be doing so. Similar observations have been made (again by leftist thinkers) of the skill with which the Republican right wing consistently seems to set the agenda, and dominate discourse, in the US 'culture wars' (Frank, 2004; Westen, 2007).

Conclusion: Ideology, discourse and the society–politics relation

In this chapter we have analysed the long history of theorising the ideational aspects of politics. We have focused in particular on the shift from accounts of ideology to discourse, and the changing status of a social referent point. We conclude once again with what this reveals about our overarching theme of the society–politics relation. The picture is complex: there are moments of apolitical/asocial analysis – as well as socio- and politico-centrism – not just between but also *within* different perspectives on the ideational. Having outlined these, in keeping with the overall argument of the book we then call for a more balanced approach. This will keep our categories of both the inescapably social and irreducibly political in view – in this case by recognising what we label the *boundedness* of ideology and discourse.

Asocial/apolitical tendencies

Classic approaches to ideology – characteristic of political philosophy, intellectual history and more traditional political theory – typically lack a conception of either the inescapably social or the irreducibly political as we have used those terms. Specifically, they underplay the sociological context of ideas, or their politically contingent and contested nature. However, we should note that such asocial/apolitical approaches are also found in aspects of the major traditions of ideology analysis we have explored in this chapter, often in surprising ways. To begin again with Marx (e.g. 1846), his key contribution is of course to have opened the way to a socialised – and indeed more politicised – contextual view of ideology: by linking it to capitalism and class power. However, the extent to which political agency generates ideology is in question in classical Marxist theory, where ideology is seen as a reflex of the economic structure. Such a structure and its associated class relations could be a platform for a socialised view of ideology. But by prioritising the economic and then jumping immediately to its political effects, there is a sense in which Marx actually bypasses what sociologists understand as society or social institutions. These are reduced to being 'merely' part of the superstructure, the political character of which is predetermined by the economic (Marx, 1859).

While Marx's reductionism is well known, there are aspects of later, supposedly more sophisticated theories that continue to marginalise both empirical social context and political contestation. The formalism of structuralism can result in highly abstract discussion about the structural preconditions and properties of language, ideology and discourse. We saw this in the earlier, archaeological method of Foucault (1966, 1969). It is also apparent in the 'total' conception of Althusser (1971), in which there is little sense of the content of either social structures or political struggles. Rather, these are treated as abstractions towards producing an all-encompassing model of the ideological production of subjects. Post-structuralists are typically characterised as being above all concerned with political agency and dynamism. But these perspectives also embody moments of a more traditional, textual analysis. This was evident in the later, genealogical approach of Foucault (e.g. 1975, 1976), and the way this was taken up in accounts of governmentality and neoliberal ideology (Brown, 2015; Rose, 1999). There are moments when considerable attention is paid to the founding texts of the leading neoliberal ideologues, as a means of tracing the lineage of key discourses such as 'freedom'.

Interestingly, in the supposedly 'fully' post-structuralist discourse theory of Laclau and Mouffe (1985), there is a sense of the theory having gone full circle, and back to the classical treatment of political ideas. This is to be found in the increasingly elaborate focus on the *mechanisms* through which discourse operates, captured in concepts such as logics of equivalence and difference. These are useful in describing the dynamics of neoliberal ideology in practice, but are nevertheless highly formalised in character. As if to confirm this sense of a return to more classical concerns, there has been a recent 'rhetorical turn' in political analysis, led by those sympathetic to post-structuralist approaches (Finlayson, 2012). Laclau's (2014) final book – *The Rhetorical Foundations of Society* – explicitly confirmed this trend.

Socio-centrism

Despite these moments of an asocial/apolitical treatment of ideas, the great contribution of social theory to the study of ideology was of course to locate it as a social product. We have seen a number of benefits across our theorists in recognising what we have called the inescapably social. The first is to move away from the view of ideas as having purely abstract, intrinsic properties, and to contextualise them as being a product either of groups and/or a wider social structure. Marx linked knowledge/ideology to the relative location of social groups. This aspect was developed in Mannheim's (1936) account of the social production of knowledge, and its relationship to the specific character (conservative/progressive) of ideologies. But the Marxist account also suggests we can understand political ideas, and 'common sense' more generally, as a reaction to more fundamental changes within the socio-economic structure. When applied to neoliberalism, we saw that this contextual approach allows us to understand a dominant ideology in terms of the interests of specific social classes, and/or the requirements posed by structural shifts or crises within the wider capitalist system.

The socialised conception also allows us to understand the role of political ideas in cohering and reproducing the social order. While not detailing a theory of ideology as such, Durkheim (1912) foregrounded the integrative role of norms and rituals, and this was taken up in more detail by the later neo-functionalists. One implication is that the manifest content of ideology may be less important than its function for system reproduction as a whole: a sentiment which, for very different, critical reasons, is also shared by Marxists. A final, related advantage of the socialised approach is to appreciate how ideologies are not just 'produced' by social structures, but are also embodied in social agents and practices dispersed throughout society. Gramsci (1971) explored this materiality of ideology as being embedded across civil society. Interestingly, despite their focus on the normative aspects of social life,

Durkheim and neo-functionalist political sociologists also draw attention to materiality in their accounts of rituals and symbolic political power. But it is Foucault who offers the most comprehensive tools for capturing the material embodiment of ideology. Of course, Foucault eschewed a fully formed conception of 'society', and was reluctant to talk of 'ideology'. However, his vision of the *dispositif* – a matrix of expertise, the institutional apparatus of power and techniques informed by political rationalities – demonstrates how the abstract ideas of ideologues become adapted into the messy business of governmental programmes.

The socialisation of the study of ideologies thus enabled a fuller conception of their production and reception. However, just as the traditional account of ideologies reifies texts and ideas in themselves, stripping them out of social context, so the socialised conception risks shifting the emphasis to a monolithic social structure. This presents a number of limitations revolving around the marginalisation of agency in theorising ideologies. The first is a lack of dynamism in the account of ideological production, which is treated as a reflex, mechanistic effect of prior social structures. While Marx's theory is certainly dynamic in capturing both historical change and class conflict, the shape and function of ideologies are predetermined by capitalist social relations. The integrative Durkheimian account is a mirror image of this same basic limitation. Mannheim's portrayal of ideologies as group product shows more promise in specifying the relationship between social actors and the character of ideologies, but it is still ultimately mechanistic. For Mannheim, it is the intelligentsia who can exercise more ideational autonomy, but he treats their outputs as technocratic and non-ideological.

The second, related limitation of a mechanistic account is that the specificity and diversity of ideologies are neglected. Ultimately, the function of ideology in Marxist theory is always to reproduce ruling class interests. This means that the contradictory, unstable or indeed ingenious combinations of ideas and practices that can constitute specific ideologies are of secondary concern. But in considering the flexible and adaptive history of neoliberalism, we saw that grasping such specificity is vital, as Foucault (2008) well understood with his genealogical approach.

The third main limitation of the over-socialised view concerns the reception of ideologies, and how they might be contested. Both Marx – and especially Durkheim – do indicate some of the institutional sites where ideologies and/ or cultural norms might be transmitted, but there is little interest in exactly how these are internalised and processed by individual agents. Ironically, the structuralist theorist who offers the most comprehensive account of the interface between individuals and ideology – Althusser (1971) – is also the one who denies agents any autonomy or creativity in that process, seeing them as 'bearers' of ideological conditioning. Given this lack of interest in the specifics of ideological production, content and reception, ideological counter-warfare is seen as either misplaced (in Marx), futile (in Althusser) or uninteresting to sociologists (Durkheim and neo-functionalists).

Politico-centrism

The remedy to the over-socialised conception of ideology is, as it has been throughout this book, to lean towards more explicitly political accounts. It was the post-structuralist turn to discourse that re-politicised our understanding of ideology, in the sense of restoring the role of agency. Foucault is often characterised as denying the agency of both those who might wield and resist powerful ideologies or discourses, focusing instead on institutional apparatus. But Foucault's emphasis on the role of expertise draws our attention to the powerful agency of those invested with 'authority' in various domains. In addition, his genealogical work stresses the agency of the researcher, while the concept of the *dispositif* highlights the specific mechanisms through which dominant ideas are constructed and implemented in a matrix of constant struggle. This vision of the social as political construct reaches its fullest expression in post-structuralist discourse theory. Laclau and Mouffe (1985: 111) starkly refuse the idea of an objective, prior society of the type that informs classic sociological theory and many accounts of ideology: '"[s]ociety" is not a valid object of discourse.' On this view, 'society' is perhaps the ultimate hegemonic intervention: it is an attempt to capture the sum total of human experience within a particular discursive imaginary, and present it as total and fixed. But, being another discursive construction, it too will be subject to a surplus of meaning, dislocation and disruption.

These politico-centric accounts of ideology are resonant of older, brutal forms of realism in the tradition of Hobbes or Machiavelli, where social life consists in the machinations and struggles between different agents. However, even if society is seen as a purely contingent political construct, it is nevertheless a remarkably stable and enduring formation, as are its core institutions such as economy, state and family. Can these really be 'merely' discursive? Does there not come a point where their sheer durability indicates they have an existence 'outside' discourse? Post-structuralists have two interesting – if controversial – responses to these objections. One is that identities (of subjects, institutions, norms) are always *signified as being prior* to the interventions of discourse, power and politics (see e.g. Butler, 1993: 209–10). Indeed, this signification is crucial to the ideological (i.e. stabilising) work of a discourse such as 'society'. A second, related strategy concerns *sedimented discourse*. Here it is claimed that however enduring an institution or social norm, for example, seems to be, it simply consists of discourses and struggles – politics – that have become 'sedimented' over time (Mouffe, 2005: 18). As Anna Marie Smith (1998: 172) summarises, '[t]he objectivity that we are confronted with, then, is like the accumulation of the traces that are left behind by power relations, and the institutionalization of these traces through regulated acts of iteration'.

The contingent, agentially created origins of institutions, norms and practices may have become masked, but post-structuralist critique seeks to reveal their political origins and character, so that they might again be contested.

Synthesis: the social boundedness of ideology and discourse

Despite these intellectually skilful post-structuralist responses to the society question, it is impossible to eliminate at least a minimal conception of the social. Institutions (whether sedimented discourse or not), dominant norms that have a structural character and entrenched patterns of social stratification – to name but a few – all set limits upon the play of discourse. But to insist on a conception of the social needn't undermine post-structuralist approaches to ideology and discourse. Instead, acknowledging the inescapably social can enhance them. A concept of the social can reveal the 'boundedness' of ideologies, and their limits in terms of making sense of the world. But it can also show how they come to be *productive* of political identities and worldviews. Post-structuralist discourse theory is criticised for presenting ideologies and discourses as if they are free floating, implying that agents simply pick and choose among them. However, since Gramsci, sociologically aware ideology theorists have offered an antidote to this. They argue that for ideologies to actually make sense to people and be identified with, they have to resonate with their prior normative assumptions, experience of social relations and everyday practices (Leggett, 2013). These social elements are related to – but analytically separate from – their activation and possible transformation through political activity.

To understand ideology and discourse is thus to understand the interplay between their social and political elements. This is why the Hall–Jessop debate over Thatcherism remains seminal (see e.g. Bruff, 2014; Worth, 2014). In debating the relative influence of material and discursive factors in accounting for Thatcherism, they were also conducting – as we have been in this chapter – a fundamental debate over what ideology, discourse and politics are when seen in their sociological context. This task is equally urgent today, as we continue to grapple with ideological flux in the face of the economic and social problems generated by the neoliberal Global Financial Crisis.

Conclusion

Restating the theoretical argument

The inescapably social and the irreducibly political

The *Themes in Social Theory* series shows how social theory can enhance empirical research across a wide range of social scientific concerns. However, we began by noting how the relationship of social theory to politics poses particularly complex challenges. The 'social' and the 'political' are mutually constitutive: where does one end and the other begin, both theoretically and empirically? Rather than avoiding this problem, we made it central to our wider theoretical contribution, offering a device for understanding the society–politics relation. In Chapter 1, we introduced and detailed the categories of the 'inescapably social' and the 'irreducibly political', and argued that both should be kept in view as distinct but interrelated elements of any analysis. The inescapably social captures the role of macro social structures, institutions, norms, relations and practices. The irreducibly political denotes the political agency, ideas, strategy and conflict that these social elements are shot through with, rendering them open-ended and contestable. We cannot decide in advance of any empirical scenario which of the social or political might predominate: by keeping both in view we can analyse their interplay in specific conjunctures. Sociology and political science have at times been guilty of neglecting the irreducibly political and inescapably social respectively. By sustaining a conception of both categories we might achieve what should be a natural and productive synergy between the two disciplines.

Social theory and empirical analysis: explanation, critique, constitution

In considering more specifically how this social–political interplay manifests itself in substantive cases, we identified three senses in which social theory relates to empirical political research and analysis – and also how these can become blurred when theory meets practice. The first is at the basic level of identification, description and explanation. We have seen throughout the book how social theory – particularly macro analysis of the development, institutions and dynamics of modernity – has provided a broad, background canvas. This has offered context to familiar motifs of political analysis, as well as gesturing towards new types of political actors and practices emerging at the increasingly complex level of the social. The second function is critique. Social theory is characterised by competing analytical and normative visions of the world that are, as post-structuralists say, always already political. Analytically, these tend to insist on political analysis giving due weight to both the structural and agential aspects of a conjuncture. Normatively, social theory's devices are varied, ranging from invoking visions of a future society, to seeking to deconstruct and reconfigure power relations or dominant discourses. Interestingly, we have found throughout that the classic traditions of social-theoretical critique – and debates between them – remain highly relevant to contemporary political analysis.

While the roles of explanation and critique are familiar, the additional dimension we identified – of social theory actually constituting its political object – is more novel. This was most visible where social-theoretical ideas have been explicitly taken up by political actors. But there is a more subtle, speculative sense in which social theory might be said to enter the political field. This is where, by virtue of its own position as part of the culture, social theory can plausibly be argued to have impacted upon the assumptions and activities of elite and lay actors, as well as wider political discourses. Sometimes this influence is present in ways that would have been unanticipated by – and even anathema to – social theorists themselves. We saw this in our argument about social theory's possible role in having provided neoliberalism with a more expansive sense of its own capacity and mission.

Summarising the substantive chapters

In our substantive chapters we examined in detail how these analytical themes play out in key areas of politics. Chapter 2 began at the familiar institutional level, by considering 'politics from above' in the form of the state and governance. Chapter 3 switched to 'politics from below' at the level of agents, and the shifting nature of political identity and participation. Finally, Chapter 4 addressed the broad field of culture and the ideational, which had loomed large throughout the book: 'politics all around'. Each chapter proceeded by firstly constructing a history of how major social theories have related to the topic; secondly illustrating this through empirical case studies (e.g. the rise of the networked, 'active state'; new modes of 'everyday' politics; the hegemony of neoliberalism), drawing out the senses in which social theory relates to empirical political research and practice; and finally evaluating the topic in terms of our overarching argument concerning the inescapably social and irreducibly political.

Despite the breadth of the material covered across the chapters, a clear picture emerged of the analytical trajectory since the nineteenth century. There has been a definite shift from describing political institutions, identities and ideas as deeply socially embedded – even socially determined – to instead capturing more dynamic social and political processes: these are complex, contingent and characterised by the very agency that the irreducibly political denotes. This mirrors how social theory more broadly has come to understand modernity, notably in Zygmunt Bauman's (2000) description of the move from a 'solid' to a 'liquid' world. This book has in large measure confirmed Bauman's metaphor, in both the development of social theory, and the nature of the political objects it captures. However, as the breaking open of socio-centric models drew more attention to political dynamics, the inescapably social element began to fade from analytical view. Thus, we have called throughout for social theory and political analysis to be re-embedded in a thicker understanding of the social. Let's review this argument in more detail, with reference to each of our substantive chapters.

Politics from above: the state and governance

In considering the state and governance (Chapter 2), we identified Max Weber as having offered the classic politico-centric account of the state as a site of individual power-seeking; notwithstanding his broader sociological concerns such as the threat of rationalisation. We then saw how more fully socio-centric perspectives, originating in Marxism, had the merit of demystifying the state: they revealed it as a product of economic and social relations. However, the most mechanistic forms of this analysis were unable to capture the increasing range of state action. This included the state promoting the long-term stability of the 'system', even against the short-term interests of the dominant classes; adopting an ideologically or nationally distinctive character, or perhaps becoming an interest group in its own right. While the class strategy and action aspect of Marxist theory could account for agency in state analysis, the politico-centric Foucauldian approach did so more fully, in some respects echoing Weber. Foucauldians focused on expertise, discourse and the diverse practices through which governing occurs at all levels of social life – including the level of individual subjectivity. However, this ultimately lent too much weight to the specific practices of political calculation and programmes, losing sight of the wider recursive power of social institutions, structures and norms in shaping the matrix – or playing field – of power it depicted. A Gramscian approach was argued to be more attuned to both these social and political aspects, acknowledging the autonomy and creativity of state power, its complex relationship to civil society, and how both are underpinned by capitalism. Significantly, Gramsci indicated a terrain of struggle which is ripe for counter-narratives and resistance, as well as ruling class domination: it is the social which both circumscribes and provides the raw materials for political action.

We set the scene for our contemporary case studies by detailing the macro-social theoretical framework of reflexive modernity and its attendant concepts: these were reflected in a shift among political analysts from describing

government to governance. The case studies then revealed a complex relationship between social theory and politics with regard to the state. In the case of
the widespread centrist Third Way politics of the 1990s and 2000s, social theory
described what it identified as the shifting form of the state in the face of external
sociological change. However, such theory also actively contributed to the state's
remaking, by appealing to and being adopted by elite political actors such as
Bill Clinton and Tony Blair: this was the most direct case – perhaps in history –
of social theory being constitutive of politics. The socio-centric assumptions of
the Third Way, presenting external social forces such as globalisation as a *fait
accompli*, had significant political consequences. Notably, it shut down alternative accounts about what a (progressive) role for the state might be in reshaping
globalisation. Marxist criticism of the Third Way curiously echoed the latter's
own reductionist account of social change. Foucauldian analytics paid more
attention to political aspects, such as the surveillance role of discourses of 'community', and the construction of new responsible citizen-consumers. But it was
the Gramscian approach which held in view both the operating environment of
a more globalised and individualised modernity, and also the ways in which this
itself could generate critique and political alternatives.

    That broad social-theoretical backdrop – of reflexive modernity – was the
starting point in our second case study on the changing face of governance.
Various contributions from Scandinavia have used this macro social theory to
describe and explain the rise of new types of citizens, and how they interface
with the state. Rather like Third Way politicians, the academics who developed
ideal-types such as 'culture governors' and 'everyday makers' (Bang, 2003,
2005) were shown to have accepted processes such as individualisation and
detraditionalisation in a socially reductionist way. By drawing on aspects of
the Marxist, Foucauldian and Gramscian critiques, we were able to unpack
how new types of political actor are emerging at an intersection of deep economic and social change, combined with state strategy. The political content of
their worldviews remains open-ended and contested: successful analysis thus
involves mapping the interplay between the social basis of new identities, and
their complex political inflections.

Politics from below: political identity and participation

The shifting nature of political identity and agency, in the face of rapid social
change, was examined in detail in Chapter 3. Here, the 'arc' of social theory
moving from images of stable wholes to those of fluid combinations became
still more evident. We saw how the contribution of classical social theory was –
in contrast to political-theoretical and philosophical approaches to 'human
nature' – to develop a socialised account of individual identity. Such theory
analysed how social arrangements were determining and/or stifling the political
identity and potential of agents. However, it typically also held out hope for the

liberation of both social structures and individuals in the future. But the most socially determinist accounts of identity called political liberation into question: what would be the motivation or mechanism for freeing identities, if identity as such was the product of a 'total' economic or ideological structure (as it seemed to be for Althusser)? We charted how both theoretical and empirical shifts – and again the complex relationship between these – dissolved the socio-centric vision. Theoretical developments included the influence of psychoana-lytic theory, discourse-theoretical approaches to subject construction and, from sociology, the individualisation thesis and a focus on hybridity and complex-ity. Empirical developments included a post-Fordist mode of production, new media and communication technologies, cultural globalisation, a decline in tra-ditional political ideologies and the growth of single-issue and identity politics.

Whereas in Chapter 2 we saw how elite political actors absorbed a particu-lar account of social change and the role of the state since the 1990s, here we traced the more subtle ways in which social theories of identity have influenced wider, oppositional social movements since the 1960s. However, such eman-cipatory accounts of identity have more recently been co-opted by traditional political actors, as mainstream parties and policymakers make increasingly individualised and niche appeals to voters, reflecting and reinforcing wide-spread consumerism. All of these developments have been complicated by the ongoing interventions of a growing, eventually hegemonic neoliberal ideology and politics. This both resonates with – and subverts – the 'spirit of liberation' that has been associated with identity politics since the late 1960s.

Our case study – on the rise of political consumerism – encapsulated these complex themes, and what is at stake by adopting different social-theoretical approaches to studying them. The concept of political consumerism captures the ways in which individuals are politicising the market (e.g. through fair trade 'buycotting'), as well as behaving more like individualised consumers with regard to their political identities. The boundaries between description/ explanation and critique here begin to be blurred, as the character of political consumerism identified in empirical work reflects wider normative stances on consumer capitalism more widely. The most socio-centric approach equates political consumerism with hyper-consumer capitalism. This results in a pes-simistic analysis, in which political consumerist practices simply represent the commodification of political identities. This is inflected through a neoliberal ideology that valorises individual choice above all else, to the extent that even mundane consumer choices are falsely read as a new, innovative form of pol-itics: 'I shop therefore I am'. Alternatively, politico-centric accounts identify political consumerism as embodying the effective agency that is a hallmark of late or reflexive modernity. This leads to a more positive appraisal, in which agents are seen as proactively linking the personal and the public, authoring their own ethically informed decisions in the market and other spheres. What emerges is the sense of individual choice – expressed here through political consumerism – as a contested space, which our categories of the inescapably social and irreducibly political can make more nuanced sense of. The claim that political consumerism simply reproduces a neoliberal monolith has critical purchase, but cannot possibly capture the full contemporary range of identity practices. Conversely, dynamic accounts of new practices of the Self – in the context of the individualisation thesis – risk overstating agential capacities and neglecting institutional and social context.

The most comprehensive empirical studies draw out the interplay between these categories. For example, we noted the role that pre-existing forms of social capital (networks, ideological repertoires, institutional commitments) play in facilitating new individualised, online or consumerist political practices. However, we also saw how participation in new practices can actually develop more traditional forms of social association and citizenship skills. In this latter case, political action enhances social capital, rather than vice versa as is often assumed. From the standpoint of critical theory and political practice, some of the most creative activists mirror this intersection. Thus, culture jamming self-consciously operates on the given social terrain of a marketised, digitised environment that constantly appeals to individual choice. However, culture jammers use those same technologies and discourses to subvert aspects of 'the system' from an ethical or political standpoint. While the political consumerism example again revealed a clear role for social theory in explaining and critiquing political practices, its constitutive influence was more complex. Both new activists (political consumers and culture jammers) as well as their targets (multinational brands and advertising) have developed in a highly educated milieu in which social scientific theory and techniques, including critical theory, will have figured strongly. But the extent to which they have consciously drawn on such a repertoire – and in what ways – is itself a further empirical question.

Politics all around: culture, ideology and discourse

In understanding the changing social context of both the state and political identities, the role of ideology in general – and contemporary neoliberalism in particular – loomed large, and this formed the focus of Chapter 4. Increasing centrality is being given to the ideational realm in social and political analysis. The metaphor of a move from 'wholeness' to 'fluidity' was sustained in our discussion of the broad theoretical transition from ideology to discourse. We charted how the social contextualisation of political ideas initially created a radical challenge to ideo-centric navel gazing, as well as speculative (and ideological) assumptions about 'human nature'. However, the socialised accounts themselves became as determinist and ossified as the theories of human nature they had supplanted. This culminated in structuralism, where agents were literally the 'bearers' of ideological subject positions. While intellectually suggestive, such an approach was unable to account for the increasingly varied and insidious ways that ideological work was being conducted throughout social life: the different assemblages of ideas, the sites and mechanisms for their dissemination, and the ways in which they were received and contested.

The need to address these irreducibly political aspects of the ideational realm – along with the rise of post-structuralist theory – opened up the broader category of discourse. The logical endpoint of this development – the completion of the arc from socio- to politico-centric accounts – was the post-structuralist, post-Marxist refusal of society itself, associated with Laclau and Mouffe. On this view, 'society' was simply a master discursive construct, the ultimate hegemonic intervention. However, we concluded by suggesting that society had to be brought back in, for both theoretical and political reasons. Theoretically, because a concept of the social is necessary to grasp real limits to the play of discourse. Politically, because for post-structuralist, discourse-oriented political strategies to work, they need to resonate with prior identities and practices: these exist at the level of something approximating society. A sense of the complex interplay between the social and the political is thus necessary for both capturing empirical variety, and developing critique and effective political strategies. It is striking that it is two older research programmes among those we considered – of Gramsci and then Foucault – that are perhaps more adept at grasping this interplay than the contemporary, fully developed politico-centrism of post-Marxists Laclau and Mouffe.

These twin theoretical and political-strategic concerns were tracked in our case study, on the hegemonic development of neoliberalism. With this example, the dividing lines between our fluid categories of description/explanation, critique and constitution arguably dissolved. This is owing to the universally critical and politically oriented nature of social-theoretical work on neoliberalism. We saw how structurally determinist accounts – seeing neoliberalism as the reflex of the latest phase of capitalism – were unable to capture its rapid development and mutation. While the core ideational tenets of neoliberalism have remained constant (individual liberty, pro-market, anti-state), its manifestations have become increasingly complex and diffuse. It has been characterised by both the aggressive destruction of oppositional forces, as well as the subtle construction of new subjectivities and sites of operation – and in ways that can disorient potential opposition (e.g. the complex status of 'choice' in contemporary feminist debates). The Foucauldian tradition made the boldest move in grasping this configuration, and in a way that could do justice to recognising the social–political interplay. Shifting the focus away from a logic of capital or modernity, it instead foregrounds the problem of order, government and 'freedom' with the category of advanced liberalism. In unpacking this, we saw how a traditional concern with the ideological origins of neoliberal discourse was combined with analysis of new modes of expertise, surveillance and also – crucially – the production of a new type of 'autonomous', choosing subject.

Post-structuralist and post-Marxist approaches fully elaborated the discourse-theoretical aspect of Foucault's project. Interestingly, while often theoretically very dense, such approaches return us to an almost Machiavellian vision of 'total politics', defined in this instance as an inherently relentless struggle to control meaning. Such an approach is adept at detailing, for example, how key contemporary signifiers such as 'choice', 'freedom' and even 'happiness' have been given an almost exclusively neoliberal content, and have colonised political discourse. It can also show how 'friends and enemies' of the neoliberal project are discursively designated through means of inclusion/exclusion. Perhaps more visibly than the Foucauldian approach, this also provides resources for thinking about how discourses might be subverted and/or reconstructed. However, for this to reach its analytical and political potential, a sense of the social needs to be reintegrated once again. Society provides the complex and uneven terrain upon which neoliberal subjectivities are constructed and contested. It presents structural, material – as well as discursive – limits upon what discourse can achieve. It also, of course, provides the opportunities for developing alternatives. In this respect, it is again a theorist of the state, capitalism and civil society long before contemporary neoliberalism – Antonio Gramsci – who continues to offer some of the best theoretical resources for understanding the interplay between the social and political in specific conjunctures.

The increasing sophistication of social-theoretical accounts of neoliberalism may have led to the most unexpected example of social theory constituting its empirical, political object. It was sociologists who first designated Thatcherism as a hegemonic project: this reaches beyond the formal sphere of politics and economic policy, into the 'hearts and minds' of citizens and the culture itself. Subsequent decades have continued this trend, with 'neoliberalism' now being a byword for the operations of capitalism – or really anything the political left objects to – in all spheres of social life. We noted the simultaneous growth of confidence, skill and ambition among neoliberal political actors, despite what many thought would be a knockout blow to their ideological project in 2008. This led us to consider if social theory had contributed to the making of a monster that neither it, nor its favoured political actors on the left, are able to tame.

Sociology, political science and a (post-?)neoliberal world

The spectre of neoliberal hegemony is an appropriate place to conclude our analysis, as it crystallises the theoretical, empirical and political themes of this book. Neoliberalism is indeed the most comprehensive and sustained economic, social and political formation that modern social theory has had to grapple with, and has haunted our account of the society–politics relation here. It has been a key driver in recasting the shape of the state, with the move from government to governance under conditions of globalisation and social complexity. It is also entangled with longer-term sociological processes of individualisation: this fragments traditional social and political identities, but also creates the terrain for new ones, including those that resist neoliberalism itself. And neoliberalism exemplifies the contemporary operation of ideology and discourse: it frames our understanding of what is taken for granted and natural in social and political life, and our capacity to imagine alternatives.

Neoliberalism does not conform to the disciplinary boundaries sometimes policed by sociology and political science. This is clear in the way that it informs the worldviews of elite, oppositional and everyday actors; extends market relations in a way that challenges the relative autonomy of the 'political' and 'social' spheres; and co-opts cultural practices to sustain markets and reinforce its ideological messages. Thus, in order for sociology and political science to serve their descriptive, explanatory and critical functions, they cannot afford to work in isolated silos. To meet this challenge, this book has introduced and deployed the categories of the inescapably social and irreducibly political, arguing that the complex interplay between these should inform theoretical and empirical work. Through this, it is hoped that the rich traditions of both social theory and political analysis can be brought to bear upon a reality that shows no respect for the disciplinary distinctions between them.

Bibliography

Abercrombie, N., Hill, S. and Turner, B.S. (1980) *The Dominant Ideology Thesis*, London: Allen & Unwin.

Adorno, T. and Horkheimer, M. (1944) *Dialectic of Enlightenment*, repr. London: Verso, 1991.

Agamben, G. (2005) *State of Exception* (trans. Kevin Attell), Chicago: University of Chicago Press.

Albrow, M. (1996) *The Global Age*, Cambridge: Polity.

Alexander, J.C. (1988) 'Culture and political crisis: "Watergate" and Durkheimian sociology', in Jeffrey C. Alexander (ed.) *Durkheimian Sociology: Cultural Studies*, Cambridge: Cambridge University Press, pp.187–224.

Alexander, J.C. (2006) *The Civil Sphere*, Oxford: Oxford University Press.

Althusser, L. (1965) *For Marx* (trans. Ben Brewster 1969), repr. London: Verso, 2005.

Althusser, L. (1968) 'The object of capital', in Althusser, L. and Balibar. E. (1970) *Reading Capital* (trans. Ben Brewster), London: New Left Books.

Althusser, L. (1971) 'Ideology and ideological state apparatus (notes towards an investigation)' in Althusser, L., *On Ideology*, repr. London: Verso, 2008, pp.1–60.

Amin, A. (ed.) (1994) *Post-Fordism: A Reader*, Oxford: Blackwell.

Andersen, J.G. and Tobiasen, M. (2004) 'Who are these political consumers anyway? Survey evidence from Denmark', in *op cit* Micheletti, Follesdal and Stolle (eds) *Politics, Products and Markets*, pp.203–21.

Anderson, P. (1976) 'The antinomies of Antonio Gramsci', *New Left Review* (I)100: 5–78.

Anderson, P. (2000) 'Renewals', *New Left Review* (II)1: 1–20.

Arato, A. (1982) 'Introduction' to 'Part II: Esthetic Theory and Cultural Criticism', in Andrew Arato and Eike Gebhardt (eds) *The Essential Frankfurt School Reader*, New York: Continuum, pp.185–224.

Archer, M. (1995) *Realist Social Theory: The Morphogenetic Approach*, Cambridge: Cambridge University Press.

Archer, M. (2000) *Being Human: The Problem of Agency*, Cambridge: Cambridge University Press.

Arnould, E.J. (2007) 'Should citizens escape the market?', *The ANNALS of the American Academy of Political and Social Science*, 611(1): 96–111.

Ashenden, S. (2005) 'Structuralism and post-structuralism' in *op cit* Harrington (ed.) *Modern Social Theory*, pp.198–214.

Atkinson, L. (2012) 'Buying in to social change: how private consumption choices engender concern for the collective', *The ANNALS of the American Academy of Social and Political Science*, 644(1): 191–206.

Atkinson, W. (2007) 'Beck, individualization and the death of class: a critique', *British Journal of Sociology*, 58(3): 349–66.

Bang, H.P. (2003) 'A new ruler meeting a new citizen: culture governance and everyday making', in Henrik P. Bang (ed.) *Governance as Social and Political Communication*, Manchester: Manchester University Press, pp.241–66.

Bang, H.P. (2004) 'Culture governance: governing reflexive modernity', *Public Administration*, 82(1): 157–90.

Bang, H.P. (2005) 'Among everyday makers and expert citizens', in *op cit* Newman (ed.) *Remaking Governance*, pp.159–78.

Bang, H.P. (2009) '"Yes we can": identity politics and project politics for a late modern world', *Urban Research and Practice*, 2(2): 117–37.

Baringhorst, S. (2004) 'Political rituals', in *op cit* Nash and Scott (eds) *The Blackwell Companion to Political Sociology*, pp. 291–301.

Barthes, R. (1957) *Mythologies*, repr. London: Vintage, 2000.

Barthes, R. (1964) *Elements of Semiology*, repr. London: Cape, 1967.

Bates, S. (2010) 'Re-structuring power', *Polity*, 42(3): 352–76.

Baudrillard, J. (1980) 'The implosion of meaning in the media and the implosion of the social in the masses', in Kathleen Woodward (ed.) *The Myths of Information: Technology and Postindustrial Culture*, Madison, WI: Coda Press, pp.137–48.

Bauman, Z. (1993) *Postmodern Ethics*, Oxford: Blackwell.

Bauman, Z. (1999) *In Search of Politics*, Cambridge: Polity.

Bauman, Z. (2000) *Liquid Modernity*, Cambridge: Polity.

Bauman, Z. (2001) *The Individualized Society*, Cambridge: Polity.

Bauman, Z. (2003) *Liquid Love*, Cambridge: Polity.

Bauman, Z. (2007) *Consuming Life*, Cambridge: Polity.

Bauman, Z. (2012) 'Fuels, sparks and fires: on taking to the streets', *Thesis Eleven*, 109(1): 11–16.

Beck, U. (1986) *Risk Society: Towards a New Modernity*, repr. London: Sage, 1992.

Beck, U. (1997) *The Reinvention of Politics: Re-Thinking Modernity in the Global Social Order*, Cambridge: Polity.

Beck, U. (1999) 'Zombie categories: an interview with Ulrich Beck', int. Jonathan Rutherford, repr. in *op cit* Beck and Beck-Gernsheim (2002) *Individualization*, pp.202–13.

Beck, U. (2000) *What is Globalization?*, Cambridge: Polity.

Beck, U. (2006) *Cosmopolitan Vision* (trans. Ciaran Cronin), Cambridge: Polity.

Beck, U. (2007) 'Beyond class and nation: reframing social inequalities in a globalising world', *British Journal of Sociology*, 58(4): 679–705.

Beck, U. (2009) *World at Risk* (trans. Ciaran Cronin), Cambridge: Polity.

Beck, U., Giddens, A. and Lash, S. (1994) *Reflexive Modernization: Politics, Tradition and Aesthetics in the Modern Social Order*, Cambridge: Polity.

Beck, U. and Beck-Gernsheim, E. (2002) *Individualization: Institutionalized Individualism and its Social and Political Consequences*, London: Sage

Beck, U., Bonss, W. and Lau, C. (2003) 'The theory of reflexive modernization: problematic, hypotheses and research programme', *Theory, Culture & Society*, 20(2): 1–33.

Beck, U. and Lau, C. (2005) 'Second modernity as a research agenda: theoretical and empirical explorations in the "meta-change" of modern society', *British Journal of Sociology*, 56(4): 525–57.

Beckett, F. and Hencke, D. (2009) *Marching to the Fault Line: The 1984 Miners' Strike and the Death of Industrial Britain*, London: Constable.

Bellah, R.N. (1967) 'Civil religion in America', in Bellah, R.N. (1991) [1970] *Beyond Belief: Essays on Religion in a Post-Traditional* World, Berkeley: University of California Press, pp.168–91.

Bellamy, R. (2004) 'Developments in pluralist and elite approaches', in *op cit* Nash and Scott (eds) *The Blackwell Companion to Political Sociology*, pp.17–28.

Benjamin, W. (1936) 'The work of art in the age of mechanical reproduction', in Benjamin, W. (1955) *Illuminations*, repr. London: Pimlico, 1999, pp.211–44.

Bennett, W.L. (2004) 'Branded political communication: lifestyle politics, logo campaigns, and the rise of global citizenship', in *op cit* Micheletti, Follesdal and Stolle (eds) *Politics, Products and Markets*, pp.101–25.

Bennett, W.L. and Lagos, T. (2007) 'Logo logic: the ups and downs of branded communication', *The ANNALS of the American Academy of Political and Social Science*, 611(1): 193–206.

Benton, T. (1999) 'Radical politics – neither Left nor Right?', in Mike O'Brien, Sue Penna and Colin Hay (eds) *Theorising Modernity: Reflexivity, Environment and Identity in Giddens' Social Theory*, Harlow: Addison Wesley Longman, pp.39–64.

Bevir, M. (2010) *Democratic Governance*, New Jersey: Princeton University Press.

Bhambra, G.K. and Demir, I. (2009) 'Introduction: 1968 in retrospect', in Gurminder K. Bhambra and Ipek Demir (eds) *1968 in Retrospect: History, Theory, Alterity*, Basingstoke: Palgrave Macmillan, pp.xi–xix.

Binkley, S. (2008) 'Liquid consumption', *Cultural Studies*, 22(5): 599–623.

Blackman, L. (2004) 'Self-help, media cultures and the production of female psychopathology', *European Journal of Cultural Studies*, 7(2): 219–36.

Blair, T. (1998) *The Third Way: New Politics for the New Century*, Fabian Society Pamphlet 588, London: College Hill.

Blair, T. (1999) Leader's Speech to the Labour Party Conference, Bournemouth, UK, 28 September 1999.

Blair, T. (2001) 'Prime Minister's speech on public service reform', 16 October (London: Downing Street Press Office).

Block, F. (1987a) 'The ruling class does not rule: notes on the Marxist theory of the state', in Block, F. (1987) *Revising State Theory: Essays in Politics and Postindustrialism*, Philadelphia: Temple University Press, pp.51–68.

Block, F. (1987b) 'Beyond relative autonomy: state managers as historical subjects', in Block, F. (1987) *Revising State Theory: Essays in Politics and Postindustrialism*, Philadelphia: Temple University Press, pp.81–97.

Boltanski, L. and Chiapello, E. (1999) *The New Spirit of Capitalism* (trans. Gregory Elliott), London: Verso, 2006.

Bonefeld, W. (2012) 'Freedom and the strong state: on German ordoliberalism', *New Political Economy*, 17(5): 633–56.

Bourdieu, P. (1990) *The Logic of Practice*, Cambridge: Polity.

Bowring, F. (2016) 'The individual and society in Durkheim: unpicking the contradictions', *European Journal of Social Theory*, 19(1): 21–38.

Brassett, J., Rethel, L. and Watson, S. (eds) (2009) Special section on the political economy of the sub-prime crisis in Britain, *British Journal of Politics and International Relations*, 11: 3.

Bratich, J.Z., Packer, J. and McCarthy, C. (eds) (2003) *Foucault: Cultural Studies and Governmentality*, Albany NY: SUNY Press.

Brown, G. (1994) *Fair is Efficient: A Socialist Agenda for Fairness*, Fabian Pamphlet 563, London: College Hill.

Brown, W. (2015) *Undoing the Demos: Neoliberalism's Stealth Revolution*, New York: Zone Books.

Bruff, I. (2014) 'The rise of authoritarian neoliberalism', *Rethinking Marxism*, 26(1): 113–29.

Budgeon, S. (2011) *Third Wave Feminism and the Politics of Gender in Late Modernity*, Basingstoke: Palgrave Macmillan.

Burawoy, M. (2003) 'For a sociological Marxism: the complementary convergence of Antonio Gramsci and Karl Polanyi', *Politics & Society*, 31(2): 193–261.

Burawoy, M. (2005) 'For public sociology', *American Sociological Review*, 70 (1): 4–28.

Burke, E. (1790) *Reflections on the Revolution in France*, repr. London: Penguin (ed. Conor Cruise O'Brien), 2004 [1968].

Butler, J. (1990) *Gender Trouble: Feminism and the Subversion of Identity*, London: Routledge.

Butler, J. (1993) *Bodies that Matter: The Discursive Limits of Sex*, London: Routledge.

Byrne, C. (2013) *Neo-Liberalisms in British Politics*, unpublished D.Phil. thesis, University of Birmingham, available at etheses.bham.ac.uk.

Byrne, C., Kerr, P. and Foster, E. (2014) 'What kind of 'Big Government' is the 'Big Society'? A reply to Bulley and Sokhi-Bulley', *British Journal of Politics and International Relations*, 16(3): 471–8.

Callinicos, A. (1999) 'Social theory put to the test of politics: Pierre Bourdieu and Anthony Giddens', *New Left Review*, (I)236: 77–102.

Callinicos, A. (2001) *Against the Third Way: An Anti-Capitalist Critique*, Cambridge: Polity.

Cammack, P. (2004) 'Giddens's way with words', in *op cit* Hale, Leggett and Martell (eds) *The Third Way and Beyond*, pp.151–66.

Castells, M. (1997) *The Information Age: Economy, Society and Culture Vol. I: The Rise of the Network Society*, Oxford: Blackwell.

Castells, M. (2000) 'Materials for an exploratory theory of the network society', *British Journal of Sociology*, 51(1): 5–24.

Chapman, J. (2007) 'Living in the machine: New Labour and public services', in Gerry Hassan (ed.) *After Blair: Politics After the New Labour Decade*, London: Lawrence and Wishart, pp.120–30.

Clarke, J. (2008) 'Living with/in and against neo-liberalism', *Focaal-European Journal of Anthropology*, 51: 135–47.

Clarke, J. (2010) 'After neoliberalism?', *Cultural Studies*, 24(3): 375–94.

Coates, D. (2005) *Prolonged Labour: The Slow Birth of New Labour Britain*, Basingstoke: Palgrave Macmillan.

Conservative Party (2010) *The Conservative Manifesto 2010: Invitation to Join the Government of Britain*, East Sussex: Pureprint Group.

Copeland, L. (2014) 'Conceptualizing political consumerism: how citizenship norms differentiate boycotting from buycotting', *Political Studies*, 62(S1): 172–186.

Coulter, A. and Ellins, J. (2006) *Patient Focused Interventions: A Review of the Evidence*, London: Health Foundation.

Craib, I. (1992) 'Parsons: theory as a filing system', in Craib, I. (1992) *Modern Social Theory: From Parsons to Habermas*, (2nd edn), repr. London: Routledge, 2014, pp.37–68.

Critchley, S. and Marchant, O. (eds) (2004) *Laclau: A Critical Reader*, London: Routledge.

Crouch, C. (2004) *Post-Democracy*, Cambridge: Polity.

Crouch, C. (2011) *The Strange Non-Death of Neoliberalism*, Cambridge: Polity.

Curtis, B. (1995) 'Taking the state back out: Rose and Miller on political power', *British Journal of Sociology*, 46(4): 575–89.

Dalton, R.J. (2014) *Citizen Politics* (6th edn), Thousand Oaks, CA: CQ Press.

Davidson, A. (2008) 'The uses and abuses of Gramsci', *Thesis Eleven*, 95(1): 68–94.

Davies, J.S. (2011) *Challenging Governance Theory: From Networks to Hegemony*, Bristol: Policy Press.

Davies, W. (2014) 'Neoliberalism: a bibliographic review', *Theory, Culture & Society*, 31(7/8): 309–17.

Davis, J.B. (2011) *Individuals and Identity in Economics*, New York: Cambridge University Press.

Dawson, M. (2010) 'Bauman, Beck, Giddens and our understanding of politics in late modernity', *Journal of Power*, 3(2): 189–207.

Dean, J. (2009) *Democracy and Other Neoliberal Fantasies*, Durham, NC: Duke University Press.

Dean, M. (2010) *Governmentality: Power and Rule in Modern Society*, (2nd edn) London: Sage.

Debord, G. (1967) *The Society of the Spectacle* (trans. Donald Nicholson-Smith), repr. New York: Zone Books, 1994.

Derrida, J. (1966) 'Structure, sign and play in the discourse of the human sciences', in Derrida, J. (1967) *Writing and Difference*, repr. London: Routledge, 1978.

Derrida, J. (1967) *Of Grammatology*, repr. Baltimore: Johns Hopkins University Press, 1976.

Devine, P. (2000) 'The conflict theory of inflation re-visited', in Jan Toporowski (ed.) *Political Economy and the New Capitalism: Essays in honour of Sam Aaronovitch*, London: Routledge, pp.23–39.

Dews, P. (1984) 'Power and subjectivity in Foucault', *New Left Review*, (I)144: 72–95.

Dixon, A., Robertson, R., Appleby, J., Burge, P., Devlin, N. and Magee, H. (2010) *Patient Choice: How Patients Choose and How Providers Respond*, London: Kings Fund.

Dreyfus, H.L. and Rabinow, P. (1982) *Michel Foucault: Beyond Structuralism and Hermeneutics*, Brighton: Harvester Press.

Driver, S. and Martell, L. (2002) *Blair's Britain*, Cambridge: Polity.

Durkheim, E. (1893) *The Division of Labour in Society*, repr. New York: Macmillan (trans. George Simpson), 1933.

Durkheim, E. (1895) *The Rules of Sociological Method*, repr. Chicago: Chicago University Press (trans. Sarah A. Solovay and John H. Mueller), 1938.

Durkheim, E. (1897) *Suicide: A Study in Sociology*, repr. Glencoe: Free Press (trans. John A. Spaulding and George Simpson), 1951.

Durkheim, E. (1898) 'Individualism and the intellectuals', in Robert N. Bellah (ed.) (1973) *Emile Durkheim: On Morality and Society*, Chicago: University of Chicago Press, pp.43–57.

Durkheim, E. (1912) *The Elementary Forms of the Religious Life*, repr. London: Allen & Unwin (trans. Joseph Ward Swain), 1915.

Durkheim, E. (1914) 'The dualism of human nature and its social conditions', in Robert N. Bellah (ed.) (1973) *Emile Durkheim: On Morality and Society*, Chicago: Chicago University Press, pp.149–63.

Durkheim, E. (1950) *Professional Ethics and Civic Morals*, repr. London: Routledge & Keegan Paul (trans. Cornelia Brookfield), 1957.

Elder-Vass, D. (2010) *The Causal Power of Social Structures: Emergence, Structure, Agency*, Cambridge: Cambridge University Press.

Elliott, E. (2008) *Concepts of the Self* (2nd edn), Cambridge: Polity.

Eriksson, K. and Vogt, H. (2013) 'On self-service democracy: configurations of individualizing governance and self-directed citizenship', *European Journal of Social Theory*, 16(2): 153–73.

Eriksson, L. (2011) *Rational Choice Theory: Potential and Limits*, Basingstoke: Palgrave.

Evans, M. (2006) 'Elitism', in *op cit* Hay, Lister and Marsh (eds) *The State*, pp.39–58.

Fairclough, N. (2000) *New Labour, New Language?*, London: Routledge.

Farrell, N. (2012) '"Conscience capitalism" and the neoliberalisation of the non-profit sector', *New Political Economy*, 20(2): 254–72.

Finlayson, A. (2003) *Making Sense of New Labour*, London: Lawrence and Wishart.

Finlayson, A. (2012) 'Rhetoric and the political theory of ideologies', *Political Studies*, 60(4): 751–67.

Finlayson, Alan and Valentine, Jeremy (eds) (2002) *Politics and Post-Structuralism: An Introduction*, Edinburgh: Edinburgh University Press.

Flew, T. (2014) 'Six theories of neoliberalism', *Thesis Eleven*, 122(1): 49–71.

Foster, E.A., Kerr, P. and Byrne, C. (2014) 'Rolling back to roll forward: Depoliticisation and the extension of government', *Policy & Politics*, 42(2): 225–41.

Foucault, M. (1963) *The Birth of the Clinic: An Archaeology of Medical Perception* (trans. A.M. Sheridan-Smith), London: Tavistock, 1973.

Foucault, M. (1966) *The Order of Things: An Archaeology of the Human Sciences*, London: Tavistock, 1970.

Foucault, M. (1969) *The Archaeology of Knowledge*, (trans. A.M. Sheridan-Smith), London: Tavistock, 1972.

Foucault, M. (1975) *Discipline and Punish: The Birth of the Prison* (trans. A.M. Sheridan-Smith), Harmondsworth: Penguin, 1977.

Foucault, M. (1976) *The History of Sexuality Vol I: An Introduction* (trans. Robert Hurley), Harmondsworth: Penguin, 1978.

Foucault, M. (1980) *Power/Knowledge: Selected Interviews and Other Writings 1972–77* (ed. Colin Gordon), Brighton: Harvester Press.

Foucault, M. (1981) 'Friendship as a way of life' (trans. John Johnston), repr. Paul Rabinow (ed.) *Michel Foucault: Ethics, Subjectivity and Truth* (Essential works of Foucault 1954–1984, Volume 1), Harmondsworth: Penguin, 2000, pp.135–40.

Foucault, M. (1982) 'Technologies of the Self', repr. Paul Rabinow (ed.) *Michel Foucault: Ethics, Subjectivity and Truth* (Essential works of Foucault 1954–1984, Volume 1), Harmondsworth: Penguin, 2000, pp.223–51.

Foucault, M. (1983) 'The subject and power', in Hubert L. Dreyfus and Paul Rabinow (eds) (1983) *Michel Foucault: Beyond Structuralism and Hermeneutics* (2nd edn), Chicago: University of Chicago Press pp.208–26.

Foucault, M. (1984) *The Care of the Self: The History of Sexuality Vol. Three* (trans. Robert Hurley), Pantheon: New York, 1986.

Foucault, M. (2007) *Security, Territory, Population: Lectures at the College de France 1977–78* (ed. Michel Senellart, trans. Graham Burchell), Basingstoke: Palgrave.

Foucualt, M. (2008) *The Birth of Biopolitics: Lectures at the College de France 1978–79* (ed. Michel Senellart, trans. Graham Burchell), Basingstoke: Palgrave.

Frank, T. (2004) *What's the Matter with Kansas? How Conservatives Won the Heart of America*, New York: Henry Holt & Co.

Freeden, M. (1996) *Ideologies and Political Theory: A Conceptual Approach*, Oxford: Clarendon.

Freund, J. (1972) *The Sociology of Max Weber* (trans. Mary Ilford, 1968), Harmondsworth: Penguin.

Fukuyama, F. (1992) *The End of History and the Last Man*, Harmondsworth: Penguin.

Gamble, A. (1983) 'Thatcherism and Conservative politics', in Stuart Hall and Martin Jacques (eds) *The Politics of Thatcherism*, pp.109–31.

Gamble, A. (1988) *The Free Economy and the Strong State: The Politics of Thatcherism*, Basingstoke: Macmillan.

Gamble, A. (2007) 'Neoliberalism', in George Ritzer (ed.) *The Blackwell Encyclopedia of Sociology Online*, Blackwell Reference Online.

Gamble, A. (2009) 'The western ideology', *Government and Opposition*, 44(1): 1–19.

Gane, N. (2014a) 'The emergence of neoliberalism: thinking through and beyond Michel Foucault's lectures on biopolitics', *Theory, Culture & Society*, 31(4): 3–27.

Gane, N. (2014b) 'Sociology and neoliberalism: a missing history', *Sociology*, 48(6): 1092–106.

Gee, J.P. and Handford, M. (eds) (2012) *The Routledge Handbook of Discourse Analysis*, Abingdon: Routledge.

Geras, N. (1987) 'Post-Marxism?', *New Left Review* (I)163: 40–82.

Gerth, H.H. and Mills, C.W. (trans. and eds) (1948) *From Max Weber: Essays in Sociology*, repr. London: Routledge, 1991.

Giddens, A. (1971) *Capitalism and Modern Social Theory: An Analysis of the Writings of Marx, Durkheim and Max Weber*, Cambridge: Cambridge University Press.

Giddens, A. (1972) *Politics and Sociology in the Thought of Max Weber*, repr. Polity, 2013.

Giddens, A. (1984) *The Constitution of Society: Outline of the Theory of Structuration*, Cambridge: Polity.

Giddens, A. (1990) *The Consequences of Modernity*, Cambridge: Polity.

Giddens, A. (1991) *Modernity and Self-Identity: Self and Society in a Late Modern Age*, Cambridge: Polity.

Giddens, A. (1994) *Beyond Left and Right: The Future of Radical Politics*, Cambridge: Polity.

Giddens, A. (1998) *The Third Way: The Renewal of Social Democracy*, Cambridge: Polity.

Giddens, A. (2000) *The Third Way and Its Critics*, Cambridge: Polity.

Giddens, A. (2002a) *Runaway World: How Globalisation is Reshaping our Lives* (2nd edn), London: Profile Books.

Giddens A. (2002b) *Where Now for New Labour?*, Cambridge: Polity.

Giddens, A. (2007) *Over to You, Mr Brown*, Cambridge: Polity.

Gilbert, J. (2000) 'Beyond the hegemony of New Labour', in Timothy Bewes and Jeremy Gilbert (eds) *Cultural Capitalism: Politics After New Labour*, London: Lawrence & Wishart, pp.223–44.

Gilbert, J. (2013) 'What kind of thing is "neoliberalism"?', *New Formations*, 80/81: 7–22.

Gill, R. and Scharff, C. (2011) 'Introduction', in Rosalind Gill and Christina Scharff (eds) *New Feminities: Postfeminism, Neoliberalism and Subjectivity*, Basingstoke: Palgrave Macmillan, pp.1–19.

Glynos, J. and Howarth, D. (2007) *Logics of Critical Explanation in Social and Political Theory*, London: Routledge.

Goes, E. (2004) 'The Third Way and the politics of community' in *op cit* Hale, Leggett and Martell (eds.) *The Third Way and Beyond*, pp.108–27.

Goldthorpe, J., Lockwood, D., Bechhofer, F. and Platt, J. (1968) *The Affluent Worker: Political Attitudes and Behaviour*, Cambridge: Cambridge University Press.

Goldthorpe, J., Lockwood, D., Bechhofer, F. and Platt, J. (1969) *The Affluent Worker in the Class Structure*, Cambridge: Cambridge University Press.

Goodwin, B. (2014) *Using Political Ideas* (6th edn), Chichester: John Wiley & Sons.

Gotlieb, M.R. and Wells, C. (2012) 'From concerned shopper to dutiful citizen: implications of individual and collective orientations toward political consumerism', *ANNALS of the American Academy of Political and Social Science*, 644(1): 207–19.

Gould, P. (1998) *The Unfinished Revolution: How the Modernisers Saved the Labour Party*, repr. London: Abacus, 2011.

Gouldner, A. (1973) *For Sociology: Renewal and Critique in Sociology Today*, London: Allen Lane.

Gramsci, A. (1971) *Selections from the Prison Notebooks* (ed. and trans. Quinton Hoare and Geoffrey Nowell-Smith), London: Lawrence and Wishart.

The Guardian (2013) 'Editorial: Margaret Thatcher: the lady and the land she leaves behind', 8 April, theguardian.com.

Habermas, J. (1987) *The Theory of Communicative Action Volume Two: Lifeworld and System: A Critique of Functionalist Reason*, Cambridge: Polity.

Hale, S. (2004) 'The communitarian 'philosophy' of New Labour', in *op cit* Hale, Leggett and Martell (eds) *The Third Way and Beyond*, pp.87–107.

Hale, S., Leggett, W. and Martell, L. (eds) (2004) *The Third Way and Beyond: Criticisms, Futures, Alternatives*, Manchester: Manchester University Press.

Hall, S. (1979) 'The great moving right show', *Marxism Today*, (January), 14–20.

Hall, S. (1982) 'Introductory essay: reading Gramsci', in *op cit* Simon *Gramsci's Political Thought*, pp.7–10.

Hall, S. (1983) 'The problem of ideology: Marxism without guarantees', in Betty Matthews (ed.) *Marx: 100 Years On*, London: Lawrence & Wishart, pp.57–84.

Hall, S. (1985a) 'Faith, hope or clarity', *Marxism Today*, January, 15–19.

Hall, S. (1985b) 'Authoritarian populism: a reply to Jessop *et al*', *New Left Review*, (I)151: 115–24.

Hall, S. (1987) 'Gramsci and Us', *Marxism Today*, June, 16–21. Also repr. in *op cit* Simon (1991) *Gramsci's Political Thought*, pp.114–30.

Hall, S. (1998) 'The great moving nowhere show', *Marxism Today: Special Edition*, Nov/Dec, 9–14.

Hall, S. (2003) 'New Labour's double shuffle', *Soundings*, 24 (Summer): 10–24.

Hall, S. (2011) 'The neo-liberal revolution', *Cultural Studies*, 25(6): 705–28.

Hall, S., Lumley, B. and McLennan, G. (1977) 'Politics and ideology: Gramsci', in *Centre for Contemporary Cultural Studies Working Paper in Cultural Studies No. 10: On Ideology*, pp.45–76, repr. as *On Ideology: Vol III, CCCS Classic Texts*, Abingdon: Routledge, 2012.

Hall, S. and Jacques, M. (1983) 'Introduction' in Stuart Hall and Martin Jacques (eds) *The Politics of Thatcherism*, London: Lawrence & Wishart, pp.9–16.

Hall, S. and Jacques, M. (eds) (1989) *New Times: The Changing Face of Politics in the 1990s*, London: Lawrence and Wishart.

Hardin, C. (2014) 'Finding the "neo" on neoliberalism', *Cultural Studies*, 28(2): 199–221.

Hardt, M. and Negri, A. (2000) *Empire*, Cambridge, MA: Harvard University Press.

Harrington, A. (2005) 'Introduction: What is social theory?' in *op cit* Harrington (ed.), *Modern Social Theory*, pp.1–15.

Harrington, A. (ed.) (2005) *Modern Social Theory: An Introduction*, Oxford: Oxford University Press.

Harvey, D. (2005) *A Brief History of Neoliberalism*, Oxford: Oxford University Press.

Hay, C. (1999) 'Crisis and political development in postwar Britain', in Marsh, D., Buller, J., Hay, C., Johnston, J., Kerr, P., McAnulla, S. and Watson, M. (1999) *Postwar British Politics in Perspective*, Cambridge: Polity, pp.87–106.

Hay, C. (2002) *Political Analysis: A Critical Introduction*, Basingstoke: Palgrave Macmillan.

Hay, C. (2006) '(What's Marxist about) Marxist state theory?', in *op cit* Hay, Lister and Marsh (eds), *The State*, pp.59–78.

Hay, C. and Lister, M. (2006) 'Introduction: theories of the state', in *op cit* Hay, Lister and Marsh (eds), *The State*, pp.1–20.

Hay, C., Lister, M. and Marsh, D. (eds) (2006) *The State: Theories and Issues*, Basingstoke: Palgrave Macmillan.

Hayward, C. and Lukes, S. (2008) 'Nobody to shoot? Power, structure and agency: a dialogue', *Journal of Power:* 1(1): 5–20.

Heelas, P., Lash, S. and Morris, P. (eds) (1996) *Detraditionalization*, Oxford: Blackwell.

Held, D. (2004) *Global Covenant: The Social Democratic Alternative to the Washington Consensus*, Cambridge: Polity.

Heywood, A. (2012) *Political Ideologies: An Introduction* (5th edn), Basingstoke: Palgrave Macmillan.

Hicks, A.M. and Lechner, F.J. (2005) 'Neopluralism and neofunctionalism in political sociology', in Thomas Janoski, Robert Alford, Alexander Hicks and Mildred A. Schwartz (eds), *The Handbook of Political Sociology: States, Civil Societies and Globalization*, Cambridge: Cambridge University Press, pp.54–71.

Hirschhorn, T. (2015) 'Gramsci monument', *Rethinking Marxism*, 27(2): 213–40.

Hobbes, T. (1651) *Leviathan*, repr. ed. Richard Tuck, Cambridge: Cambridge University Press, 1991.

Hochschild, A.R. (2012) [1983] *The Managed Heart: Commercialization of Human Feeling*, Berkeley: University of California Press.

Holzer, B. and Sorensen, M.P. (2003) 'Rethinking subpolitics: beyond the 'iron cage' of modern politics?', *Theory, Culture & Society*, 20(2): 79–102.

Howarth, D. (2000) *Discourse*, Buckingham: Oxford University Press.

Howarth, D. (2004) 'Hegemony, political subjectivity, and radical democracy', in *op cit* Critchley and Marchant (eds), *Laclau*, pp.256–76.

Howarth, D., Norval, A.J. and Stavrakakis, Y. (eds) (2000) *Discourse Theory and Political Analysis: Identities, Hegemonies and Social Change*, Manchester: Manchester University Press.

Inglehart, R. and Welzel, C. (2005) *Modernization, Cultural Change and Democracy*, Cambridge: Cambridge University Press.

Jaeggi, R. (2014) *Alienation* (trans. and ed. Frederick Neuhouser, trans Alan E. Smith), New York: Columbia University Press.

Jaenicke, D. (1999) 'New Labour and the Clinton presidency', in David Coates and Peter Lawler (eds), *New Labour in Power*, Manchester: Manchester University Press, pp.34–48.

Jay, M. (1996) [1973] *The Dialectical Imagination: A History of the Frankfurt School and the Institute of Social Research 1923–1950*, Berkeley: University of California Press.

Jenkins, P. (1987) *Mrs Thatcher's Revolution*, London: Jonathan Cape.

Jessop, B. (1990) *State Theory: Putting Capitalist States in Their Place*, Cambridge: Polity.

Jessop, B. (2004) 'Developments in Marxist theory', in *op cit* Nash and Scott (eds), *The Blackwell Companion to Political Sociology*, pp.7–16.

Jessop, B. (2007) *State Power: A Strategic-Relational Approach*, Cambridge: Polity.

Jessop. B., Bonnett, K., Bromley, S. and Ling, T. (1984) 'Authoritarian populism, two nations and Thatcherism', *New Left Review*, (I)147: 32–60.

Jessop. B., Bonnett, K., Bromley, S. and Ling, T. (1985) 'Thatcherism and the politics of hegemony: a reply to Stuart Hall', *New Left Review*, (I)153: 87–101.

Joll, J. (1977) *Gramsci (Fontana Modern Masters Series*, ed. Frank Kermode), Glasgow: Fontana.

Jones, O. (2014) *The Establishment: And How They Get Away With It*, London: Penguin.

Kaldor, M. (2012) *New and Old Wars: Organised Violence in a Global Era* (3rd edn), Cambridge: Polity.

Kavanagh, D. and Morris, P. (1994) *Consensus Politics from Atlee to Major*, Oxford: Blackwell.

Keat, R. and Abercrombie, N. (1991) 'Introduction: Starship Britain or universal enterprise?', in Russell Keat and Nicholas Abercrombie (eds), *Enterprise Culture*, London: Routledge, pp.1–17.

Kellner, D. (1989) *Critical Theory, Marxism and Modernity*, Cambridge: Polity.

Kennedy, E. (1978) *A Philosophe in the Age of Revolution: Destutt de Tracy and the Origins of Ideology*, Philadelphia: American Philosophical Society.

Kerr, C., Dunlop, J., Harbison, F. and Myers, C. (1960) *Industrialism and Industrial Man: The Problems of Labour and Management in Economic Growth*, Cambridge, MA: Harvard University Press.

Kerr, P. (2001) *Postwar British Politics: From Conflict to Consensus,* London: Routledge.

Kerr, P., Byrne, C. and Foster, E. (2011) 'Theorising Cameronism', *Political Studies Review,* 9(2): 193–207.

King, A. (1975) 'Overload: problems of governing in the 1970s', *Political Studies,* 23(2/3): 284–96.

King, A. (1999) 'Legitimating post-Fordism: a critique of Anthony Giddens' later works', *Telos,* 115 (Spring): 61–77.

Kisby, B. (2010) 'The Big Society: power to the people?', *The Political Quarterly,* 81(4): 484–91.

Kolarz, P. (2016) *Giddens and Politics beyond the Third Way: Utopian Realism in the Late Modern Age,* Basingstoke: Palgrave Macmillan.

Kooiman, J. (2003) *Governing as Governance,* London: Sage.

Kumar, K. (2006) 'Ideology and sociology: reflections on Karl Mannheim's *Ideology and Utopia*', *Journal of Political Ideologies,* 11(2): 169–81.

Labour Party (2010) *A Future Fair For All: The Labour Party Manifesto 2010,* London: Labour Party.

Lacan, J. (1949) 'The mirror stage as formative of the *I* function as revealed in psycho-analytic experience', in Lacan, J. (2006) *Ecrits* (trans. Bruce Fink), New York: W.W. Norton & Co., pp.75–81.

Laclau, E. (1990) 'New reflections on the revolution of our time', in Laclau, E. (1990) *New Reflections on the Revolution of our Time,* London: Verso, pp.3–87.

Laclau, E. (1994) 'Why do empty signifiers matter to politics?', in Laclau, E. (1996) *Emancipation(s),* pp.36–46.

Laclau, E. (1996) 'The death and resurrection of the theory of ideology', *Journal of Political Ideologies,* 1(3): 201–20.

Laclau, E. (2005) *On Populist Reason,* London: Verso.

Laclau, E. (2006) 'Ideology and post-Marxism', *Journal of Political Ideologies,* 11(2): 103–14.

Laclau, E. (2014) *The Rhetorical Foundations of Society,* London: Verso.

Laclau, E. and Mouffe, C. (1985) *Hegemony and Socialist Strategy: Towards a Radical Democratic Politics,* London: Verso.

Laclau, E. and Mouffe, C. (1987) 'Post-Marxism without apologies', *New Left Review* (I)166: 79–106.

Lechner, F.J. (2009) *Globalization: The Making of World Society,* Oxford: Wiley-Blackwell.

Leggett, W. (2005) *After New Labour: Social Theory and Centre-Left Politics,* Basingstoke: Palgrave Macmillan.

Leggett, W. (2009) 'Prince of modernisers: Gramsci, New Labour and the meaning of modernity', in Mark McNally and John Schwarzmantel (eds), *Gramsci and Global Politics: Hegemony and Resistance,* London: Routledge, pp.137–55.

Leggett, W. (2013) 'Restoring society to post-structuralist politics: Mouffe, Gramsci and radical democracy', *Philosophy & Social Criticism,* 39(3): 299–315.

Leggett, W. (2014) 'The politics of behaviour change: nudge, neoliberalism and the state', *Policy & Politics,* 42(1): 3–19.

Levitas, R. (2010) 'Back to the future: Wells, sociology, utopia and method', *The Sociological Review,* 58(4): 530–47.

Li, Y. and Marsh, D. (2008) 'New forms of political participation: searching for expert citizens and everyday makers', *British Journal of Political Science*, 38(2): 247–72.

Little, A. (2002) 'Community and radical democracy', *Journal of Political Ideologies*, 7(3): 369–82.

Lopes, A. (2014) 'The University as power or counter–power? May 1968 and the emergence of a new learning subject', *European Journal for Research on the Education and Learning of Adults*, 5(1): 31–49.

Lowndes, V. and Roberts, M. (2013) *Why Institutions Matter: The New Institutionalism in Political Science*, Basingstoke: Palgrave Macmillan.

Ludlam, S. and Smith, M.J. (eds) (2004) *Governing as New Labour: Policy and Politics under Blair*, Basingstoke: Palgrave Macmillan.

Lukes, S. (1974) *Power: A Radical View*, London: Macmillan Press.

McDonald, K. (2006) *Global Movements: Action and Culture*, Oxford: Blackwell.

Macdonald, M. (2003) *Exploring Media Discourse*, London: Hodder Arnold.

Machiavelli, N. (1532) *The Prince*, repr. London: Penguin (trans. George Bull), 1999.

McLennan, G. (2006) *Sociological Cultural Studies: Reflexivity and Positivity in the Human Sciences*, Basingstoke: Palgrave Macmillan.

McLennan, G., Molina, V. and Peters, R. (1977) 'Althusser's theory of ideology', in *Centre for Contemporary Cultural Studies Working Paper in Cultural Studies No. 10: On Ideology*, pp. 77–105, repr. as *On Ideology: Vol III, CCCS Classic Texts*, Abingdon: Routledge, 2012.

McNay, L. (1994) *Foucault: A Critical Introduction*, Cambridge: Polity.

De Maio. F. (2010) *Health and Social Theory*, Basingstoke: Palgrave Macmillan.

Mannheim, K. (1936) *Ideology and Utopia: An Introduction to the Sociology of Knowledge*, London: Routledge & Kegan Paul.

Marcuse, H. (1956) *Eros and Civilization: A Philosophical Inquiry into Freud*, London: Routledge & Kegan Paul.

Marcuse, H. (1964) *One-Dimensional Man: Studies in the Ideology of Advanced Industrial Society*, repr. London: Routledge, 1991.

Marcuse, H. (1969) *An Essay On Liberation*, Boston: Beacon Press.

Marquand, D. (2004) *Decline of the Public*, Cambridge: Polity.

Marshall, G. (1990) *In Praise of Sociology*, London: Unwin Hyman.

Marske, C.E. (1987) 'Durkheim's "cult of the individual" and the moral reconstitution of society', *Sociological Theory*, 5(1): 1–14.

Marttila, T. (2015) *Post-Foundational Discourse Analysis: From Political Difference to Empirical Research*, Basingstoke: Palgrave Macmillan.

Marx, K. (1844) *Economic and Philosophic Manuscripts of 1844*, repr. London: Lawrence & Wishart (5th revsd edn), 1977.

Marx, K. (1845) 'Theses on Feuerbach', in *op cit* Tucker (ed.) *The Marx-Engels Reader*, pp.143–5.

Marx, K. (1846) *The German Ideology*, in *op cit* Tucker (ed.) *The Marx-Engels Reader*, pp.146–200.

Marx, K. (1849) *Wage Labour and Capital* (ed. Friedrich Engels, 1891) in *op cit* Tucker (ed.) *The Marx-Engels Reader*, pp.203–17.

Marx, K. (1859) 'Preface' to *A Contribution to the Critique of Political Economy*, in *op cit* Tucker (ed.) *The Marx-Engels Reader*, pp.3–6.

Marx, K. (1867) *Capital: A Critique of Political Economy, Volume One*, repr. London: Penguin (trans. Ben Fowkes), 1976.

Marx, K. (1875) *Critique of the Gotha Program* (repr. Friedrich Engels, 1891), in *op cit* Tucker (ed.) *The Marx-Engels Reader*, pp.525–41.

Marx, K. and Engels, F. (1848) *Manifesto of the Communist Party*, in *op cit* Tucker (ed.) *The Marx-Engels Reader*, pp.469–500.

Matthewman, S. (2011) *Technology and Social Theory*, Basingstoke, Palgrave Macmillan.

May, V. (2013) *Connecting Self to Society: Belonging in a Changing World*, Basingstoke: Palgrave Macmillan.

May, T. and Perry, B. (2011) *Social Research and Reflexivity: Content, Consequences and Context*, London: Sage.

Mayes, C. (2016) *The BioPolitics of Lifestyle: Foucault, Ethics and Healthy Choices*, Abingdon, Oxon: Routledge.

Mennell, S. (2014) 'What economists forgot (and what Wall Street and the City never learned): a sociological perspective on the crisis in economics', *History of the Human Sciences*, 27(3): 20–37.

Mestrovic, S. (1998) *Anthony Giddens: The Last Modernist*, London: Routledge.

Micheletti, M. (2003) *Political Virtue and Shopping: Individuals, Consumerism, and Collective Action*, New York: Palgrave.

Micheletti, M., Follesdal, A. and Stolle, D. (eds) (2004) *Politics, Products and Markets: Exploring Political Consumerism Past and Present*, New Brunswick NJ: Transaction Publishers.

Micheletti, M. and Stolle, D. (2008) 'Fashioning social justice through political consumerism, capitalism and the internet', *Cultural Studies*, 22(5): 749–69.

Miliband, R. (1965) 'Marx and the state', in Miliband, R. (1983) *Class Power and State Power*, London: Verso, pp.3–25.

Miliband, R. (1969) *The State in Capitalist Society: An Analysis of the Western System of Power*, London: Weidenfeld & Nicholson.

Miliband, R. (1970) 'The Capitalist State – Reply to Poulantzas', *New Left Review*, (I)59: 53–60.

Miliband, R. (1973) 'Poulantzas and the capitalist state', *New Left Review* (I)82: 83–92.

Miliband, R. (1977) *Marxism and Politics*, Oxford: Oxford University Press.

Miller, J.H. (2004) '"Taking up a task": moments of decision in Ernesto Laclau's thought', in *op cit* Critchley and Marchant (eds) *Laclau*, pp.217–25.

Miller, P. and Rose, N. (2008) *Governing the Present: Administering Economic, Social and Personal Life*, Cambridge: Polity.

Mills, C. Wright (1959) *The Sociological Imagination*, repr. Harmondsworth: Pelican, 1973.

Moran, J. (2005) 'The strange birth of Middle England', *Political Quarterly* (76) 2: 232–40.

Morley, D. and Chen, K-H (eds) (1996) *Stuart Hall: Critical Dialogues in Cultural Studies*. London: Routledge.

Morton, A.D. (2007) *Unravelling Gramsci: Hegemony and Passive Revolution in the Global Economy*, London: Pluto Press.

Mouffe, C. (1993) *The Return of the Political*, London: Verso.

Mouffe, C. (2000) *The Democratic Paradox*, London: Verso.

Mouffe, C. (2005) *On the Political*, London: Routledge.

Mouffe, C. (2013) *Agonistics: Thinking the World Politically*, London: Verso.

Mouzelis, N. (1991) *Back to Sociological Theory*, Basingstoke: Macmillan.

Mouzelis, N. (2008) *Modern and Postmodern Social Theorizing: Bridging the Divide*, Cambridge: Cambridge University Press.

Murray, C. (1990) *The Emerging British Underclass (IEA Choice in Welfare Series No. 2)*, London: Institute of Economic Affairs.

Nash, K. (2001) 'The "cultural turn" in social theory: towards a theory of cultural politics', *Sociology*, 35(1): 77–92.

Nash, K. (2010) *Contemporary Political Sociology: Globalization, Politics and Power* (2nd edn), Oxford: Wiley-Blackwell.

Nash, K. and Scott, A. (eds) (2004) *The Blackwell Companion to Political Sociology*, Oxford: Blackwell.

Negri, A. (2005) *The Politics of Subversion: A Manifesto for the Twenty-First Century*, Cambridge: Polity.

Nelson, M.R., Rademacher, M.A. and Paek, H-J. (2007) 'Downshifting consumer = upshifting citizen? An examination of a local Freecycle community', *The ANNALS of the American Academy of Political and Social Science*, 611(1): 141–56.

Newman, J. (2001) *Modernising Governance: New Labour, Policy and Society*, London: Sage.

Newman, J. (2005) 'Participative governance and the remaking of the public sphere', in *op cit* Newman (ed.) *Remaking Governance*, pp.119–38.

Newman, J. (ed.) (2005) *Remaking Governance: Peoples, Politics and the Public Sphere*, Bristol: Policy Press.

Ohmae, K. (1995) *The End of the Nation State*, New York: Free Press.

Ollman, B. (1971) *Alienation: Marx's Conception of Man in Capitalist Society*, Cambridge: Cambridge University Press.

O'Neill, J. (1986) 'The disciplinary society: from Weber to Foucault', *British Journal of Sociology*, 37(1): 42–60.

O'Reilly, K. (2012) *International Migration and Social Theory*, Basingstoke: Palgrave Macmillan.

Olsaretti, A. (2014) 'Beyond class: The many facets of Gramsci's theory of intellectuals', *Journal of Classical Sociology*, 14(4): 363–81.

Pahl, R. (1995) *After Success: Fin-de-Siecle Anxiety and Identity*, Cambridge: Polity.

Parkin, F. (2002) *Max Weber* (revsd. edn), London: Routledge.

Parry, G. (1969) *Political Elites*, London: George Allen & Unwin.

Parsons, T. (1949) *The Structure of Social Action*, Glencoe, IL: The Free Press.

Parsons, T. (1951) *The Social System*, Glencoe, IL: The Free Press.

Parsons, T. (1969) *Politics and Social Structure*, New York: The Free Press.

Peck, J. (2010) *Constructions of Neoliberal Reason*, Oxford: Oxford University Press.

Pels, D. (2003) *Unhastening Science: Autonomy and Reflexivity in the Social Theory of Knowledge*, Liverpool: Liverpool University Press.

Peretti, J. (2004) 'The Nike sweatshop email: political consumerism, internet and culture jamming' (with Michelle Micheletti), in *op cit* Micheletti, Follesdal and Stolle (eds) *Politics, Products and Markets*, pp.127–42.

Perri 6, Fletcher-Morgan, C. and Leyland, K. (2010) 'Making people more responsible: The Blair governments' programme for changing citizens' behaviour', *Political Studies*, 58(3): 427–49.

Pierre, J. and Peters, B.G. (2000) *Governance, Politics and the State*, New York: St Martin's Press.

Plamenatz, J. (1963) 'Introduction' in Plamenatz, J., *Man and Society: A Critical Examination of Some Important Social and Political Theories from Machiavelli to Marx*, Harlow: Longman, pp.ix–xxii.

Poulantzas, N. (1968) *Political Power and Social Classes*, Eng. trans. London: New Left Books, 1973.

Poulantzas, N. (1969) 'The problems of the capitalist state', *New Left Review* (I)58: 67–78.

Poulantzas, N. (1976) 'The capitalist state: a reply to Miliband and Laclau', *New Left Review* (I)95: 63–83.

Poulantzas, N. (1978) *State, Power, Socialism,* London: New Left Books.

Prabhakar, R. (2004) 'New Labour and the reform of public services', in *op cit*, Ludlam and Smith (eds) *Governing as New Labour*, pp.161–76.

Purvis, T. and Hunt, A. (1993) 'Discourse, ideology, discourse, ideology, discourse, ideology…', *British Journal of Sociology*, 44(3): 473–99.

Rawls, J. (1999) *A Theory of Justice* (revsd. edn), Harvard, MA: Harvard University Press.

Rice, J.S. (2013) 'Homo economicus and consumer activist subjectivity: anti-capitalist activism through alternative trade', *New Political Economy*, 18(6): 845–61.

Rhodes, R.A.W. (1994) 'The hollowing out of the state', *The Political Quarterly*, 65(2), 138–51.

Rhodes, R.A.W. (1997) *Understanding Governance: Policy Networks, Governance, Reflexivity and Accountability*, Buckingham: Open University Press.

Ritzer, G. (2001) *Explorations in Social Theory: From Metatheorizing to Rationalization*, London: Sage.

Ritzer, G. (2015) *The McDonaldization of Society* (8th edn), Thousand Oaks, CA: Sage.

Roberts, B. (2006) *Micro Social Theory*, Basingstoke: Palgrave Macmillan.

Rose, N. (1999) *Powers of Freedom: Reframing Political Thought*, Cambridge: Cambridge University Press.

Rose, N. (2001) 'Community, citizenship and the Third Way', in Denise Meredyth and Jeffrey Minson (eds) *Citizenship and Cultural Policy*, London: Sage, pp.1–17.

Rose, N. and Miller. P (1992) 'Political power beyond the state: problematics of government', *British Journal of Sociology*, 43(2): 173–205, repr. in *op cit* Miller and Rose (2008) pp.53–83.

Rosenberg, A. (2015) *Philosophy of Social Science* (5th edn), Boulder: Westview Press.

Rostow, W.W. (1960) *The Stages of Economic Growth: A Non–Communist Manifesto*, Cambridge: Cambridge University Press.

Rottenberg, C. (2014) 'The rise of neoliberal feminism', *Cultural Studies*, 28(3): 418–37.

Runciman, W.G. (ed.) (1978) *Weber: Selections in Translation*, Cambridge: Cambridge University Press.

Rustin, M. (1989) 'The politics of post-Fordism: or, the trouble with 'New Times', *New Left Review* (I)175: 54–77.

Salvik, B. and Crewe, I. (1983) *Decade of Dealignment*, Cambridge: Cambridge University Press.

Saunders, R. (2012) 'Crisis? What crisis? Thatcherism and the Seventies', in Ben Jackson and Robert Saunders (eds) *Making Thatcher's Britain*, Cambridge: Cambridge University Press, pp.25–42.

Saussure, F. de (1916) *Course in General Linguistics*, repr. London: Peter Owen, 1960.

Savage, M. and Majima, S. (2007) 'Have there been culture shifts in Britain?: A critical encounter with Ronald Inglehart', *Cultural Sociology*, 1(3): 293–315.

Sawicki, J. (1991) *Disciplining Foucault: Feminism, Power and the Body*, New York: Routledge.

Schumpeter, J.A. (1943) *Capitalism, Socialism and Democracy*, London: Allen & Unwin.

Scott, J. (1991) *Who Rules Britain?*, Cambridge: Polity.

Scott, S. (2009) *Making Sense of Everyday Life*, Cambridge: Polity.

Sennett, R. (1998) *The Corrosion of Character: The Personal Consequences of Work in the New Capitalism*, New York: W.W. Norton & Co.

Shah, D.V., McLeod, D.M., Kim, E., Lee, S.Y., Gotlieb, M., Ho, S.S. and Breivik, H. (2007) 'Political consumerism: how communication and consumption orientations drive "lifestyle politics"', *The ANNALS of the American Academy of Political and Social Science*, 611(1): 217–35.

Shah, D.V., Friedland, L.A., Wells, C., Kim, Y.M and Rojas, H. (2012) 'Communication, consumers, and citizens: revisiting the politics of consumption', *The ANNALS of the American Academy of Political and Social Science* 644(1): 6–19.

Shils, E. and Young, M. (1953) 'The meaning of the coronation', *Sociological Review*, 1(1): 63–81.

Sigelman, L. (2010) 'Terminological interchange between sociology and political science', *Social Science Quarterly*, 91(4): 883–905.

Simon, R. (1991) *Gramsci's Political Thought: An Introduction* (revsd edn) London: Lawrence & Wishart.

Sklair, L. (2001) *The Transnational Capitalist Class*, Oxford: Blackwell.

Smith, A.M. (1998) *Laclau and Mouffe: The Radical Democratic Imaginary*, London: Routledge.

Smith, D. (1988) *The Chicago School: A Liberal Critique of Capitalism*, Basingstoke: Macmillan.

Smith, M. (2006) 'Pluralism', in *op cit* Hay, Lister and Marsh (eds) (2006) *The State*, pp.21–38.

Sorensen, E. and Torfing, J. (eds) (2007) *Theories of Democratic Network Governance*, Basingstoke: Palgrave Macmillan.

Spours, K. (2015) *The Osborne Supremacy: Why Progressives Have to Develop a Hegemonic Politics for the Twenty-First Century*, London: Compass, available at compassonline.org.

Staten, H. (1984) *Wittgenstein and Derrida*, Lincoln NB: University of Nebraska Press.

Stedman Jones, D. (2012) *Masters of the Universe: Hayek, Friedman and the Birth of Neoliberal Politics*, Princeton, NJ: Princeton University Press.

Stiglitz, J.E. (2013) *The Price of Inequality*, New York: W.W. Norton & Co.

Stolle, D. and Micheletti, M. (2013) *Political Consumerism: Global Responsibility in Action*, New York: Cambridge University Press.

Sunstein, C.R. (2014) *Why Nudge? The Politics of Libertarian Paternalism*, New Haven, CT: Yale University Press.

Suskind, R. (2004) 'Faith, certainty and the presidency of George W. Bush', *New York Times Magazine*, 17 October.

Swartz, D.L. (2013) *Symbolic Power, Politics and Intellectuals: The Political Sociology of Pierre Bourdieu*, Chicago: University of Chicago Press.

Talshir, G. (2005) 'The intellectual as a political actor? Four models of theory/praxis', *Critical Review of International Social and Political Philosophy*, 8(2): 209–24.

Thornhill, C. (2009) 'The autonomy of the political: A socio-theoretical response', *Philosophy & Social Criticism*, 35(6): 705–35.

Thompson, J.B. (1990) *Ideology and Modern Culture: Critical Social Theory in the Age of Mass Communication*, Cambridge: Polity.

Thorson, K. (2012) 'What does it mean to be a good citizen? Citizenship vocabularies as resources for action', *The ANNALS of the American Academy of Political and Social Science*, 644(1): 70–85.

Torfing, J. (1999) *New Theories of Discourse: Laclau, Mouffe and Zizek*, Oxford: Blackwell.

Torfing, J. (2005) 'Poststructuralist discourse theory: Foucault, Laclau, Mouffe and Zizek', in Thomas Janoski, Robert Alford, Alexander Hicks and Mildred A. Schwartz (eds) *The Handbook of Political Sociology*, Cambridge: Cambridge University Press, pp.153–71.

Touraine, A. (2014) *After the Crisis*, Cambridge: Polity.

Tucker, R.C. (ed.) (1978) *The Marx-Engels Reader* (2nd edn), London: W.W. Norton & Co.

Turner, C. (2010) *Investigating Sociological Theory*, London: Sage.

Unger, R. (2001) *False Necessity: Anti-Necessitarian Social Theory in the Service of Radical Democracy* (2nd edn), London: Verso.

Venugopal, R. (2015) 'Neoliberalism as concept', *Economy and Society*, 44(2): 165–87.

Verba, S. (1965) 'The Kennedy assassination and the nature of political commitment', in Bradley S. Greenberg and Edwin B. Parker (eds) *The Kennedy Assassination and the American Public: Social Communication in Crisis*, Stanford: Stanford University Press, pp.348–60.

Vighi, F. and Feldner, H. (2007) 'Ideology critique or discourse analysis? Zizek against Foucault', *European Journal of Political Theory*, 6(2): 141–59.

de Vreese, C.H. (2007) 'Digital renaissance: young consumer and citizen?', *The ANNALS of the American Academy of Political and Social Science*, 611 (1): 207–16.

Wagner, P. (2002) 'The project of emancipation and the possibility of politics, or, what's wrong with post-1968 individualism?', *Thesis Eleven*, 68(1): 31–45.

Weber, M. (1904–5) *The Protestant Ethic and the Spirit of Capitalism* (trans. Talcott Parsons, 1930), London: Allen & Unwin.

Weber, M. (1917) 'Value judgements in social science', in *op cit* Runciman, *Weber*, pp.69–98.

Weber, M. (1918a) 'Politics as a vocation' in *op cit* Gerth and Mills, *From Max Weber*, pp.77–128.

Weber, M. (1918b) 'Science as a vocation', in *op cit* Gerth and Mills, *From Max Weber*, pp.129–56.

Weber, M. (1922a) 'The nature of social action', in *op cit* Runciman, *Weber*, pp.7–32.

Weber, M. (1922b) 'The nature of charismatic domination', in *op cit* Runciman, *Weber*, pp.226–50.

Weber, M. (1922c) 'Bureaucracy', in *op cit* Gerth and Mills, *From Max Weber*, pp.196–244.

Weber, M. (1922d) 'Classes, status groups and parties', in *op cit* Runciman, *Weber*, pp.43–56.

Weir, M. (2001) 'The collapse of Bill Clinton's Third Way', in Stuart Weir (ed.) *New Labour: The Progressive Future?*, Basingstoke: Palgrave Macmillan, pp.137–48.

Westen, D. (2007) *The Political Brain: The Role of Emotion in Deciding the Fate of the Nation*, New York: Public Affairs.

Williams, R. (1981) *Culture*, Glasgow: Fontana.

Willis, M.M. and Schor, J.B. (2012) 'Does changing a lightbulb lead to changing the world? Political action and the conscious consumer', *The ANNALS of the American Academy of Political and Social Science*, 644(1): 160–90.

Wood, B. (1998) 'Stuart Hall's cultural studies and the problem of hegemony', *British Journal of Sociology*, 49(3): 399–414.

Wood, E.M. (1986) *The Retreat from Class: A New 'True', Socialism*, London: Verso.

Worth, O. (2014) 'Stuart Hall, Marxism without guarantees, and "The hard road to renewal"', *Capital & Class*, 38(3): 480–7.

Index